Lecture Notes
in Business Information Processing 337

More information about this series at http://www.springer.com/series/7911

Malu Castellanos · Panos K. Chrysanthis ·
Konstantinos Pelechrinis (Eds.)

Real-Time Business Intelligence and Analytics

International Workshops
BIRTE 2015, Kohala Coast, HI, USA, August 31, 2015
BIRTE 2016, New Delhi, India, September 5, 2016
BIRTE 2017, Munich, Germany, August 28, 2017
Revised Selected Papers

 Springer

Editors
Malu Castellanos
Teradata
Santa Clara, CA, USA

Panos K. Chrysanthis (iD)
University of Pittsburgh
Pittsburgh, PA, USA

Konstantinos Pelechrinis (iD)
University of Pittsburgh
Pittsburgh, PA, USA

ISSN 1865-1348   ISSN 1865-1356 (electronic)
Lecture Notes in Business Information Processing
ISBN 978-3-030-24123-0   ISBN 978-3-030-24124-7 (eBook)
https://doi.org/10.1007/978-3-030-24124-7

This Springer imprint is published by the registered company Springer Nature Switzerland AG
The registered company address is: Gewerbestrasse 11, 6330 Cham, Switzerland

Real-Time Business Intelligence and Analytics (BIRTE)

Preface

This LNBIP special volume on the BIRTE workshops serves as the proceedings of the last two editions of its first decade. Since its inception in 2006, BIRTE evolved its focus and its name to more accurately capture its scope but kept its acronym. This volume reflects its new name "Real-Time Business Intelligence & Analytics" and includes extended versions of selected papers presented in the 2015 and 2016 editions: The 9th International Workshop on Business Intelligence for the Real-Time Enterprise (BIRTE 2015) was held on August 31, 2015, in conjunction with the VLDB 2015 Conference that took place during September 1–4, 2015 in Kohala Coast, Hawaii. The 10th International Workshop on Enabling Real-Time Business Intelligence (BIRTE 2016) was held on September 4, 2016, in conjunction with the VLDB 2016 Conference that took place during September 5–9, 2016 in New Delhi, India.

Following the previous workshop editions, these two editions of the BIRTE workshop aimed at providing a forum for presentation of the latest research results, new technology developments, and new applications in the areas of business intelligence and analytics in the real-time enterprise. To ensure the quality of the program, each paper was reviewed by three or four reviewers who provided their feedback to authors. Authors of a conditionally accepted paper had to address the reviewers' comments and provide a summary of each improvement done to their paper. All authors had the opportunity to further improve their papers with the feedback received at the workshop.

The two BIRTE editions presented in this volume were as successful as their predecessors, with a high-quality program, evidenced by having full room in most sessions. Both had the traditional structure of a blend of research paper presentations, keynotes, and invited presentations from industry and academia as well as panel discussions.

During the first decade, the BIRTE workshops had post-proceedings published after the event by Springer as LNBIP volumes. Starting with the 11th International Workshop on Real-Time Business Intelligence and Analytics (BIRTE 2017), which took place on August 28, 2017, again in conjunction with the VLDB 2017 Conference, held on August 28–September 1, in Munich, Germany, the BIRTE workshop switched to regular proceedings, published at the time of the workshops (ACM ICPS 2017). This switch to regular proceedings reflected the feedback from the authors and participants during BIRTE 2016. However, keeping with the tradition, the presenters of BIRTE 2017 were invited to submit extended versions of their papers for this LNBIP special issue. The three selected papers, one from the keynote talk and two research papers, from BIRTE 2017 are included as an extension to the post-proceedings of BIRTE 2015 and 2016.

In the following we present a summary of the BIRTE 2015, BIRTE 2016, and BIRTE 2017 programs with emphasis on the papers included in this volume.

BIRTE 2015

BIRTE 2015 was organized in four sessions, of which the first session was devoted to the four accepted research papers. The other three sessions were the keynote talk on "Real-Time Analytics: The Third Time's a Charm?" by Michael Franklin, and the invited talks "Twitter Heron: Stream Processing at Scale" from Tweeter, "High-Availability at Massive Scale: Building Google's Data Infrastructure for Ads" from Google, and "Apache Flink: Scalable Stream and Batch Data Processing" from TU Berlin. The closing session included the panel on the topic "Can Big Data Platforms EVER Deliver Real-Time Analytics?" moderated by Guy Lohman. We briefly describe next the four research papers and the invited paper from Google, which appear in this volume.

The first paper titled "A Federated In-Memory Database System for Life Sciences" was from the Enterprise Platform and Integration Concepts group at Hasso Plattner Institute and Max Delrück Center. The authors present their hybrid cloud computing approach that integrates decentralized computing resources to form a federated in-memory database system that combines cloud computing with local storage and processing of highly sensitive data and huge amounts of data that would be too costly to transfer. The authors illustrate their approach on a real-world life sciences use case.

The second paper "An Integrated Architecture for Real-Time and Historical Analytics in Financial Services" was a short paper from Datometry Inc. The authors propose adaptive data virtualization (ADV) as an approach to satisfy the contradicting requirements of high-speed real-time analytics by some applications like analysis of ticker data, and scale by other applications like daily reporting. The authors illustrate how ADV breaks data silos by letting applications use different data management technologies without the need for database migrations or re-configuration of applications.

In the third paper, "Processing of Aggregate Continuous Queries in a Distributed Environment," the authors from the University of Pittsburgh explore how the sharing of partial aggregations can be implemented in the challenging environment of distributed data stream management systems (DSMSs) performing on-line analytics where the efficient execution of large numbers of aggregate continuous queries (ACQs) is crucial. They formulate the problem as an optimization that combines sharing of partial aggregations and assignment to servers to produce high-quality plans that keep the total cost of execution of ACQs low and balance the load among the computing nodes. The authors classify, implement, and compare optimizers and present their conclusions.

The fourth paper titled "Collecting and Analyzing User-Behavior Information in Instant Search Using Relational DBMS" is a short one from the University of California at Irvine where the authors study how to systematically collect information about user behaviors when they interact with an instant search engine, especially in a real-time environment. They present a solution, called RILCA, which uses front-end techniques, instead of methods based on traditional Web servers, to keep track of rich information about user activities, a relational DBMS to store and analyze the log records efficiently, and a dashboard to monitor and analyze log records in real time.

In the invited industrial talk "High-Availability at Massive Scale: Building Google's Data Infrastructure for Ads" from Google, the authors described the evolution of the high availability strategies of the ads infrastructure from the first generation to today's approach based on multi-homed systems. These systems run hot in multiple datacenters all the time, and adaptively move load between datacenters, with the ability to handle outages of any scale transparently. The authors described their approaches for, and experiences with, availability and consistency in multi-homed data storage and processing systems. They shared details of the large-scale streaming systems Mesa and Photon and a new system, Ubiq, a highly-available multi-homed system, that scales to extremely high throughput by continuously processing events in small batches in near real-time.

BIRTE 2016

The 10th BIRTE 2016 was a special workshop edition, celebrating ten years of bridging academic and industrial innovation, as such it featured three keynote talks in addition to the traditionally invited talks from academia and industry. The overall program was organized into five sessions that included the keynotes "A Tale of Quest for Real-Time Business Intelligence" by Rakesh Agrawal (Data Insight Labs), "Data Exploration Challenges in the Age of Big Data" by Surajit Chaudhuri (Microsoft) and "Hybrid Transaction and Analytics Processing (HTAP): State of the Art" by C. Mohan (IBM); three invited talks and the closing panel which debated the key question, "The Singularity of Real-Time Analytics, Are We There Yet?" moderated by Panos K. Chrysanthis; and presentation of two research papers, and one research demo.

This volume includes extended versions of the two research papers and the demo paper, which covered the broad spectrum from the use of real-time analytics for recommendations (the PolyRecs system), to enabling real-time analytics over raw XML data, to scheduling complex analytical workflows executing over multi-engine environments (the IReS system). It also includes two papers of the invited talks from Harvard University on "Data Systems That Are Easy to Design, Tune and Use in Real-Time", and from Google on "Ubiq: A Scalable and Fault-tolerant Log Processing Infrastructure".

In their presentations, the authors of "PolyRecs: Improving Page-View Rates Using Real-Time Data Analysis" from the University of Athens, Greece, outlined their effort to enhance the pageview rates of e-content in order to achieve higher market penetration and gains in advertisements. They presented the design decisions underlying PolyRecs, which enable PolyRecs to be both effective on-the-fly calculations of what might be interesting to the browsing individuals at specific points in time as well as produce accurate results capable of improving the user-experience. They finally shared the experimental results of the real deployment of PolyRecs, pointing out that PolyRecs is a domain-agnostic hybrid-recommendation system that successfully functions regardless of the underlying data and/or content infrastructure.

In the second research paper, titled "Enabling Real Time Analytics over Raw XML Data," its authors from Microsoft Bing, IIT Bombay, and Flipkart pointed out that transforming data from a semi-structured format, such as XML, to a structured one is often time consuming and inappropriate for real-time analytics. To avoid losing, or rendering unactionable crucial, time-sensitive insights, they posed the question of how to expose analytical insights in the raw XML data. They proposed the idea of extracting complementary information (CI) from the raw semi-structured data repository for a given user query to enhance users' ability to better comprehend the original query response. CI examples include the context of the user query and the hidden patterns in the underlying XML data. Their solution is based on the node categorization model and a new ranking function for candidate entity nodes based on the underlying XML data structure. Crowd-sourced feedback on the CI discovered by their solution showed its ability to reveal useful CI in real-world XML data repositories with high precision and recall.

The demo presentation was on the Intelligent Resource Scheduler (IReS) from the National Technical University of Athens, Greece. The details of the resource allocation, optimizations and decision making of IReS are described in the developers' demo paper titled "Robust and Adaptive Multi-Engine Analytics Using IReS." During the demo, the attendees observed how to create, optimize, and execute workflows that match real use cases over multiple compute and data engines, imposing their preferred optimization objectives. Furtermore, the attendees had a chance to confirm the resilience and adaptability of IReS in the presence of failed nodes, unavailable engines, and load surges.

The paper "Data Systems That Are Easy to Design, Tune and Use in Real-Time" captures the invited talk by Stratos Idreos, from Harvard University. In his thought-provoking talk, the speaker discussed the vision of a future where businesses are driven by explosive amounts of data, where data becomes readily available and its power can be harnessed by everyone in real-time. He made the point that for this to happen, it is crucial that data systems be easy to design, tune, and use in real-time, and then described his group's efforts towards this vision. These efforts include the development of (1) adaptive data systems that can adjust to data and access patterns on-the-fly, (2) self-designing data systems that make it easy to spin-off and test new data system architectures in near real-time, and (3) curious data systems that make it easy to explore data in real-time, even if we do not know what queries to ask.

The second invited paper from Google presents "Ubiq: A Scalable and Fault-Tolerant Log Processing Infrastructure." This infrastructure has been in production for Google's advertising system for many years, and has served as a critical log processing framework for several dozen pipelines. During his talk, Manpreet Singh, Ubiq's lead developer, described Ubiq's architecture ability to continuously process log files in real time, while fully tolerating infrastructure degradation and data center-level outages without any manual intervention. He pointed out that Ubiq guarantees exactly-once semantics for application pipelines and provides an end-to-end latency of under a minute.

BIRTE 2017

The overall program of the 11th edition of BIRTE, BIRTE 2017, was organized into four sessions that included a keynote, an invited talk, five research paper presentations, an industrial paper presentation, and a closing panel. Extended versions of two of the research papers and the keynote paper were selected to be included in this volume. We briefly describe these three papers below.

The paper titled "Towards Interactive Data Exploration" corresponds to the keynote talk in the workshop under the same title. In this talk, Carsten Binning from TU Darmstadt and Brown University made the point that even though technology has been a key enabler of the ongoing big data trend toward datafication of almost every research field and industry with open-source tools like R and Hadoop and the advent of cheap, abundant computing and storage in the cloud, the current big data tool set is ill-suited for interactive data exploration. Consequently, the knowledge discovery process is a major bottleneck in our data-driven society. He gave an overview of challenges for interactive data exploration on large data sets and then presented current research results that revisit the design of existing data management systems, from the query interface to the underlying hardware, to enable interactive data exploration.

The paper titled "DCS: A Policy Framework for the Detection of Correlated Data Streams" is an extended version of the paper "Detection of Highly Correlated Live Data Streams" presented in the workshop. This is a product of a research collaboration. The authors from the Universities of Pittsburgh, USA, and of Queensland, Australia, proposed a solution, called DCS (Detection of Correlated Data Streams), which quickly identifies windows of highly correlated data streams and provides results in real-time. DCS achieves this by combining priority scheduling, pruning, and early termination to maximize the detection of correlated pairs within a micro-batch. DCS uses the Pearson correlation coefficient as a metric of correlation of two sliding windows of data streams and supports two modes of operation, "cold start" and "warm start." In the former mode, the analysis of a micro-batch starts with no prior knowledge of correlated pairs of streams and initializes the parameters of the priority scheduler $PriCe$'s utility function to its default values, whereas in the latter mode, the utility function is initialized based on the results of the latest micro-batch analysis for deeper exploration.

The second extended research paper reported the results of a collaboration among University of Toronto, Brown University, Intel Labs, and MIT. In their paper, titled "Towards Dynamic Data Placement for Polystore Ingestion," the authors proposed a streaming ETL architecture to support heterogeneous workloads with data ingestion and analytical queries, which are executed with strict performance guarantees. Their prototype system consists of a transactional streaming engine (S-Store), an OLAP back-end engine (Postgres), and a middleware (Big-DAWG) that controls the data migration and execution of the queries. Using this prototype, the authors studied the ingestion performance in terms of latency of various data placement and migration (Copy and Move) strategies between S-Store and OLAP engines under different mixed (read and write) ETL workloads.

February 2018   Malu Castellanos
                                                     Panos K. Chrysanthis

Organization

BIRTE 2015 and 2016

General Chair

Meichun Hsu · Hewlett-Packard, USA

Program Chairs

Malu Castellanos · Hewlett-Packard, USA
Panos K. Chrysanthis · University of Pittsburgh, USA

Program Committee (BIRTE 2015)

Christof Bornhoevd · RMS, USA
Alejandro Buchmann · Technische Universität Darmstadt, Germany
Badrish Chandramouli · Microsoft Research, USA
Shimin Chen · Chinese Academy of Sciences, China
Ben Chin Ooi · National University of Singapore, Singapore
Howard Ho · IBM, USA
Wolfgang Lehner · Dresden University of Technology, Germany
Fatma Ozcan · IBM Almaden, USA
Torben B. Pedersen · Aalborg University, Denmark
Kostantinos Pelechrinis · University of Pittsburgh, USA
Evaggelia Pitoura · University of Ioannina, Greece
Karthik Ramasamy · Twitter, USA
Elke Rundensteiner · Worcester Polytechnic Institute, USA
Mohamed Sharaf · Queensland University, Australia
Eric Simon · SAP-BO, France
Nesime Tatbul · Intel Labs and MIT, USA

Program Committee (BIRTE 2016)

Roger Barga · Amazon, USA
Christof Bornhoevd · RMS, USA
Alejandro Buchmann · Technische Universität Darmstadt, Germany
Shimin Chen · Chinese Academy of Sciences, China
Howard Ho · IBM, USA
Wolfgang Lehner · Dresden University of Technology, Germany
Olga Papaemmanouli · Brandeis University, USA
Evaggelia Pitoura · University of Ioannina, Greece
Krithi Ramamrithan · IIT Bombay, India
Karthik Ramasamy · Twitter, USA
Mohamed Sharaf · Queensland University, Australia

Eric Simon   SAP-BO, France
Nesime Tatbul   Intel Labs and MIT, USA

Sponsor and Student Travel Scholarships Chair

Panos K. Chrysanthis   University of Pittsburgh, USA

Proceedings Chair

Kostantinos Pelechrinis   University of Pittsburgh, USA

Webmaster

Anatoli Shein   University of Pittsburgh, USA

Sponsors

HP VERTICA
Google Inc.

BIRTE 2017

General and Program Chairs

Malu Castellanos   Hewlett-Packard, USA
Panos K. Chrysanthis   University of Pittsburgh, USA

Program Committee (BIRTE 2017)

Stefan Appel   Siemens, Germany
Alejandro Buchmann   Technische Universität Darmstadt, Germany
Shimin Chen   Chinese Academy of Sciences, China
Avrilia Floratou   Microsoft, USA
Ashish Gupta   Google, USA
Howard Ho   IBM Almaden, USA
Wolfgang Lehner   Dresden University of Technology, Germany
Marco Mellia   Politecnico di Torino, Italy
Themis Palpanas   Paris Descartes University, France
Panickos Neophytou   NetBeez, USA
Olga Papaemmanouil   Brandeis University, USA
Evaggelia Pitoura   University of Ioannina, Greece
Mohamed Sharaf   Queensland University, Australia
Nesime Tatbul   Intel Labs and MIT, USA

Sponsor and Student Travel Scholarships Chair

Panos K. Chrysanthis   University of Pittsburgh, USA

Proceedings Chair

Damianos Chatziantoniou   Athens University of Economics and Business, Greece

Webmaster

Anatoli Shein   University of Pittsburgh, USA

Sponsors

National Science Foundation
Google Inc.

Contents

BIRTE 2015

RILCA: Collecting and Analyzing User-Behavior Information in Instant Search Using Relational DBMS

Taewoo Kim[✉] and Chen Li

University of California, Irvine, CA 92697, USA
{taewookim,chenli}@ics.uci.edu

Abstract. An instant-search engine computes answers immediately as a user types a query character by character. In this paper, we study how to systematically collect information about user behaviors when they interact with an instant search engine, especially in a real-time environment. We present a solution, called RILCA, which uses front-end techniques to keep track of rich information about user activities. This information provides more insights than methods based on traditional Web servers such as Apache. We store the log records in a relational DBMS system, and leverage the existing powerful capabilities of the DBMS system to analyze the log records efficiently. We study how to use a dashboard to monitor and analyze log records in real time. We conducted experiments on real data sets collected from two live systems to show the benefits and efficiency of these techniques.

Keywords: Instant search · User-behavior collection · Log analysis

1 Introduction

Instant search is different from traditional search in that it immediately presents results as a user types in a query. In contrast, traditional search systems show results only when a user explicitly sends a complete query. For example, if a user wants to find information about *Michael Jackson* in an instant-search engine, as the user types in characters, say "michael", results will be returned even if the user does not finish typing the entire query. This search paradigm saves users not only typing efforts but also time. Google claims that their instant search saves users an average of two to five seconds per search [1].

It is well known that query log can be analyzed to not only monitor the query workload on the server, but also obtain rich information about user behaviors and intentions. In this paper we study how to collect information about user queries in instant search, and analyze the information effectively and efficiently. Compared to log records of traditional search engines, the records of instant search have several unique characteristics. First, in traditional search, each query received by the server has completed keywords. In instant search, every keystroke

© Springer Nature Switzerland AG 2019
M. Castellanos et al. (Eds.): BIRTE 2015/2016/2017, LNBIP 337, pp. 3–18, 2019.
https://doi.org/10.1007/978-3-030-24124-7_1

can generate a query and a log record. When doing log analysis, we cannot treat each log record as a complete query since it can have a query prefix. For example, suppose a user types in the query "`michael`" character by character. The process can generate multiple log records, namely "`m`", "`mi`", "`mic`", "`mich`", "`micha`", "`michae`", and "`michael`". As a consequence, log records of instant search have a larger volume, with many records corresponding to keyword prefixes. Second, due to unique characteristic above, it becomes necessary to detect the "boundaries" between different information needs. In other words, we want to answer the following question: which of these log records can be regarded as a complete query that a user intended to type in? Along this line, we want to detect sessions in the log records corresponding to different information needs of users.

In this paper we study how to tackle these problems with a solution called "RILCA," which stands for "Real-time Instant-search Log Collector and Analyzer." Figure 1 shows the architecture of this approach. In RILCA, we have a separate server next to the search engine, and the purpose of this server is to collect rich information about user activities on the results from the search engine. The server is also used to analyze and visualize the collected log data.

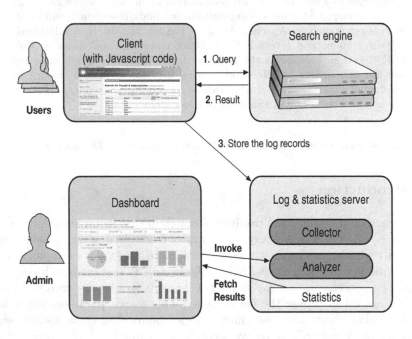

Fig. 1. Architecture of RILCA

Specifically, RILCA uses client-side techniques to collect information about user activities (Sect. 2), such as search results from the search engine, URLs clicked by the user, etc. Instead of using an ad hoc solution for storing and analyzing the collected log data, RILCA uses a relational DBMS to do the storage and analysis. Since many requests will be sent to RILCA server simultaneously, it is important to process these requests without errors. Since a relational DBMS provides concurrency control and transaction support, we can utilize these features to store our log records in a relational DBMS and use the system for analytics. Also, we study how to use built-in capabilities of DBMS such as stored procedures to process and analyze log. In particular, we show how to use SQL to analyze log records to identify sessions, and the most important query in each session. This method can not only fully utilize existing indexing and query processing functionality of DBMS based on SQL, but also support real-time analysis on log records. We develop various optimization techniques to improve the efficiency. The analyzed results are displayed on a dashboard, which can be used by the system administrator to do real-time monitoring and analysis.

We have deployed RILCA to analyze two instant-search engines we developed in the past few years, namely PSearch[1] and iPubmed[2]. PSearch is a system that supports instant search on the directory at UC Irvine, with about 70,000 records. iPubmed is an instant-search system on more than 24 million medical publications licensed from MEDLINE. We report our experiences of using RILCA to do log collection and analysis on these two systems, and conduct experiments to evaluate the techniques.

1.1 Related Work

Collecting and Analyzing Log Records in Real Time: Log records can be generated and collected through Web servers such as Apache [3]. These log records contain access information for the resource on a Web server. They also contain other information not relevant to the search, such as accessing Cascading Style Sheets (CSS), static HTML files, unrelated JavaScript files, or image files. The RILCA approach can collect additional information about user behaviors using Javascript. A similar, proprietary approach is taken by a company called Elicit Search [4], which collects user activities in real time by embedding a Javascript program on the Web server. This Javascript code sends information about user activities to a server that stores the data as log records, and analysis is done on the server. Our approach to collecting and analyzing log records in real time is similar. However, the internal structure and functionality of our method is different from that of Elicit Search, in that we collect other relevant event information, and we also use DBMS to do log analysis.

Instant Search Log Analysis: Log analysis of traditional search systems is a well-studied area [5–8]. On the contrary, instant search log analysis is new. In [9], the authors showed how to analyze instant search log records by identifying sessions and query patterns. We extend the session-identification algorithm by collecting and using additional information that is relevant to user queries. Specifically, our focus is to develop a RDBMS-based method to identify

---

[1] psearch.ics.uci.edu.
[2] ipubmed.ics.uci.edu.

sessions, the most important query in each session, and unique statistics about log records. We also focus on how to do optimization in this approach (Sect. 3).

Instant-Fuzzy Search: Instant-fuzzy search is studied in [10–12]. The authors developed a solution by incorporating data structures, namely a trie, an inverted index, and a forward index. Traversing a trie with a fuzzy method is also described in [11,12]. This method provides the combined effect of fetching certain prefixes with a fuzzy search and finding entries that start with the fetched prefixes.

2   Collecting User Search Activities

In this section we discuss how RILCA collects information about an instant-search engine and its user behaviors using client-side techniques. We first explain the limitation of log records in a traditional search server. When a client submits a request to a search engine, the search server keeps track of information such as the client's IP address, date, time, return status, size of returned object, and accessed URL. While this information is very valuable, it does not include the "big picture" of the user behavior, when the front end is interacting with multiple servers, including servers maintained by other organizations. For instance, in the iPubmed system, after a user types in a few characters, the server returns a list of publication results. After clicking a result, the user is directed to a page with detailed information about the publication. This page is generated by an external server maintained by NIH, which is beyond the control of our team. In other words, the user behaviors generate log records at multiple servers managed by different organizations, making it hard to do global information collection and analysis.

To overcome this limitation, RILCA uses client-side Javascript code to gather more information about user behaviors. As shown in Fig. 1, we embed a Javascript program in each Web page returned by the search engine. This step can be done by adding an HTML "<javascript>" tag in the page that indicates the path to the Javascript program residing on the RILCA server, so the change made on the search engine server is minimal. When the initial result page from the search engine is returned, the embedded program sends to the RILCA server a log record with relevant information, such as the search query and number of results. After that, this program monitors interesting user activities in the browser, such as copying a text string on the page and clicking a URL. For each event, the program sends a log record to the RILCA server. All these interactions with the server are happening "behind the scene," since they can be implemented using AJAX to minimize the impact on the user search experience. Specifically, since we send the log data to the RILCA server after the user receives the initial query results from the search engine, search queries are not blocked by the logging activities.

Table 1 shows sample log records of Apache and RILCA in the iPubMed search engine [2]. The Apache log records do not indicate the user actions after receiving the queries. In the RILCA log records, we can know that the user

Table 1. Comparison of search log records produced by Apache and RILCA

Apache (time, query)	RILCA (time, query)
20:19:32 imp	20:19:32.324 imp
20:19:32 impro	20:19:32.569 impro
20:19:32 improv	20:19:32.802 improv
20:19:32 improve	20:19:33.034 improve
20:19:33 improve pa	20:19:33.231 improve pa
20:19:33 improve pat	20:19:33.426 improve pat
... ...	... ...
20:19:34 improve patient co	20:19:34.404 improve patient co
20:19:34 improve patient comp	20:19:34.657 improve patient comp
20:19:34 improve patient compli	20:19:34.912 improve patient compli
20:19:34 improve patient complian	20:19:35.157 improve patient complian
20:19:35 improve patient compliance	20:19:35.395 improve patient compliance
20:19:39 improve mepatient compliance	20:19:40.263 improve mepatient compliance
20:19:40 improve medicapatient compliance	20:19:40.705 improve medicapatient compliance
20:19:40 improve medication patient compliance	20:19:40.970 improve medication patient compliance
(no more log records)	20:20:34.282 (clicked an outbound link: http://www.ncbi.nlm.nih.gov/pubmed/19182563)

clicked an outbound link that guided them to another Web site. This log record provides more insights about whether the query results included what the user was looking for. The log records also include the number of results for each query (not shown in the table).

3 Analyzing Log Records

In this section, we study how to utilize the collected query log data in RILCA. We first present a dashboard that shows the statistics of user queries, which can help the system administrator monitor and understand the workload on the search engine server, as well as gain insights of the performance of the engine. The next question is how to generate the data for the dashboard efficiently. We study how to achieve the goal by leveraging the existing query capabilities of relational DBMS systems.

3.1 Dashboard for Monitoring and Analyzing Search Queries

It is important for the system administrator of the search engine to monitor the status of the engine and understand the search behaviors of users. Figure 2 shows a dashboard interface that can achieve the goal. It allows the administrator to specify a time range, then analyze the query records collected during

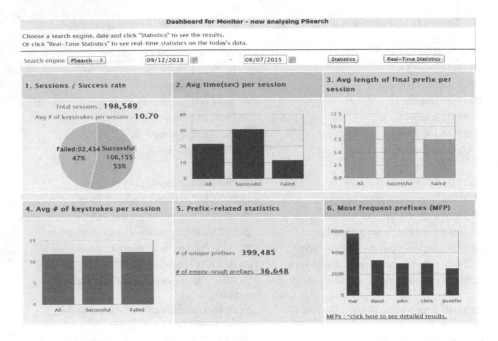

Fig. 2. Monitoring user queries using a dashboard

this period and visualize the statistical results. If the administrator clicks the "Real-time statistics" button, the system will run the computation tasks on the latest query records, such as the last one hour, 12 h, or one day, and the time duration is configurable. Compared to dashboards of traditional search engines, this dashboard is unique in two aspects due to the instant queries from users: (1) it needs new solutions to identify a session in a search, and (2) it also shows statistics related to query prefixes.

The dashboard shows the statistics about sessions, time and typing effort spent per session, and query prefixes. Formally, a session is a sequence of keystroke queries by a user issued without a major interruption to fulfill a single information need. For example, suppose a user is looking for a person named John Doe by typing in the name character by character. After receiving the first seven letters, the system can find the related record, and the user clicks the corresponding link for this person. In this case, the log records of these keystrokes form a session, indicating the process of finding this relevant answer. A session is called "successful" if the system can find the answer the user was looking for.

The dashboard shows the number of sessions, number of successful sessions, and the number of unsuccessful sessions. These numbers tell the administrator how successful the engine is to find right answers expected by the users. The dashboard includes the average number of keystrokes, the average length of query strings, and the average duration per session. These numbers indicate how much time and effort a user spent to find answers. The dashboard also shows the

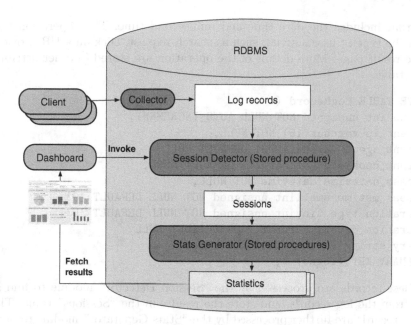

Fig. 3. Log analysis flow using a RDBMS

number of unique prefixes and empty-result prefixes. The prefixes with empty results are very useful to reveal abnormal search behaviors of the engine. As an example, by using this feature for the PSearch system, we were able to easily detect a bug in the engine. In particular, we noticed that many empty-result queries had two spaces in their keywords. By doing an investigation, we found that the client-side Javascript program had a bug related to how space was handled in keywords. This bug was fixed, and user search experience was improved. This example shows the value of this feature on the dashboard.

3.2   Generating Dashboard Statistics Using RDBMS

The next question is how to use the collected query log data to generate the statistics used in the dashboard. Instead of using ad-hoc solutions, RILCA uses relational database systems (RDBMS) to store and analyze the log data to achieve the goal. This approach can not only avoid the cost of duplicating the data at different places (e.g., the storage place and the analyzer module), but also leverage the powerful capabilities of RDBMS, including the SQL language, indexing, query processing and optimization.

Figure 3 shows how we use an RDBMS to analyze query log records to generate tables with statistical information. A module called "Collector" receives log records from clients, and stores the data into a table called "Log records." The following shows the schema of this table. It has a primary key ("logno"), IP address, agent (browser), and cookie id of the client. It also stores the access time that includes the date time and millisecond time. The "operation_type" shows the type of user activity, such as search request, click on a URL, or copy on the result page. More details of the operation are stored in other attributes in the table.

```
CREATE TABLE LogRecord (
   logno int unsigned NOT NULL AUTO_INCREMENT,
   client_ip varchar(15) NOT NULL,
   client_agent varchar(200) DEFAULT NULL,
   client_cookieid varchar(50) DEFAULT NULL,
   access_datetime datetime NOT NULL,
   access_mstime smallint unsigned NOT NULL DEFAULT '0',
   operation_type tinyint unsigned NOT NULL DEFAULT '0',
   operation_detail varchar(200) DEFAULT NULL,
   query_string varchar(200) NOT NULL,
   PRIMARY KEY (logno) );
```

These records are processed by the "Session Detector" module to find sessions from the log records, and store the results in the "Sessions" table. These session records are further processed by the "Stats Generator" module to obtain statistical information to be used by the dashboard. In our implementation of RILCA on the two live systems, we used 10 stored procedures and 6 functions for the analysis process.

3.3   Identifying Sessions Using SQL

We will focus on how to use SQL stored procedures to identify sessions from the raw query log records. We also need to detect whether a session was successful. There have been many studies on this topic (e.g., [9,13]). The main difference in this work is how to use SQL to analyze records with query prefixes, and understand whether those queries were successful or not. Specifically, we mainly consider newly available, rich information in the log records about user activities, such a click on a URL, copying a text from the result page, or closing/opening a new tab of a browser. In our analysis, we view a session as successful when the user clicked a link in the results, copied a text in the current search results, or closed the tab within a certain amount of time after the user entered the last query in the session.

Figure 4 shows the sketch of this process as a SQL stored procedure. It first declares a cursor on a query that sorts the log records in an ascending order based on the client IP and access time, so that we can process the records in the order they were received per IP. For each log record, we compare it with the previous one. A new session is started when the current IP address is different from the previous IP address, the time difference between the current record and the previous one is more than five minutes, or the current record is opening a new tab in the browser (boxes 1 to 3). Otherwise, a new session is still considered to be started if the current record is a search request and the previous record was not (box 4), or the current and previous records are both search requests with dissimilar query strings based on edit distance (box 5). After detecting a new session has started, we assign a new session ID and insert a new session record into the "Sessions" table.

The following is part of the stored procedure that includes the cursor declaration and **IF** statements that are used to identify new sessions.

```
DECLARE cursor1 CURSOR FOR
SELECT logno, ... FROM LogRecord WHERE
TIMESTAMPDIFF(SECOND, clientaccesstime, currenttime)
<= 500 ... ORDER BY client_ip, clientaccesstime logno;

FETCH cursor1 into c_logno, c_accesstime, ...

// #1. If the IP address of the current log record and
// the previous log record do not match: a new
// session has started
IF (c_client_ip != pre_client_ip) THEN
SET startnewsession = 1; ...

// #2. If the time difference between the current log
// record and the previous log record is greater than
// 5 minutes: a new session has started
ELSEIF ( timestampdiff(SECOND, pre_accesstime,
c_accesstime) > 300 ) THEN
SET startnewsession = 1; ...

// #3. If the current operation is opening a new tab:
// a new session has started
ELSEIF ( c_operationtype = 5 ) THEN
SET startnewsession = 1; ...

// #4. If the previous operation is in (clicking a
// link, copying a text, closing the tab) and the
// current operation is querying: a new session has
// started
ELSEIF ( (pre_operationtype = 2 OR pre_operationtype = 3
OR pre_operationtype=4) AND c_operationtype=1 ) THEN
SET startnewsession = 1; ...

% // #5. If both of the previous and current operation is
% // querying and the two queries are not similar: a new
% // session has been started
% ELSEIF ( pre_operationtype = 1 AND c_operationtype = 1
% AND rawlog_issimilar(pre_operation, c_operation) = 0 )
% THEN
```

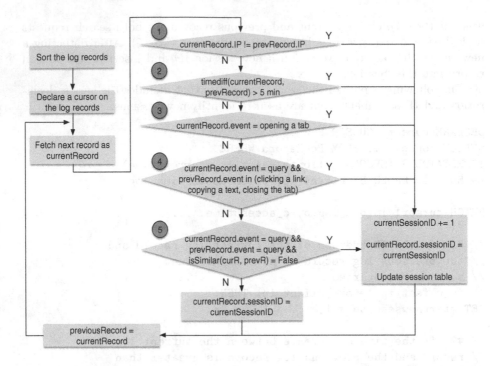

Fig. 4. Detecting sessions from log records using a stored procedure

```
%  SET startnewsession = 1; ...

% // #6. Otherwise, keep the current session.
% ELSE
%  SET startnewsession = 0; ...

% // #7. If a new session has been started, process
% // the necessary information
% IF (startnewsession = 1) THEN
%  SET new_sessionno = current_sessionno + 1; ...
```

3.4   Optimizing SQL Queries

Our experiences on the two real systems suggested that a simple implementation of the stored procedures can be slow, especially for large amounts of log records. To solve the problem, we develop several optimization techniques to improve the performance.

- *Splitting tables*: For those log records that are already processed by the session detector, we move them into a separate table. In this way, we can reduce the size of the table that is used to store newly arrived records and detect sessions. Similarly, the sessions of those processed log records are also moved to a separate table. This approach is similar to the idea used in Apache that stores query log records into different files.
- *Using the MEMORY storage for the "Sessions" table*: In this way, this table can be stored in memory for fast access and low latency.
- *Database tuning*: When detecting sessions, initially we need to declare a cursor by sorting a large number of log records based on their IP address and access time. The default DBMS setting may not be efficient for such queries. We can solve the problem by tuning system parameters such as cache size, buffer-pool size, log file size, and sort-buffer size, which can greatly affect the performance of the sorting process.

After identifying each session, we extract the final query as the most important query in the session, since a user stopped typing in more keywords after that. We also add this information to the session-related statistics. According to [9], 61% of PSearch [14] log records show a so called "L-shaped pattern" such as "c", "ca", "can", "canc", "cance", and "cancer". In this L-shaped pattern, a user gradually creates a new query by adding one more character to the previous query. Therefore, we can choose the most important query in the session by selecting the final query. There can be some sessions where the length of the intermediate query is greater than that of the final query. We choose the final query as the most important query in the session, since the user did not stop querying after checking the results of the intermediate query. For instance, the most important query for the session in Table 1 is "improve medication patient compliance".

4   Experiments

In this section, we present experimental results of RILCA on the two live instant search systems. Table 2 shows the data sets. The MEDLINE data set had information about 24 million medical publications. We extracted about 1.9 million records and used them for the experiments. We also collected log records from the live iPubMed [2] Web server. We first deployed the Javascript code on iPubMed in September 2013, and since then we collected additional log data from the RILCA server as well as Apache log records. The PSearch data set contained information about the UCI directory including their name, e-mail address, department, and office phone number, all of which were open to the public. The backend search engine supports instant, error-tolerant search. We collected log records by embedding a Javascript program on its returned pages. In addition, we also had log records from its Apache server.

For both systems, we installed a MySQL database on the server to store and analyze log records. All experiments were done on a server with 94 GB of RAM and four Intel Xeon CPUs. Each CPU had six cores with a clock speed of 2.93 GHz.

Table 2. Two data sets

Data set	MEDLINE	PSearch
Number of query log records	1,004,886	1,026,435
Number of sessions	65,260	102,743
Average character number per query	19.9	9.6
Average word number per query	2.8	1.7

4.1   Generating Query Workloads

To measure the performance of the log collector and session detector, we simulated an environment with multiple concurrent users. We set the number of concurrent users to be 5, 10, 15, and 20, respectively. We used Jmeter to simulate a user who sent about 14,000 queries sequentially. We used the real PSearch log records collected by RILCA. Table 3 shows the setting. Note that even though the number of concurrent users was between 5 and 20, the environment inserted 200 to 500 queries per second with a high insertion rate. For the live PSearch query session, on average each session had 11.64 keystroke queries with a duration of 20.56 s. Each user on average sent 0.6 queries per second, which corresponds to the case where 20 users inserted 12 queries per second, not 496 queries per second in the simulation setting. Thus, we can say that the simulation environment was approximately equivalent to a situation where there were 800 concurrent users in the live system.

Table 3. Query workload for PSearch

User number	Query number	Duration	Inserted record number per second
5	70,556	352 sec	200
10	141,893	400 sec	354
15	213,598	535 sec	399
20	283,941	572 sec	496

4.2   Log-Collection Overhead on Search Time

We evaluated the overhead of RILCA by measuring the execution time of a query when the number of concurrent users increased from 15 to 20. The purpose of this experiment was to check if RILCA can introduce a significant amount of overhead to a search process. As we can see in Fig. 5, the performance degradation of the search process was small. For instance, when there were 15 concurrent users, RILCA increased the average search time from 215 ms to 225 ms.

This low additional overhead is due to the fact that RILCA uses AJAX to do asynchronous communication with its server. The search time was a bit high because of the simulated environment with many concurrent users. We observed a similar minor time increase in the setting where the number of users is smaller and the search time was lower.

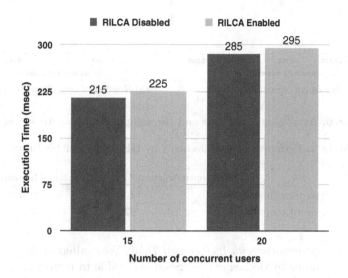

Fig. 5. RILCA overhead on search performance

4.3 Scalability of Log Analyzer

Figure 6 shows the time of the query analyzer (including the session detector and statistics generator) on different numbers of log records. (Note that we applied the optimizations in the experiments, and the effect of each optimization will be covered in the following subsection.) As the figure shows, when the number of query records increased, the total analyzer time also increased linearly, with a constant initial cost. For instance, when there were 82,500 log records with 10 concurrent users, it took about 6.7 s to analyze these records.

4.4 Effect of Optimization Techniques

Performance Improvement with RDBMS Tuning: We did an experiment to show the effect of DBMS tuning. We first used the default MySQL setting. In this case, when the number of concurrent users was 5, it took 376 s to analyze 17,000 log records. After adjusting a few database parameters (cache size, buffer-pool size, log-file size, and sort-buffer size), the analysis time decreased to 27.8 s to analyze 20,000 log records. Table 4 shows the results of this optimization.

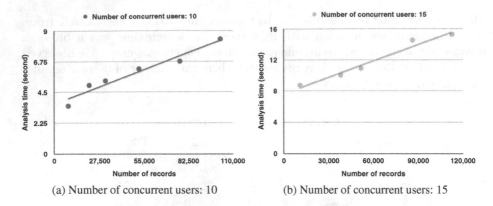

(a) Number of concurrent users: 10   (b) Number of concurrent users: 15

Fig. 6. Average analysis time and throughput from the stress test

Table 4. Performance improvement by DBMS parameter tuning

Content	Before optimization	After optimization	Improvement
Average analysis time (msec)	22	1.3	20.7
Throughput (record/sec)	45	720	675

Performance Improvement with In-memory Table: We evaluated the effect on the analysis performance by declaring the "Sessions" table in memory. As shown in Fig. 7, this approach can reduce the analysis time significantly. For example, for 100K log records, it took 134,000 ms to do the log analysis, while the time decreased to 33,570 ms after we declared the table to be in memory, with a reduction about 75%.

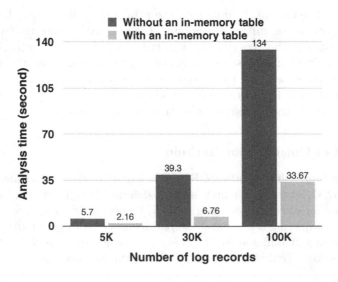

Fig. 7. The benefits of using an in-memory "Session" table

Table 5. Statistics about two search engines

Content	iPubMed	PSearch
Duration	9/'13–5/'15	9/'13–5/'15
# of sessions	4,347	197,814
# of successful sessions	649	105,726
# of unsuccessful sessions	3,698	92,088
Avg. number of queries per session	12.26	10.70
Avg. duration of a session (seconds)	56.65	21.70
Avg. time per each query (seconds)	3.58	0.63
Avg. # of keystrokes per successful session	22.98	11.45
Avg. length of the final query in a session	21.55	7.50
Avg. number of keystrokes per session	26.29	11.83
# of queries that generated no search results	5,172	36,536
# of unique queries	25,461	398,417
Most popular keywords whose length is equal to or greater than 3	cancer, practical clinical competence, brain	david, john, chris, jennifer

4.5   Comparison of Two Systems

We use RILCA to analyze the results collected from the two live systems in the past two years, and the results are shown in Table 5. As we can see, the average duration of a session on iPubMed was larger than that in PSearch. The difference is due to the fact that the average length of a query for iPubMed was nearly twice the size of that for PSearch.

5   Conclusions

In this paper, we studied how to collect information about user queries in instant search. In our proposed approach called RILCA, we embed a Javascript program in the result page of the search engine to collect user activities on the client side. RILCA includes more information in the instant search log that is relevant to a user's search activities than a traditional logging system. Then we studied how to use a relational database system to store this information and analyze the log records. In particular, we showed how to leverage the querying capabilities of RDBMS to detect sessions and produce insightful statistics that can be displayed on a dashboard, which can be used by a system administrator to do real-time monitoring of the server. We discussed several techniques to improve the performance of this analysis task. Our experiments on the real data sets collected from two live instant-search systems demonstrated the effectiveness and efficiency of these techniques. A possible future work would be utilizing the collected log records and statistics to provide useful query suggestions or provide auto-complete a query based on a query that a user typed so far.

References

1. Search: now faster than the speed of type. http://googleblog.blogspot.com/2010/09/search-now-faster-than-speed-of-type.html
2. iPubMed Search. http://ipubmed.ics.uci.edu
3. Apache. http://httpd.apache.org/
4. Elicit Search. http://elicitsearch.com/
5. Jansen, B.: Search log analysis: what it is, what's been done, how to do it. Libr. Inf. Sci. Res. **28**(3), 407–432 (2006)
6. Jansen, B.: The methodology of search log analysis. In: Handbook of Research on Web Log Analysis, pp. 99–121 (2008)
7. Anderson, J.: Analyzing clickstreams using subsessions. In: DOLAP, pp. 25–32 (2000)
8. Dogan, R., Murray, G., Neveol, A. Lu, Z.: Understanding PubMed user search behavior through log analysis. In: Database 2009 (2009)
9. Cetindil, I., Esmaelnezhad, J., Chen, L., Newman, D.: Analysis of instant search query logs. In: WebDB, pp. 7—12 (2012)
10. Cetindil, I., Esmaelnezhad, J., Kim, T., Li, C.: Efficient instant-fuzzy search with proximity ranking. In: ICDE, pp. 328–339 (2014)
11. Ji, S., Li, G., Li, C., Feng, J.: Efficient interactive fuzzy keyword search. In: WWW, pp. 371–380 (2009)
12. Li, G., Wang, J., Li, C., Feng, J.: Supporting efficient top-k queries in type-ahead search. In: SIGIR, pp. 355–364 (2012)
13. Silverstein, C., Marais, H., Henzinger, M., Moricz, M.: Analysis of a very large web search engine query log. SIGIR Forum **33**(1), 6–12 (1999)
14. Psearch. http://psearch.ics.uci.edu
15. MEDLINE Data. http://www.nlm.nih.gov/bsd/licensee/medpmmenu.html
16. IMDB Data. http://www.imdb.com/interfaces

A Federated In-memory Database System
for Life Sciences

Matthieu-P. Schapranow[1(✉)], Cindy Perscheid[1], Alf Wachsmann[2],
Martin Siegert[2], Cornelius Bock[1], Friedrich Horschig[1], Franz Liedke[1],
Janos Brauer[1], and Hasso Plattner[1]

[1] Hasso Plattner Institute, Enterprise Platform and Integration Concepts,
August-Bebel-Str. 88, 14482 Potsdam, Germany
{schapranow,cindy.perscheid,plattner}@hpi.de,
{cornelius.bock,friedrich.horschig,franz.liedke,
janos.brauer}@student.hpi.de
[2] Max Delbrück Center, Robert-Rössle-Str. 10, 13125 Berlin, Germany
{alf.wachsmann,martin.siegert}@mdc-berlin.de

Abstract. Cloud computing has become a synonym for elastic provision of shared computing resources operated by a professional service provider. However, data needs to be transferred from local systems to shared resources for processing, which might results in significant process delays and the need to comply with special data privacy acts. Based on the concrete requirements of life sciences research, we share our experience in integrating existing decentralized computing resources to form a federated in-memory database system. Our approach combines advantages of cloud computing, such as efficient use of hardware resources and provisioning of managed software, whilst sensitive data are stored and processed on local hardware only.

Keywords: Federated in-memory database · Cloud computing · Distributed data processing

1 Introduction

Cloud computing has been an emerging trend in information technology in the recent years, which abstracts computing power from physical hardware. Entities with limited or no physical hardware were early adapters of cloud computing, e.g. private households and Small and Mid-size Enterprises (SMEs) [29]. However, large companies and research facilities are reservedly moving their core business processes towards cloud computing environments due to legal regulations and various concerns although they would benefit equally from advantages, such as consolidation of hardware and improved use of available resources [16].

In the given work, we introduce a Federated In-Memory Database (FIMDB) system using unique hybrid cloud approach eliminating the need for transferring data to central cloud infrastructures. We focus on the specific requirements of large enterprises and research facilities with the example of a concrete use case

© Springer Nature Switzerland AG 2019
M. Castellanos et al. (Eds.): BIRTE 2015/2016/2017, LNBIP 337, pp. 19–34, 2019.
https://doi.org/10.1007/978-3-030-24124-7_2

taken form life sciences, i.e. data processing and analysis of Next-Generation Sequencing (NGS) data. We share experiences of providing managed services through our cloud platform we.analyzegenomes.com whilst storing sensitive data on local, on-premise computing resources in our FIMDB. Instead of data, we move algorithms and database queries, maintain a single source of truth, eliminate data duplication through data copying, and incorporate existing, local on-premise computing resources for data processing.

Figure 1 depicts our FIMDB software architecture modeled as Fundamental Modeling Concepts (FMC) block diagram [15]. The sum of all local database instances forms the FIMDB system whilst sensitive data and computing resources reside locally. In the remainder of the work, we use the terms customer and service provider. We refer to a customer as the user of a service provided by a service provider. Examples for customers are hospitals or research sites whilst central computing or bioinformatics centers are examples for service providers.

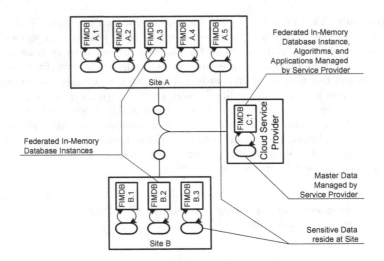

Fig. 1. Data reside at local computing resources whilst the service provider manages algorithms and apps remotely in the FIMDB system.

Our contribution is structured as follows: In Sect. 2 our work is set in the context of related work whilst we define cloud computing methods in Sect. 3. We introduce our FIMDB approach in Sect. 4 and share real-world experiences for a concrete life science application example in Sect. 5. In Sect. 6 we discuss our findings and our work concludes with an outlook in Sect. 7.

2   Related Work

The National Institute of Standards and Technology (NIST) defines cloud computing as "...a model for enabling ubiquitous, convenient, on-demand network access to a shared pool of configurable computing resources [. . .] that can be rapidly provisioned and released with minimal management effort or service provider interaction" [19]. We follow this definition and believe that cloud computing is the transition from individual physical resources, e.g. servers, CPUs, and cores, to virtually infinitely available, scalable computing resources. Furthermore, the NIST distinguishes between the service models: Software as a Service (SaaS), Platform as a Service (PaaS), and Infrastructure as a Service (IaaS). We focus on the service model SaaS as we believe managed services help to reduce Total Costs of Ownership (TCO) of complex applications, e.g. NGS data processing as described in Sect. 5.

Gartner research expects hybrid cloud computing to reach its plateau within the next two to five years [9]. We concentrate on a hybrid cloud-computing approach bridging the gap between the provision of managed cloud apps and data that resides on local on-premise computing resources. It is driven by (a) legal requirements restricting the exchange of sensitive data, e.g. patient data, and (b) the sheer amount of data, e.g. hundreds of GB, which consume a significant amount of time for data transfer to centralized cloud resources.

A spectrum of grid middleware systems was developed during the peak of the grid-computing era. They were prominently used by researchers but rarely by business users. Meanwhile, only a small fraction of them is still used, e.g. Globus or UNICORE, whilst others were discontinued, e.g. gLite [3,5,27]. For example, the Globus Genomics project is a middleware for the compute-intensive data processing of genomic data on top of Amazon's Elastic Computing Cloud (EC2) incorporating Galaxy as workflow management system [1,3,10]. It addresses researchers with a certain IT and bioinformatics background requiring them to move acquired raw data from local sequencing centers to cloud-computing resources. It is a beneficial alternative if no local computing resources are available as discussed in Sect. 6.2. However, we consider research centers and hospitals with existing on-premise computing resources and motivate the provision of managed algorithms to them.

Table 1 compares physical locations of selected infrastructure components per cloud category. Our approach extends the flexible hybrid cloud approach by processing data on existing on-premise infrastructure components whilst enabling provision of managed serviced by a managed service provider. The remaining infrastructure components reside either locally or remotely or both locally and remotely comparable to the hybrid cloud approach.

3 Transferring Data to Computing Resources

Today, cloud computing is often used as a metaphor for consolidation of hardware resources by major public cloud service providers, e.g. Microsoft, Google, Backspace, and Amazon [6,26]. We define the user groups as depicted in Fig. 2 consuming cloud services to understand their different requirements:

A: Large enterprises maintain their existing on-premise server systems and use cloud computing for outsourcing of selected services that typically do not involve sensitive data,

Table 1. Physical location of selected IT components per cloud category (L = Local on premise, R = Remote off premise, / = Either or, + = And).

Component	Public	Private	Hybrid	FIMDB
Apps	R	L	L/R	L+R
Data	R	L	L/R	L
Runtime environment	R	L	L/R	L+R
Middleware	R	L	L/R	L+R
Operating system	R	L	L/R	L+R
Virtualization	R	L	L/R	L+R
Physical servers	R	L	L/R	L+R
Storage subsystem	R	L	L/R	L+R
Network	R	L	L/R	L+R

Table 2. User characteristics ($\searrow$ = Low, $\rightarrow$ = Medium, $\nearrow$ = High).

User group	Hardware		Software		Band-width	Cat.
	Local	Cloud	Local	Cloud		
Large enterprises	$\nearrow$	$\searrow$	$\nearrow$	$\searrow$	$\nearrow$	I
Universities or healthcare providers	$\nearrow$	$\searrow$	$\nearrow$	$\rightarrow$	$\nearrow$	
Small and mid-size enterprises	$\rightarrow$	$\rightarrow$	$\rightarrow$	$\rightarrow$	$\rightarrow$	II
Private households	$\searrow$	$\searrow$	$\rightarrow$	$\rightarrow$	$\searrow$	

B: Universities or healthcare providers have existing on-premise server systems but need to consolidate software and hardware across multiple sites,

C: Small and Mid-size Enterprises (SMEs) might have limited set of local hardware resources or outsource specific software services, such as financials, from the beginning, and

D: Private households do not have any server systems on premise and consume cloud services for their private purposes only.

Table 2 compares the aforementioned user groups of cloud services and their requirements, which can be subsumed in the following categories:

I: Users are characterized by existing on-premise hardware resources, high computing power, a variety of local software apps, and high network bandwidth, e.g. large enterprises, universities, and healthcare providers, and

II: Users are characterized by medium or low local hardware resources, a mix of local and cloud-based apps, and low to medium Internet bandwidths, e.g. SMEs and private households.

Currently, cloud service providers mainly focus on customers of Cat. II and customers of Cat. I that aim to reduce local hardware, software, and personnel. Cat. I user with specific legal restrictions regarding exchange and processing of

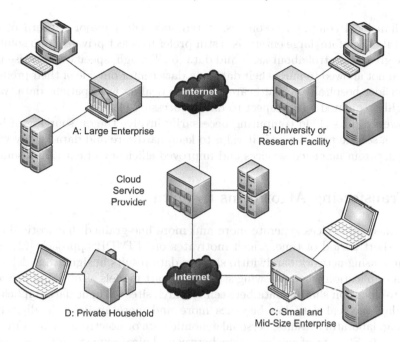

Fig. 2. Categories of cloud service users.

data are not addressed, yet. We focus on the latter group in the remainder of the work focusing on how to enable them to benefit from cloud services, integrating their existing computing resources, and keeping their data on premise.

From an engineering perspective, consolidation of existing hardware resources in data centers, improved use of asset utilization, and near-instantaneous increase and reductions in capacity are obvious benefits of cloud computing [16]. From a business perspective, TCO are optimized by incorporating cloud computing since the service provider is able to deploy processes and tools that enable management of hundreds or thousands of similar systems at the same time, e.g. to perform regular software updates on all systems in parallel. Cloud computing provides a moderate way of scaling for end users, i.e. they can transparently extend their hardware resources for a selected period of time without the need to have the maximum capacity of required hardware permanently available [2]. For example, consider an online shop of a department house, which needs additional resources during seasonal sales.

A major concern of private and enterprise consumers equally to use cloud computing infrastructure is the privacy of their data once they are moved to the cloud, e.g. accidental disclosure or targeted attacks [22]. For private users, it might be acceptable to move photos, videos, or music to cloud storages since they believe these data only have individual value. For enterprises, it would be a fiasco if confidential data stored in cloud storage is exposed to unauthorized persons, e.g. competitors. Although the cloud storages are often maintained at a higher level than local computer resources, it remains still a major concern of end-users [14]. Therefore, large enterprises still prefer to select private cloud solutions to have greater control about asset and data [6]. Though, specific enterprise users are even not allowed to move their data to a data center outside of their premises, e.g. consider hospitals or healthcare providers dealing with patient data, which are highly regulated with respect to data processing [4].

However, does cloud computing necessarily involve the outsourcing of hardware to a service provider or is it valid to keep hardware and data locally whilst benefiting from managed services and improved efficiency of existing resources?

4   Transferring Algorithms to Data

Latest medical devices generate more and more fine-grained diagnostic data in a very short period of time, which motivates our FIMDB approach [21]. Even with increasing network bandwidth, sharing data results in significant delay due to data duplication when following state-of-the-art models as outlined in Sect. 6. Thus, we focus on sharing data between research sites without data duplication.

Today, medical data has becomes more and more available in digital formats, e.g. laboratory results, personal genomic data or Electronic Health Records (EHR) [13]. Sharing of medical data between clinical experts and the integration into clinical software systems is the foundation for discovery of new medical insights [28]. However, personal data requires very specific handling and exchange is limited, e.g. due to legal and privacy regulations, such as the Data Protection Directive of the European Union [8]. The collaboration of international life science research centers and hospitals all over the globe is important to support the finding of new scientific insights, e.g. by sharing of selected knowledge about existing patient cases. However, collaborations face today various IT challenges, e.g. heterogeneous data formats and requirements for data privacy.

4.1   Interconnecting International Genomic Research Centers

What is the meaning of sharing data in the era of cloud computing? To discuss this, we consider the following real-world example. A clinician needs to choose the optimal chemotherapy for a tumor patient once the tumor has been removed. Therefore, the clinician orders whole genome sequencing of the tumor sample to identify driver mutations. The tumor sample is sent to the pathology department to perform the required wet lab work. Data acquired from NGS devices result in up to 750 GB of raw data per single patient, which requires data pre-processing steps, such as alignment of chunks to a reference and variant calling, prior to its use in context of clinical decision support [25]. The latter requires dedicated bioinformatics expertise, hardware and software expertise, and trained staff on site, which results in additional costs for hospitals. Instead of the local department of pathology, a cloud service provider can provide tools for data analysis, trained staff, and required hardware in a more efficient way by offering the same service to multiple clients.

When considering an exclusively available 1 Gb network connection between the local site and the cloud service provider and a payload bandwidth ratio of 75 %, it consumes 8,000 s or approx. 2 h 14 m to transfer the data from the local site to the cloud service before any processing can start.

Our FIMDB system builds on the observation that a significant amount of time is consumed by transferring big medical data sets to computing resources before the actual processing can start. If the time for data transfer exceeds the execution time of the algorithms by far, it might be more efficient to transfer algorithms or database queries to the local site instead and process data locally. Thus, only the algorithms need to be transferred, which is typically orders of magnitudes smaller in size than the data to be processed. Examples for algorithms are alignment and variant calling tools in the size of some MB instead of hundreds of GB of raw data per tumor sample. For example, 14 MB for GATK 3.1.1 variant calling algorithm is exchanged within approx. 0.15 s in our real-world example.

However, does the idea of transferring algorithms instead of data conflicts with sharing data? We define "data sharing" as the process of granting access to a data set without the need to replicate it, i.e. sharing does not involve copying. Eliminating the need for data replication results in the following advantages when dealing with big medical data sets:

- No latency for data processing as big medical data resides locally,
- Single source of truth eliminating data redundancy, and
- Changes are applied directly to original data eliminating sync conflicts.

4.2 Patient Data vs. Master Data

In the following, we distinguish data in regard to their privacy as patient and master data. Patient data subsumes all kinds of personal data referring to an individual, e.g. name, birth date or personal genome, which involve specific steps to guarantee privacy. In contrast, master data refers to all kinds of sharable data required for various data operations, e.g. disease classifications, publications, or genomic annotations, which are not translational nature. As master data is rarely updated, existing caching approaches are efficient, which keeps master data transfer at a minimum, e.g. local file system cache or database result caches.

Based on this classification, patient data is considered as sensitive data that needs to reside at their current locations, e.g. at the local hospital site, to comply with privacy regulations. In contrast, master data will be managed at the central site to optimize maintenance, but can also be shared across and accessed by various sites, e.g. the genome annotations that can be incorporated to perform local genome data analysis.

4.3 Managed Services

Cloud-based infrastructures also offer managed services, e.g. which are hosted, configured and maintained by the service provider keeping the costs for operation minimal from the customers perspective. This approach is also referred to as SaaS or hosted software, where the complete maintenance effort for the software is handled by the service provider [2]. Providing access to managed services requires the isolation of customer-specific data, e.g. the execution details of specific genome data analyses. As patient data are not copied to the service provider there is no need for additional data privacy and security measures.

With regards to complexity of genome data processing and analysis, the advantages of hosted services should also be available for a federated system. As a result, we consider the provision of managed services as an integral aspect for a next-generation genome data processing and analysis platform [21]. The provider of the managed services has the required expertise in bioinformatics, software engineering as well as access to infrastructure and hosting structures. It manages algorithms for processing of medical data and maintains all master data incorporated by the algorithms at the central site.

Consuming Managed Services. A customer accesses the managed service of the service provider, e.g. a web application provided via an internal web page. The customer uses her/his credentials for authentication and to protect customer-specific data and results. The service provider manages the web application and the logon centrally. The customer needs to specify additional input parameters, e.g. local patient data, depending on the application's purpose. In the aforementioned NGS use case, a clinician wants to process the raw NGS data acquired by a sequencing device in the department of pathology. The clinician creates a new task using the web application. Reference genome and genetic annotation data are considered as master data whilst patient-specific NGS data obtained from the tumor sample are considered as patient data. The service provider manages the master data and the web application whilst patient data must reside at the local site within the department of pathology.

Data Processing. We refer to hardware at the customer site as local computing resources whilst we refer to remote computing resources for infrastructure physically hosted at the service provider. Processing of sensitive, patient-specific data is performed on the local computing resources only. All local and remote computing resources together form the FIMDB system, which might also involve multiple distributed sites connected to a single infrastructure provided by a service provider. Local hard- and software needs to be configured once to connect to the existing FIMDB system using existing infrastructure components, e.g. Virtual Private Network (VPN). Furthermore, apps need to be configured, e.g. to incorporate master data provided by the service provider. Master data are shared using established network protocols, which implement caching strategies to minimize network traffic, e.g. Common Internet File System (CIFS), Server Message Block (SMB), or Network File System (NFS).

Setup and Configuration to Access Managed Service. The site administrator performs the following steps once during setup phase to connect a local site to the FIMDB system:

- Establish site-to-site VPN connection with the service provider [20],
- Configure services directory exposed by the services provider locally, which contains managed algorithms for execution on local data,
- Install local IMDB instances and join them to the FIMDB system,
- Subscribe to selected app, and
- Configure app, e.g. user accounts, home directory, and access rights.

The application user performs the following steps to consume managed services from the FIMDB as part of their daily work:

- Log in to managed app with personal credentials,
- Application-specific configuration, e.g. specify FASTQ files for processing,
- Trigger service execution, e.g. submit request to process local files, and
- Investigate results, e.g. use genome browser to analyze genetic variants.

5   Use Case: Processing and Analysis of Genome Data

In the following, we outline the required steps (a) performed once to join our FIMDB and (b) configure a managed service as defined in Sect. 4.3. Our use case focuses on processing and analyzing of NGS data provided as managed service. NGS data is created at decentralized research sites or sequencing centers and must reside locally due to legal restrictions for patient-specific data. However, to assess treatment alternatives, the comparison of the concrete patient case with similar patient cases stored at individual partner sites is required. Both, research and managed services sites, may consist of multiple computing nodes, e.g. in our real-world use case the research site was equipped with 150 and the service provider with 25 computing nodes.

5.1   VPN Connection

The network team of the local IT department needs to install and configure the VPN client. For the application scenario, OpenVPN version 2.3.5 was used and configured to establishing a secured bidirectional site-to-site VPN tunnel. The VPN tunnel connects the Local Area Networks (LANs) at site A and site B via the public Internet as depicted in Fig. 3. In the typical VPN setup multiple VPN clients connect to a corporate network via a single VPN server, i.e. the corporate network is extended and clients consume corporate services in the same way they would access them being physically connected to the corporate network. In contrast, the site-to-site setup connects multiple LANs with each other, i.e. multiple LANs are connected forming a dedicated virtual network across all network topologies being able to create any kind of point-to-point connections. In the given application scenario, the local research site configured a single system as gateway system for the VPN connection while the updated network routes were pushed to individual computing nodes. Thus, the configuration efforts were minimized while a single point of maintenance was established.

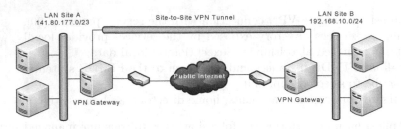

Fig. 3. Site-to-site VPN interconnecting LANs of site A and site B.

5.2   Configure Remote Services Directory

In the application scenario, services are either file- or database-based. File-based services, e.g. the alignment algorithms Burrows Wheeler Aligner (BWA) or Bowtie, are exposed as runtime binaries via a NFS share [17,18]. Therefore, the service consumer needs to create a local mount point and add the configuration for automatically mounting the remote service directory to its local computing nodes. In our given scenario, local sites integrated the configuration in their puppet scripts to automatically deploy configuration to all computing nodes. Database-based services, e.g. stored procedures or analytical queries, are deployed via the database layer of the FIMDB system. They are accessible once local database instances are connected to the FIMDB landscape without additional configuration.

5.3   Install Local IMDB Database Instance

For each local computing node, a dedicated database instance needs to be installed and configured to connect to the FIMDB landscape. We incorporated SAP HANA version 1.00.82.394270 as our in-memory database system in landscape mode to form a distributed database [7]. The required database software is provided via the dedicated remote services directory. Thus, after mounting the services directory, the installation of the local database instance needs to be performed. For minimizing the efforts of installing the database instances, we incorporated the parameter-based installation, i.e. all parameters for the installation were predefined and provided as command parameters, which was executed in parallel across all nodes at the same time using the Linux tool Parallel Distributed SHell (PDSH) version 2.29 [11]. As a result, the required binaries were copied to the local database nodes, the local instances started, and registered online with the SAP HANA master server without any configuration downtime of the FIMDB system. In the concrete use case, the service provider invokes the SAP HANA Database Lifecycle Manager with the addhosts command [23]:

```
./hdblcm --action=add_hosts --addhosts=node-01,...,node-25
```

5.4   Subscribe to Managed Service

In the given application scenario, the managed service for processing and analysis of genome data was provided as a web application, which was accessible via any Internet browser. The web application was hosted at the site of the service provider and can be accessed by users using the URL of the application. The service provider supports the use of local user accounts and the integration of existing authentication providers, e.g. OAuth 2.0, for authentication [12].

Customer. The application administrator of the research site subscribes to the managed services for the entire site or research department and access is granted to administer the application and settings. She/he is responsible to maintain user groups and access rights for users of the research site within the application. The application administrator performs the mapping of application users to corresponding database users and roles while the service provider maintains users and roles in the database.

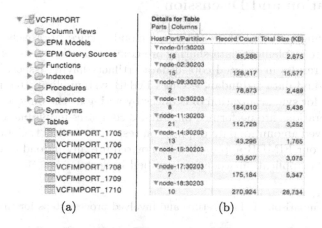

(a)   (b)

Fig. 4. Screenshots: (a) Database schema of the FIMDB grouping tables, functions, and stored procedures; (b) partitioning details of a FIMDB table.

Service Provider. The service provider defines a dedicated database schema per site. A database schema is a container for a set of database tables, functions, and stored procedures as depicted in Fig. 4 on the left. Each database schema is kept isolated, i.e. tenant-specific data is separated to ensure data privacy [24]. The database administrator maintains specific user roles per tenant and grants them access to their tenant-specific database schemes. Each database schema is partitioned across a tenant-specific resource set, i.e. a local subset of the overall computing nodes, which are used for storing and processing the data. The database administrator can update the list of computing nodes online without interfering running operations, i.e. data is repartitioned without any database downtime. Furthermore, the FIMDB administrator can assign additional resources to a resource set, e.g. to ensure scalability by adding resources of the service provider. Figure 4 on the right depicts selected details of a database table partitioned across the FIMDB. For example, the first line describes that database table chunk 16, which has a cardinality of 85,286 entries and a size of 2.6 MB, is stored on the computing resource named node-01.

5.5   Configure Selected Service

The user of the research site accesses the managed service using the URL of the web application. The web application is accessed via the VPN connection, i.e. all data is exchanged via the secured tunnel. The end user is able to maintain her/his personal profile and configure application settings. In the application scenario, each end user was able to define her/his local home directory, which contains all genome data they were working on.

6   Evaluation and Discussion

In the following, selected state-of-the-art cloud service approaches and their applicability to implement data sharing are compared. We are focusing on data sharing as it results in isolated copied data artifacts having issues, e.g. conflict management and data redundancy. Our FIMDB system eliminates redundancy and the need for synchronization of changes by acting as the only source of data where all operations are performed on. Table 3 compares individual cloud setups and the involved amount of data duplication resp. data transfer. Compared to all other setups, our FIMDB approach does not require any upload of data, which is shown in the application scenario described in Sect. 5.

Table 3. Comparison of cloud setups and involved process steps for sharing data.

Description	Sect. 6.1	Sect. 6.2	Sect. 6.3	Sect. 6.4	Sect. 6.5
Export data from local system at site A	✓	✓	✗	✗	✗
Upload local data to shared cloud storage or cloud app resp	✓	✓	✓	✓	✗
Sync data between shared cloud services or cloud apps resp	✓	✗	✓	✗	✗
Sync data from cloud service B to local site B	✓	✓	✗	✗	✗
Import local data at site B to local system B	✓	✓	✗	✗	✗

6.1   Local Systems and Multiple Cloud Service Providers

Sharing data from a local system, e.g. a Hospital Information System (HIS), via a single cloud service involves individual cloud service provider per local site as depicted in Fig. 5. Local site A uses cloud provider A whilst local site B uses cloud provider B. Synchronization between local sites and their cloud service provider as well as between multiple cloud service providers is required.

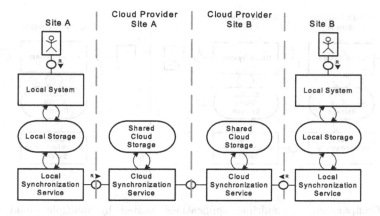

Fig. 5. Multiple sites interconnected via individual cloud providers.

6.2 Local Systems and Single Cloud Service Provider

The current configuration incorporates a single cloud provider used by all involved local sites instead of multiple cloud service provides as given in Sect. 6.1. Regular data synchronization between local sites A, B, and the shared cloud storage of the cloud provider occurs. It involves data ex- and import from local systems, i.e. data duplication requiring conflict management. A single cloud service provider is usually in place when you need to rely on locally installed software at various sites. It can be considered as a first transition towards a cloud-based software deployment model [19].

6.3 Cloud-Based Software of Different Cloud Service Providers

Sharing data between apps of different cloud providers requires data synchronization as described in Sect. 6.2. Figure 6 on the left depicts two sites A and B interconnected via individual cloud service providers hosting individual apps. Data synchronization is performed transparently between cloud service centers of individual providers using high-speed interconnections. Due to higher network bandwidth, data exchange requires less time than data exchanged between cloud provider and local site. This approach offers full flexibility in terms of incorporated cloud software and local IT optimization. However, it requires high-speed interconnections between cloud providers and still results in data duplication.

6.4 Cloud-Based Software of a Single Service Provider

Figure 6 on the right depicts two sites A and B using one app provided by a single cloud service provider. Working with a cloud-based application of a single provider does not eliminate the initial upload and import of data from the local site. However, the need for synchronization and conflict management are eliminated. Thus, only a single data transfer from all participating local sites to the cloud service provider is required.

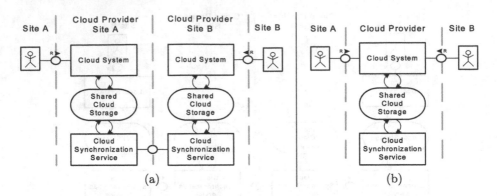

Fig. 6. Comparison: (a) multiple applications hosted by multiple cloud service providers; (b) single application hosted by the same cloud service provider.

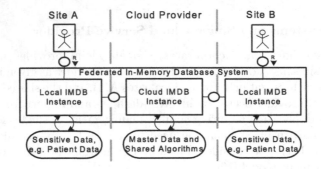

Fig. 7. Multiple IMDB instances forming the FIMDB.

6.5   Federated In-memory Database Systems

Our FIMDB system eliminates even the initial data transfer to the cloud as discussed in Sect. 6.4 by importing data directly into the local database instance as depicted in Fig. 7. When incorporating our FIMDB system, there is no need to upload data via the Internet connection to a central cloud provider. Required algorithms and methods are either downloaded from the service directory, e.g. software executed by the OS, or accessed via the FIMDB system, e.g. stored database procedures. For distributed execution of the algorithms and management of results, we incorporate our worker framework [21]. It is a dedicated runtime environment for executing arbitrary programs on either the operating system or database level. Thus, the FIMDB system eliminates processing latency due to data transfer while offering full access control for sensitive data by keeping them always on local hardware.

7   Conclusion and Outlook

In the given work, we presented details about our unique hybrid cloud computing approach enabling (a) the use of cloud service even if legal requirements do not allow exchange of sensitive data with traditional cloud apps and (b) the processing of huge data sets locally when their exchange would significantly delay the processing of data even with latest network bandwidths.

Based on a real-world scenario, we shared experiences implementing our cloud approach in a concrete life sciences use case. As a result, we were able to provide managed apps for research without moving high volume NGS data to central computing resources. For that, all local sites were interconnected via the Internet to our service infrastructure using secured VPN connection. Data was processed decentralized and results stored only in local database systems, which were configured to form our distributed FIMDB system.

We are convinced that sharing knowledge is the foundation to support research cooperation and to discover new insights cooperatively. Thus, our future work will focus on how to use our FIMDB system to encourage sharing of huge dataset in life sciences between research facilities without the need to create duplicates of sensitive data at partner sites.

References

1. Amazon Web Services, Inc.: Amazon Elastic Computing Cloud (EC2), July 2015. http://aws.amazon.com/ec2/Jul27. Accessed 10 Dec 2018
2. Armbrust, M., et al.: A view of cloud computing. Commun. ACM **53**(4), 50–58 (2010)
3. Bhuvaneshwar, K., et al.: A case study for cloud-based high-throughput analysis of NGS data using the globus genomics system. Comput. Struct. Biotechnol. J. **13**, 64–74 (2015)
4. Bundesärztekammer und Kassenärztliche Vereinigung: Empfehlungen zur ärztlichen Schweigepflicht, Datenschutz und Datenverarbeitung in der Arztpraxis. Deutsche Ärzteblatt **111**(21), A963–A972 (2014)
5. CERN: gLite - Lightweight Middleware for Grid Computing, April 2014. http://grid-deployment.web.cern.ch/grid-deployment/glite-web/introductionJul27. Accessed 10 Dec 2018
6. Everest Global, Inc.: Enterprise Cloud Adoption Survey, March 2014. http://www.everestgrp.com/wp-content/uploads/2014/03/2014-Enterprise-Cloud-Adoption-Survey.pdfDec17. Accessed 10 Dec 2018
7. Färber, F., et al.: SAP HANA database: data management for modern business applications. SIGMOD Rec. **40**(4), 45–51 (2012)
8. Fears, R., et al.: Data protection regulation and the promotion of health research: getting the balance right. QJM **107**(1), 3–5 (2013)
9. Gartner, Inc.: 2014 Hype Cycle for Emerging Technologies Maps the Journey to Digital Business, August 2014. http://www.gartner.com/newsroom/id/2819918Dec11. Accessed 10 Dec 2018
10. Goecks, J., Nekrutenko, A., Taylor, J., The Galaxy Team: Galaxy: a comprehensive approach for supporting accessible, reproducible, and transparent computational research in the life sciences. Genome Biol. **11**(8), R86 (2010)

11. Grondona, M.A.: Parallel Distributed Shell (PDSH), August 2011. https://code.google.com/p/pdsh/wiki/UsingPDSHNov26. Accessed 10 Dec 2018
12. Hardt, D.: RFC6749: The OAuth 2.0 Authorization Framework, October 2012. http://tools.ietf.org/html/rfc6749/Nov26. Accessed 10 Dec 2018
13. Jensen, P.B., Jensen, L.J., Brunak, S.: Mining electronic health records: towards better research applications and clinical care. Nat. Rev. Genet. **13**(6), 395–405 (2012)
14. Kalloniatis, C., Manousakis, V., Mouratidis, H., Gritzalis, S.: Migrating into the cloud: identifying the major security and privacy concerns. In: Douligeris, C., Polemi, N., Karantjias, A., Lamersdorf, W. (eds.) I3E 2013. IAICT, vol. 399, pp. 73–87. Springer, Heidelberg (2013). https://doi.org/10.1007/978-3-642-37437-1_7
15. Knöpfel, A., Grone, B., Tabeling, P.: Fundamental Modeling Concepts: Effective Communication of IT Systems. Wiley, Hoboken (2006)
16. Kundra, V.: Federal Cloud Computing Strategy, February 2011. http://www.whitehouse.gov/sites/default/files/omb/assets/egov_docs/federal-cloud-computing-strategy.pdfDec15. Accessed 10 Dec 2018
17. Langmead, B., Salzberg, S.L.: Fast gapped read alignment with bowtie 2. Nat. Methods **9**, 357–359 (2012)
18. Li, H., Durbin, R.: Fast and accurate short read alignment with burrows-wheeler transformation. Bioinformatics **25**, 1754–1760 (2009)
19. National Institute of Standards and Technology: The NIST Definition of Cloud-Computing: Recommendations of the National Institute of Standards andTechnology. NIST Special Publication 800-145, September 2011
20. OpenVPN Technologies, Inc.: Site-to-Site Layer 3 Routing Using OpenVPNAccess Server and a Linux Gateway Client, February 2012. https://docs.openvpn.net/. Accessed 10 Dec 2018
21. Plattner, H., Schapranow, M.-P. (eds.): High-Performance In-Memory Genome Data Analysis: How In-Memory Database Technology Accelerates Personalized Medicine. IDMR. Springer, Cham (2014). https://doi.org/10.1007/978-3-319-03035-7
22. Ryan, M.D.: Cloud computing privacy concerns on our doorstep. Commun. ACM **54**(1), 36–38 (2011)
23. SAP SE: Add Hosts Using the Command-Line Interface (2014). http://help.sap.com/saphelp_hanaplatform/helpdata/en/0d/9fe701e2214e98ad4f8721f6558c34/content.htm. Accessed 10 Dec 2018
24. Schaffner, J.: Multi Tenancy for Cloud-Based In-Memory Column Databases: Workload Management and Data Placement. Springer, Heidelberg (2014). https://doi.org/10.1007/978-3-319-00497-6
25. Schapranow, M.P., et al.: In-memory computing enabling real-time genome data analysis. Int. J. Adv. Life Sci. **6**(1 and 2), 11–29 (2014)
26. Srinivasan, S.: Cloud computing evolution. In: Srinivasan, S. (ed.) Cloud Computing Basics. SECE, pp. 1–16. Springer, New York (2014). https://doi.org/10.1007/978-1-4614-7699-3_1
27. The UNICORE Forum e.V.: UNICORE - Documentation, July 2015. https://www.unicore.eu/documentation/Jul27. Accessed 10 Dec 2018
28. Wicks, P., et al.: Sharing health data for better outcomes on PatientsLikeMe. J. Med. Internet Res. **12**(2), e19 (2010)
29. Zhang, Q., Cheng, L., Boutaba, R.: Cloud computing: state-of-the-art and research challenges. J. Internet Serv. Appl. **1**(1), 7–18 (2010)

An Integrated Architecture for Real-Time and Historical Analytics in Financial Services

Lyublena Antova, Rhonda Baldwin, Zhongxian Gu, and F. Michael Waas[✉]

Datometry Inc., 795 Folsom St Ste 100, San Francisco, CA 94107, USA
{lyublena,rhonda,zgu,mike}@datometry.com

Abstract. The integration of historical data has become one of the most pressing issues for the financial services industry: trading floors rely on real-time analytics of ticker data with very strong emphasis on speed, not scale, yet, a large number of critical tasks, including daily reporting and backtesting of models, put emphasis on scale. As a result, implementers continuously face the challenge of having to meet contradicting requirements and either scale real-time analytics technology at considerable cost, or deploy separate stacks for different tasks and keep them synchronized—a solution that is no less costly.

In this paper, we propose *Adaptive Data Virtualization*, as an alternative approach, to overcome this problem. ADV lets applications use different data management technologies without the need for database migrations or re-configuration of applications. We review the incumbent technology and compare it with the recent crop of MPP databases and draw up a strategy that, using ADV, lets enterprises use the right tool for the right job flexibly. We conclude the paper summarizing our initial experience working with customers in the field and outline an agenda for future research.

1 Introduction

The value of Big Data has been recognized universally in recent years, but, truly integrating Big Data technology with existing IT infrastructure and business processes has often remained an elusive goal. In particular, in the financial services industry, the combination of real-time data processing and historical data analysis poses a number of unsolved challenges, see e.g., [1].

Financial institutions have developed sophisticated systems that consume massive amounts of trade-and-quote (TAQ) data at a rapid pace and make split-second decisions in what is called real-time or high frequency trading. In-memory technology, often proprietary and highly specialized, has proven its mettle in this space and is widely accepted as the standard methodology, see e.g., [3,6,7].

However, technology developed for low latency data management cannot be extended easily to tackle Big Data challenges and institutions found themselves facing the uneasy choice between one of the following approaches: (1) use a single

© Springer Nature Switzerland AG 2019
M. Castellanos et al. (Eds.): BIRTE 2015/2016/2017, LNBIP 337, pp. 35–44, 2019.
https://doi.org/10.1007/978-3-030-24124-7_3

architecture, built on in-memory principles and attempt to scale it, or, (2) use a Big Data stack, e.g., MPP databases, Hadoop, or like products in addition to in-memory systems and duplicate all application logic and constantly switch between both architectures. The former entails significant hardware expenses and complexity, the latter poses all sorts of deployment and data management issues and, on top of this, is highly error-prone. In short, both approaches are highly impractical, resource intensive, and economically unattractive. What institutions are really looking for is the ability to access both, real-time and historical data with exactly the same tools and exactly the same applications. And not only the same tool chain but literally the same tools they have developed over the past decades.

Even though the urgency of the problem has accelerated recently, not last because of regulatory and security concerns, vendors have been trying for quite some time already to address the chasm between low-latency and scalable processing. Unfortunately, these approaches focused either on making low-latency in-memory systems scale, or, making scalable, distributed systems respond faster [2,4]. And while the results are respectable in their own right, they continue to fall short of a workable solution, and reconciling the different processing paradigms has long been considered the *Holy Grail* of data processing [1].

In this paper, we devise a research agenda for a radically different approach which we call *Adaptive Data Virtualization (ADV)*. ADV abstracts and impersonates systems: instead of pursuing a "one size fits all approach", ADV enables users to access different data management technologies using the same query language and the same APIs. This way, users can leverage any data management technology—be it in-memory or MPP database systems—within the same application and without interruption of business processes. ADV eliminates the need for costly database migrations and lets business users tap into a variety of data sources, e.g., in-memory, MPP databases, NoSQL systems etc., *without* having to change or re-configure their applications.

Naturally, a complete ADV solution takes considerable effort to build and has yet to reach commercial viability. In this paper, we describe our experience in investigating the space and present learnings regarding use cases, technical difficulties, and desiderata for such a platform. We describe our first experiences with ADV, the challenges we anticipate, and opportunities for future research.

Roadmap. The remainder of this paper is organized as follows. In Sect. 2, we briefly survey the relevant basics of data processing in financial services and present current alternatives on how to address the historical data challenge in Sect. 3. In Sect. 4, we present the concept and benefits of Adaptive Data Virtualization including a catalog of desiderata for successful implementation and adoption.

2   Background

Financial applications, such as *High-Frequency Trading (HFT)*, utilize a specialized environment and proprietary algorithms to profit from the trade of stocks at scale. The HFT world is highly competitive and those that have the fastest access to information and the most sophisticated algorithms are at an advantage. In this section, we describe the general building blocks required by financial applications and introduce the problem of integrating real-time and historical data in financial services.

2.1 Market Data

Market data is the time-series data produced by an entity like a stock exchange. For specification and samples, we refer the reader to the New York Stock Exchange Trades and Quotes (NYSE's TAQ) dataset [5]. Market data is used in real-time to make time-sensitive decisions about trading equities and is also used for historical data applications like predictive modeling, e.g., projecting pricing trends and calculating market risk, and backtesting of trading strategies.

2.2 Environment Building Blocks

A typical trade processing environment is illustrated in Fig. 1.

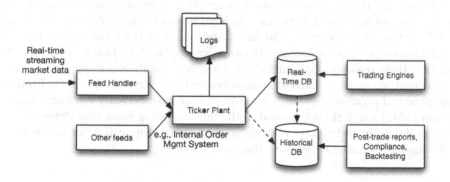

Fig. 1. Typical trade order processing infrastructure

The *feed handler* processes data as it streams in live from an exchange or other data provider. Processing in the feed handler generally includes simple adjustments to the data that are required by the ticker plant, e.g., data type conversion, formatting, removing unnecessary information, etc.

Upon receiving data from the feed handler and other internal feeds, e.g., from an Order Management System, the *ticker plant* logs all data and publishes relevant data to subscribing processes. Clients query the databases for different purposes, including actual trading decisions, post-trade reports, enforcement of regulations (compliance), and backtesting to name just the most prominent.

2.3   Real-Time and Historical Databases

The *real-time database* stores the current day's data in memory to avoid the latency of fetching data from disk. Periodically throughout the day, or in some cases at the end of day, the data is either discarded or saved to disk, freeing up memory to store the latest data from the ticker plant.

In addition to a real-time database, newer environments also include a *historical database* to store several years' worth of data for analytic workloads. In the not-so-distant past, market data was thrown away at the end of the day, after the market closed, but now market data is stored for much longer. Typically data comes directly from the ticker plant or is exported from the real-time database.

2.4   Integration Problem

The need to integrate real-time and historical data is accute in every financial services firm. For example, in an industry where a financial model can make (or cost) the firm millions of dollars, much attention is paid to backtesting: the testing of predictive models using historical data. Given a trading strategy, backtesting predicts the performance of a strategy as if it had been employed in the past. In reality, financial models are very sophisticated, the quantitative researchers who build these models have access to multiple years worth of historical data, and those that backtest and course-correct the fastest have a significant competitive advantage. In other words, the firm that can seamlessly integrate their real-time and historical data, sets itself up for success. In the next section, we consider current approaches to the integration problem. From a more practical point of view, however, compliance with Security Exchange Commission (SEC) regulations is probably the most pressing issue that demands an integrated data infrastructure with cleanly separated responsibilities in the form of checks-and-balances between trading and reporting.

3   Current Approaches

In practice, we see several solution patterns emerging that attempt to solve the integration problem described in the previous section, including the addition of more resources to real-time databases, periodic export of data from real-time to historical databases, and migration to an entirely new technology stack. In this section, we discuss the pros and cons for each of these approaches.

3.1   Scaling In-memory Technology

Scaling an existing in-memory analytics engine by adding memory and CPU cores allows more than the current day's data to fit in memory for analyses, which may be sufficient for a given real-time/historical data integration scenario. This solution seems simple and straight-forward at first, however, it comes with a number of severe drawbacks:

1. Most importantly this approach quickly becomes prohibitively expensive, as the hardware costs associated with expanding real-time systems easily exceed more than 10x the cost of conventional RDBMS technology on commodity hardware.
2. The IT effort required to manage these systems when sharding of data across multiple instances is substantial. In this case, a whole slew of highly challenging distributed systems problems need to be addressed by IT to guarantee flawless operation.
3. Finally, since real-time database systems were built for a very different use case than analytics on historical data, they often lack the compliance, management utilities, and tools required by enterprises when storing massive volumes of historical data, which RDBMS and BI vendors have taken 20–30 years to perfect.

3.2 Multi-stack Environments

Most real-time databases provide export functionality to "integrate" with conventional or MPP database systems.

Freeing up expensive in-memory resources to focus only on real-time analytics and using less-expensive data stores for historical data is a significant cost-saver. Many financial firms are considering options like moving archival data to Hadoop and historical data that will be used heavily for analytics to a shared-nothing MPP database. Over the past years, MPP databases have further improved with regards to performance, scalability, and manageability and continue to provide major innovations, such as Pivotal Greenplum Database's recent advances in query optimization [8].

One of the big detractors to this approach is the additional intermediate steps required to aggregate result sets from different interfaces for real-time and historical databases. Also, since the interfaces and technology stacks are different, the people and skills required to manage and use both stacks are very different. This is a limiting factor in the case of backtesting financial models, for example, where a "quant"/statistician may write the real-time model in a language that he/she is familiar and not have the experience or desire to use a separate interface for back-testing. Moreover, it may a substantial amount of non-trivial work to translate a model or query written for one database to work on another.

In financial institutions, a single source of truth is especially critical for compliance; another concern is the risk associated with exporting data. Movement of data introduces risk of loss or unavailability and the existence of multiple data copies introduces risk of mis-management.

3.3 Migration to Latest Technology

Starting over from scratch and building out a new environment could be the answer in some situations. Certainly the opportunity to retire old infrastructure to bring in new technology, may be advantageous for financial institutions to keep up with the pace of innovation and competitors, especially new fin-tech startups.

Unfortunately it is difficult to migrate from one environment to another. It causes substantial disruptions to the business over extended periods of time. While moving data between database systems is relatively easy, migration of applications can take up to one or more years in practice, depending on the number of applications that need to be migrated.

Given institutions' investment of 20+ years in the incumbent technology, migrating is highly unattractive from a cost perspective. Not last, a migration is a big bet and runs the risk to stunt innovation over extended periods of time with uncertain outcome. The next innovation cycle may make the newly adopted systems obsolete in only a few years.

4   Adaptive Data Virtualization

Adaptive Data Virtualization (ADV) is the concept of abstracting a data management system in a way that, simply put, lets a native application written for system X run on system Y. It eliminates the problems detailed above and enable business users to access data across the enterprise readily. Using ADV, IT gets to choose the appropriate backend database based on requirements such as scalability, performance, or cost etc., but, importantly, independent of the choice of application business users make. Figure 2 highlights the basic components and their interplay. In the financial services industry, this means workloads like reporting, compliance, or backtesting, for which in-memory technology was an accidental choice at best, can now be off-loaded to systems that are much better suited while real-time use cases continue to run on in-memory systems.

We propose ADV as the natural extension of *data virtualization* in general. DV is loosely defined as the concept of making different data sources accessible to a central component. However, DV does not *adapt* to the existing applications and therefore requires business users to migrate to new APIs and query language—this time the APIs and query language of the DV system, not of a specific back-end database. Commercial DV products are available and have seen uptake in the industry wherever data federation is needed, i.e., the combining of data from different data sources, see for example [9].

4.1   Approach

The idea to ADV arose from our work with customers and frequently recurring requests by customers wanting to access data or migrate applications to different databases to meet additional requirements such as scalability, availability or simply reduce cost. However, migrations rank among the most costly and disruptive IT operations imaginable. In particular, having witnessed countless migrations in the data warehousing space, we are keenly aware of where most of the effort in a migration needs to be placed.

Fig. 2. Architecture overview (example Q/KDB+ to PostgreSQL compatible DBs)

We set out to accomplish the vision of ADV by reviewing and investigating the technical underpinnings needed for this undertaking. The following is a list of desiderata and an architectural blueprint for an implementation:

Platform Architecture. One of the most important requirements from a practitioner's point of view is that neither the application nor the backend databases need to be re-configured. This prohibits not only the recompiling of applications but also re-configurations such as loading different database connectors, including ODBC/JDBC drivers. Hence, ADV needs to be implemented as an *independent platform* completely transparent to the applications and the underlying database systems (see Fig. 2).

Trade-offs in Performance. To be successful, an ADV platform must provide acceptable performance. We deliberately use the term *acceptable* instead of, say, comparable. Replacing in-memory technology with a disk-based system trades off latency with throughput and scale. As emphasized above, ADV enables choosing the right technology for a workload rather than replacing databases wholesale. On top of this, the overhead incurred by the ADV platform must be insignficant.

Expressivity. Enabling an application to run on any other database than the one it was written for requires a sufficiently complete implementation of all critical query and command language elements. In preparations for our undertaking we classified workloads that we obtained from customers by the feature surface they are using. Not surprisingly a non-trivial number of features in the source system are virtually unused. In contrast, the lion share of queries in a workload use only a astonishingly small portion of the available features.

Security. For practical viability, ADV has to be able to integrate with security and other IT services. We found this usually requires a deep integration with the wire protocols of source and target systems in addition to a language integration.

The above is by no means a complete list, however, in our research we found these to be the most pressing requirements as emphasized by prospects and customers.

5   State of Development

In this paper we report on ongoing research. A first implementation of a complete ADV system is currently underway at Datometry under the product name Datometry Hyper-Q. In its present state, the system supports applications written using Q and KDB+, the market leader and most prevalent real-time analytics engine in the financial services industry (see e.g., [3]) and backend databases of the PostgreSQL family, including PostgreSQL 9.x [12], AWS Redshift [10], IBM Netezza [11], Pivotal Greenplum Database and HAWQ [8], etc.

Our system accepts connection request in Q's wire-protocol QIPC, parses query and command language requests, represents them in a more powerful extensible algebra before converting them into one or more requests in SQL for the target system and encodes it using the PGv3 wire protocol. Results retrieved from the database are translated back into the QIPC data format.

5.1   Challenges

The above sketched translation on-the-fly poses various challenges, most of which are highly intricate and in the intrest of space we can only briefly survey the most prominent categories. In the following, we enumerate the categories which in our exprience have solicited the most frequently asked questions in discussions with prospects and customers:

Query Language. KDB+'s query language Q descends from APL and while a functional programming language like SQL is quite different from the latter. Yet, despite significant syntax differences, both languages are Turing complete and for practical purposes can express the same queries. For a discussion of Q see e.g., [3].

Data Model. The PostgreSQL family's traditional row-based model stands in stark contrast to KDB+'s column model. Being a physical design choice, however, it is of little relevance for the language translation but must be taken into account in translation of the wire protocol, see below.

Wire Protocol. RDBMS's support elaborate protocols that are often burdened with support for esoteric connection details. KDB+'s protocol supports a much smaller number of use cases and therefore meshes well with a more elaborate protocol.

ACID properties. Given the primary use cases for which KDB+ was developed, it has little need for the classic ACID properties. However, implementing the same semantics—in particular the reliance on being single-threaded to ensure transactional semantics—on a full-fledge ACID system is quite straightforward.

Data Types. Data types are often proprietary to a given database, yet, in practice the vast majority of workloads we have dealt with, including our 20+ years of experience in implementing database technology, rely on a small number of universally available types. The ability to nest types or enforce total order on objects are usually sufficiently supported by the target systems–be it directly or in the form of workarounds.

Naturally, most of our work has been invested in the language cross-compilation but suffice it to say, for the product to be successful all dimensions of the problem need to be addressed accordingly.

In its current development, Hyper-Q supports Q applications to run on PostgreSQL-compatible systems. Support for additional systems including support for PostgreSQL applications to run on KDB+ will be added based on market demand.

5.2 State of Product

Datometry Hyper-Q is currently in private beta with well-known customers in the financial services industry and initial feedback has been overwhelmingly positive. We expect to be able to report on initial field experience with the system in production soon.

6 Summary

In this paper we presented the concept of *Adaptive Data Virtualization*, a novel type of data virtualization that enables applications to run on alternative database systems. ADV is the result of our experience of over 15 years in implementing commercial database systems and the realization that breaking open data silos requires an approach that enables applications to move freely between different data management systems without the painful burden of re-compiling or re-configuring them.

We reported on ongoing work, including the primary requirements for the success of this type of platform. However, the initial success of the platform we created, indicates a strong interest in the market for this type of technology—not only in the financial services industry.

We firmly believe ADV is the starting point of fundamental transformation of the database industry, moving away from an market place in which databases dictate one of the strongest vendor lock-ins in the IT industry, to an open environment where databases become an interchangeable commodity.

References

1. Garland, S.: Big Data Analytics: Tackling the Historical Data Challenge. Wired Magazine, Innovation Insights, October 2014
2. SAP HANA, May 2015. http://hana.sap.com/abouthana.html
3. Kx Systems, May 2015. http://kx.com
4. MemSQL, May 2015. http://www.memsql.com
5. New York Stock Exchange: Market Data, Data Products-Daily TAQ, May 2015. http://www.nyxdata.com/Data-Products/Daily-TAQ
6. Security Technology Analysis Center: STAC Benchmark Council-Various Benchmark Results, May 2015. http://stacresearch.com/research
7. Shasha, D.: KDB+ Database and Language Primer. Kx Systems, May 2005. http://kx.com/q/d/primer.htm

8. Soliman, M., et al.: Orca: a modular query optimizer architecture for big data. In: ACM SIGMOD Conference, May 2014
9. Informatica, May 2015. http://www.informatica.com
10. Amazon Redshift, May 2015. http://aws.amazon.com/redshift
11. IBM Netezza, May 2015. www.ibm.com/software/data/netezza
12. PostgreSQL, May 2015. http://www.postgresql.org

Processing of Aggregate Continuous Queries in a Distributed Environment

Anatoli U. Shein$^{(\boxtimes)}$, Panos K. Chrysanthis, and Alexandros Labrinidis

Department of Computer Science, University of Pittsburgh,
Pittsburgh, PA 15260, USA
{aus,panos,labrinid}@cs.pitt.edu

Abstract. Data Stream Management Systems (*DSMSs*) performing online analytics rely on the efficient execution of large numbers of Aggregate Continuous Queries (*ACQs*). In this paper, we study the problem of generating high quality execution plans of *ACQs* in *DSMSs* deployed on multi-node (multi-core and multi-processor) distributed environments. Towards this goal, we classify optimizers based on how they partition the workload among computing nodes and on their usage of the concept of *Weavability*, which is utilized by the state-of-the-art *WeaveShare* optimizer to selectively combine *ACQs* and produce low cost execution plans for single-node environments. For each category, we propose an optimizer, which either adopts an existing strategy or develops a new one for assigning and grouping *ACQs* to computing nodes. We implement and experimentally compare all of our proposed optimizers in terms of (1) keeping the total cost of the *ACQs* execution plan low and (2) balancing the load among the computing nodes. Our extensive experimental evaluation shows that our newly developed *Weave-Group to Nodes* (WG_{TN}) and *Weave-Group Inserted* (WG_I) optimizers produce plans of significantly higher quality than the rest of the optimizers. WG_{TN} minimizes the total cost, making it more suitable from a client perspective, and WG_I achieves load balancing, making it more suitable from a system perspective.

1 Introduction

Nowadays, more and more applications are becoming available to wider audiences, resulting in an increasing amount of data being produced. A large volume of this generated data often takes the form of high velocity streams. At the same time, online data analytics have gained momentum in many applications that need to ingest data fast and apply some form of computation, such as predicting outcomes and trends for timely decision making.

In order to meet the near-real-time requirements of these applications, Data Stream Management Systems (*DSMS*) [4,5,18,24,25] have been developed to efficiently process large amounts of data arriving with high velocities in the form of streams. In *DSMSs*, clients register their analytics queries, which consist of one or more *Aggregate Continuous Queries* (*ACQs*). *ACQs* continuously aggregate streaming data and periodically produce results such as *max*, *count*, *sum*, and *average*.

© Springer Nature Switzerland AG 2019
M. Castellanos et al. (Eds.): BIRTE 2015/2016/2017, LNBIP 337, pp. 45–62, 2019.
https://doi.org/10.1007/978-3-030-24124-7_4

A representative example of online analytics can be found in stock market web applications where multiple clients monitor price fluctuations of stocks. In this setting, a system needs to be able to answer analytical queries (i.e., average stock revenue or profit margin per stock) for different clients, each one with potentially different relaxation requirements in terms of accuracy.

Another example is the monitoring of personal health data (e.g., heart beats per minute) and physical activity data (e.g., number of steps walked, number of miles ran) of individuals, along with location and environmental data (e.g., barometric pressure), generated by devices such as Fitbit, Apple iWatch, etc. This data serves as input to a set of monitoring applications, which are implemented as *ACQs* that may execute for a user or on behalf of a user such as by the user's primary care physician or health insurance companies to which the user may have only allowed aggregate-level queries.

The accuracy of an *ACQ* can be thought of as the window in which the aggregation takes place and the period at which the answer is recalculated. Periodic properties that are used to describe *ACQs* are *range* (**r**) and *slide* (**s**) (sometimes also referred to as *window* and *shift* [13], respectively). A slide denotes the interval at which an *ACQ* updates its result; a range is the time window for which the statistics are calculated. For example, if a stock monitoring application has a slide of 3 s and a range of 5 s, it means that the application needs an updated result every 3 s, and the result should be derived from data accumulated over the past 5 s.

DSMSs are required to maintain *ACQs'* state over time, while performing aggregations. *ACQs* with a larger range will have a higher cost to maintain its state (memory) and compute its results (CPU). The most space and time efficient method to compute aggregations is to run partial aggregations on the data while accumulating it, and then produce the answer by performing the final aggregation over the partial results (Sect. 2).

In order to cope with the sheer volume of information, enterprises move to distributed processing infrastructures such as local clusters or the *Cloud*. The deployment of *DSMSs* to *Cloud* results in multi-tenant settings, where multiple *ACQs* with even more diverse periodic properties are executed on the same hardware.

Problem Statement. It is safe to say that the efficiency of *DSMSs* deployed on multiple multi-core computing nodes depends on the *intelligent* collocation of *ACQs* operating on the same data streams and calculating similar aggregate operations. If such *ACQs* have similarities in their periodic properties, the opportunity to share final and partial results arises, which can reduce the overall processing costs.

Typically, the number of *ACQs* with similar aggregation types for a given data stream can be overwhelming in online systems [5]. Therefore, it is crucial for the system to be able to make decisions quickly on combining different *ACQs* in such a way that would benefit the system. Unfortunately, this has been proven to be NP-hard [27], and, currently, only approximation algorithms can produce acceptable execution plans. For instance, the state-of-the-art *WeaveShare* optimizer [12], which selectively combines *ACQs* and produces high quality plans, is theoretically guaranteed to approximate the optimal cost-savings to within a factor of four for practical variants of the problem [8].

Under these circumstances, *it is vital to develop efficient data sharing schemes among ACQs that lead to an effective assignment of ACQs to computing nodes.*

Our Approach. The state-of-the-art *WeaveShare* optimizer is a cost-based *ACQ* optimizer that produces low cost execution plans by utilizing the concept of

Weavability [12]. Since *WeaveShare* is targeting single-node *DSMSs*, it is oblivious to distributed processing capabilities, and as our experiments have revealed, *WeaveShare* cannot produce *ACQ* execution plans of equivalent cost that can be assigned to the various computing nodes. This motivated us to address the problem of generating high quality execution plans of *ACQs* in *DSMSs* deployed on multi-node (multi-core and multi-processor) distributed environments with a *Weavability*-based optimizer.

Formally, given a set $\mathcal{Q}$ of all *ACQs* submitted by all clients and a set $\mathcal{N}$ of all available computing nodes in the distributed *DSMS*, our goal is to find an execution plan $\mathcal{P}(\mathcal{Q}, \mathcal{N}, \mathcal{T})$ that maps $\mathcal{Q}$ to $\mathcal{N}$ ($\mathcal{Q} \rightarrow \mathcal{N}$) and generates a set $\mathcal{T}$ of local *ACQ* execution trees per node, such that the total cost of the *ACQs* execution is low and the load among the computing nodes is balanced.

The rationale behind these two optimization criteria is (Sect. 3):

- *Minimizing the total cost* of the execution plan allows the system to support more *ACQs*. In the case of the *Cloud*, since *Cloud* providers charge money for the computation resources, satisfying more client requests using the same resources results in less costly client requests.
- *Balancing the workload* among computation nodes saves energy while still meeting the requirements of the installed *ACQs*, which directly translates to monetary savings for the distributed infrastructure providers. Additionally, it is advantageous for the providers to maintain load balancing, because it prevents the need to over-provision in order to cope with unbalanced workloads.

Contributions. We make the following contributions:

- We explore the challenges of producing high quality execution plans for distributed processing environments and categorize possible *ACQ* optimizers for these environments based on how they utilize the concept of Weavability for cost-based optimization as shown in Table 1 (Sect. 4).
- We propose an *ACQ* optimizer for each category. These optimizers either adopt an existing strategy or develop a new one for assigning and grouping *ACQs* to computing nodes. (Sects. 5 and 6)
- We experimentally evaluate our optimizers and show that our newly developed *Weave-Group to Nodes* optimizer is the most effective in terms of minimizing the total cost of the execution plan, making it more suitable from the clients' perspective, and our *Weave-Group Inserted* optimizer is the most effective in terms of achieving load balance, making it more suitable from a system perspective. Both produce quality plans that are orders of magnitude better than the other optimizers (Sect. 7).

2 Background

In this section we briefly review the underlying concepts of our work, namely *partial aggregation* and *Weavability*.

Partial aggregation was proposed to improve the processing of *ACQs* [10, 15–17]. The idea behind partial aggregation is to calculate partial aggregates over a number of partitions, then assemble the final answer by performing the final aggregation over these aggregates. As opposed to partial aggregation in traditional database systems where partitioning is value-based, partial aggregation in *DSMSs* uses time-based (or tuple-based) partitioning.

Partial aggregations, as shown in Fig. 1, are implemented as *two-level operator trees*, consisting of the partial- or sub-aggregator and the final-aggregator. The *Paired Window* technique, [15], also shown in Fig. 1, is the most efficient implementation of partial aggregations. This technique does not assume any relation between range and slide and uses two fragment lengths, g_1 and g_2, where $g_1 = range\%slide$ and $g_2 = slide - g_2$. Partial aggregations are computed at periods of fragment g_1 and fragment g_2 interchangeably.

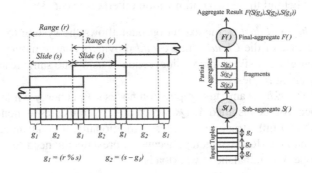

Fig. 1. Paired Window technique

Shared Processing of ACQs. Several processing schemes, as well as multiple *ACQ* optimizers, utilize the *Paired Windows* technique [12, 15]. To show the benefits of sharing partial aggregations, consider the following example:

Example 1. Assume two *ACQs* that perform *count* on the same data stream. The first *ACQ* has a slide of 2 s and a range of 6 s, the second one has a slide of 4 s and a range of 8 sec. That is, the first *ACQ* is computing partial aggregates every 2 s, and the second is computing the same partial aggregates every 4 s. Clearly, the calculation producing partial aggregates only needs to be performed once every 2 s, and both *ACQs* can use these partial aggregates for their corresponding final aggregations. The first *ACQ* will then run each final aggregation over the last three partial aggregates, and the second *ACQ* will run each final aggregation over the last 4 partial aggregates.

To determine how many partial aggregations are needed after combining n *ACQs*, we need to first find the length of the new combined (composite) slide, which is the *Least Common Multiple* (*LCM*) of all the slides of combined *ACQs*. Each slide is then repeated *LCM/slide* times to fit the length of the new composite slide. All partial aggregations happening within each slide are also repeated and marked in the composite slide as *edges* (to mark the times at which partial aggregations will be happening). If two *ACQs* mark the same location, it means that location is a *common edge*.

To count how many partial aggregations (*edges*) are scheduled within the composite slide we can use either the *Bit Set* technique [12] or the *Formula F1* technique [23].

Weavability. [12] is a metric that measures the benefit of sharing partial aggregations between any number of *ACQs*. If it is beneficial to share computations between these *ACQs*, then these *ACQs* are known to *weave* well together and are combined into the same shared execution tree. Intuitively, two *ACQs* *weave* perfectly when their *LCM* contains only *common edges*.

The following formula can be used to calculate the cost (*C*) of the execution plan before and after combining *ACQs* from their own trees into shared trees. The difference between these costs tells us if the combination is a good choice.

$$C = m\lambda + \sum_{i=1}^{m} E_i \Omega_i \qquad (1)$$

Where m is the number of the trees in the plan, λ is input rate in tuples per second, E_i is *Edge rate* of tree i, and Ω_i is the overlap factor of tree i. *Edge rate* is the number of partial aggregations performed per second, and the overlap factor is the total number of final-aggregation operations performed on each fragment.

The WeaveShare optimizer utilizes the concept of *Weavability* to produce an execution plan for a number of *ACQs*. It selectively partitions the *ACQs* into multiple disjoint execution trees (i.e., groups), resulting in a dramatic reduction in total query plan processing cost. *WeaveShare* starts with a no-share plan, where each *ACQ* has its own execution tree. Then, it iteratively considers all possible pairs of execution trees and combines those that reduce the total plan cost the most into a single tree. *WeaveShare* produces a final execution plan consisting of multiple disjoint execution trees when it cannot find a pair that would reduce the total plan cost further.

3 System Model and Execution Plan Quality

In this paper, we assume a typical *DSMS* deployed over a set of servers (i.e., computing nodes). These servers can be a local cluster or on the *Cloud* and are capable of executing any *ACQs* using partial aggregation. Submitted *ACQs* are assumed to be independent of each other and have no affinity to any server. Furthermore, without a loss of generality, we target *ACQs* that perform similar aggregations on the same data stream.

In a single node system, the main metric defining the quality of an execution plan is the *Cost* of the plan. The *Cost* of the plan is measured in operations per second. That is, if the plan cost is X, then we would need a server that can perform at least X operations per second in order to execute this plan and satisfy all users by returning the results of their *ACQs* according to their specified range and slide.

In the context of the distributed environment, we have to split our workload between the available nodes. Since our workload consists of *ACQs*, we can assign them to the available computing nodes in the system and group them into execution trees within these nodes. Thus, in any distributed environment, the *Total Cost* of a plan P is calculated as a sum of all costs C_i (according to the Eq. 1) of all n nodes in the system:

$$TotalCost(P) = \sum_{i=1}^{n} C_i$$

Table 1. Optimizer categories

		Optimizers				
		Non-Cost-based		Cost-based		
		Random	Round Robin	to Lowest	to Nodes	inserted
	Group Only	G_{RAND}	G_{RR}	G_{TL}	-	-
Categories	Weave Only	W_{RAND}	W_{RR}	W_{TL}	W_{TN}	W_I
	Weave + Group	WG_{RAND}	WG_{RR}	WG_{TL}	WG_{TN}	WG_I

This metric is important for the *Cloud* environment, because lowering the total cost T allows *DSMSs* to handle larger numbers of different *ACQs* on the same hardware, which in turn can potentially lower the monetary cost of each *ACQ* for the clients.

Another important metric in a distributed environment is the *Maximum node cost* of all computational nodes. The maximum node cost of a plan P is calculated by finding the highest cost C_i of all n nodes in the system:

$$MaxCost(P) = Max_i^n C_i$$

Minimizing the *Max Cost* is vital for distributed *DSMSs* with heavy workloads. In such a case, if we optimize our execution plans purely for the *Total Cost*, due to the heavy workload, the *Max Cost* can become higher than the computational capacity of the highest capacity node in the system, and the system will not be able to accommodate this execution plan. Furthermore, it is advantageous for the providers to maintain load balancing, because it prevents the need for over-provisioning in order to cope with unbalanced workloads.

Additionally, good load balancing could enable power management that executes *ACQs* at lower CPU frequency. This could lead to significant energy savings, ergo monetary savings, given that the energy consumption is at least a quadratic function of CPU frequency [26].

4 Taxonomy of Optimizers

As mentioned in the Introduction, in order to structure our search for a suitable multi-*ACQ* optimizer for a distributed *DSMS* in a systematic way, we categorize possible *ACQ* optimizers based on how they utilize the concept of *Weavability* for both non-cost-based and cost-based optimization. This taxonomy is shown in Table 1. Below, we highlight the underlying strategy of each category.

Group Only. This category allows for the grouping of *ACQs* on different computation nodes. No sharing of final or partial aggregations between *ACQs* is allowed. Optimizers in this category are expected to be effective in environments where sharing partial aggregates is counter productive, for example, when there are no similarities between periodic properties of *ACQs*. Even though there is no sharing between *ACQs* in this category, it is still essential to maintain the load balance between computation nodes in a distributed environment. Since node costs in this case are calculated trivially by adding together separate costs of *ACQs* running on this node, there can be many analogies (such as CPU scheduling in OS) to optimizers from this category.

Weave Only. This category allows the sharing of final and partial aggregations between *ACQs*. The *Weavability* concept is used in this category to generate the number of execution trees matching the number of available nodes. As a result, only one execution tree can be present on each computation node in the resulting plan. Optimizers in this category are expected to be effective in the environments where partial result sharing is highly advantageous, for example, if the submitted *ACQs* all have similar periodic properties (*ACQ* slides are the same or multiples of each other).

Weave and Group. This category allows both the sharing of aggregations between *ACQs* within execution trees and the grouping of them on different computation nodes. Thus, multiple execution trees can be present on any node. Optimizers in this category are attempting to be adaptive to any environment and produce high quality execution plans in different settings by collocating and grouping *ACQs* in an intelligent way.

5   Non-Cost-Based Optimizers

In this section, we provide the details on the *Non-Cost-based* optimizers, which we further classified as *Random* and *Round Robin* optimizers. Random and Round Robin optimizers iterate through a set of input *ACQs*, selecting a node for each *ACQ* in a random or round robin fashion respectively.

Depending on the way *ACQs* on a node are woven,

- G_{RAND} & G_{RR} (*GroupOnly*) add the *ACQs* to the selected node as a separate tree.
- W_{RAND} & W_{RR} (*WeaveOnly*) *weave* the *ACQs* into a single, shared tree on the node.
- WG_{RAND} & WG_{RR} (*WeaveandGroup*) choose (in random or round robin fashion) whether to add this *ACQ* as a separate tree, or to *weave* it with one of the available trees on this node.

6   Cost-Based Optimizers

In this section, we provide the details on the second class of optimizers: *Cost-based* optimizers (Table 1), which includes three categories: "To Lowest", "To Nodes", and "Inserted". Note that no representatives for the "Group Only – Insert" and "Group Only – To Nodes" categories are listed in Table 1 because in both cases the representative is effectively G_{TL} without weaving. In all optimizers, we consider the initial cost of each node to be zero.

6.1   Category "To Lowest"

Optimizers in this category follow the "To Lowest" algorithm shown in Algorithm 1.

Group to Lowest (G_{TL}). This optimizer is a balanced version of a *No Share* generator, which assigns each *ACQ* to run as a separate tree and that are then assigned to available nodes in a cost-balanced fashion.

Algorithm: The trees are first sorted by their costs, then, starting from the most expensive one, each tree is assigned to the node that currently has the lowest total cost.

Algorithm 1. The *"To Lowest"* Algorithm

Input: A set of Q Aggregate Continuous Queries, N computation nodes, and *Category*
Output: Execution plan P
Create an execution tree $(t_1, t_2, \ldots, t_Q)$ for each query
Calculate costs for all execution trees $(c_1, c_2, \ldots, c_Q)$
Sort all execution trees from expensive to cheap
Assign N most expensive trees to N nodes $(n_1, n_2, \ldots, n_N)$ ▷ assign one tree per node
$T \leftarrow Q - N$ ▷ T is the number of remaining trees to be grouped/weaved
for $i = 0$ *to* T **do**   ▷ iterate over the trees until all are grouped/weaved to nodes
    $MinNode \leftarrow findMinNode()$ ▷ determine the node with the current smallest cost
    switch *Category* **do**
        case *GroupOnly*   ▷ each node can have multiple trees
            $group(t_i, MinNode)$ ▷ group t_i as a separate tree to *MinNode*
        case *WeaveOnly*   ▷ each node can have only one tree
            $weave(t_i, MinNode)$ ▷ weave t_i to the tree in *MinNode*
        case *WeaveAndGroup*   ▷ each node can have multiple trees
            $Cost_1 \leftarrow group(t_i, MinNode)$ ▷ new cost of *MinNode* if t_i is grouped to *MinNode*
            $MinTree \leftarrow findMinTree(MinNode)$ ▷ minimal costing tree in *MinNode*
            $Cost_2 \leftarrow weave(t_i, MinNode)$ ▷ new cost of *MinNode* if t_i is weaved to *MinTree*
            if $Cost_1 < Cost_2$ **then**
                $group(t_i, MinNode)$ ▷ group t_i as a separate tree to *MinNode*
            else
                $weave(t_i, MinNode)$ ▷ weave t_i to *MinTree*
            end if
    end switch
end for
end (Return P)

Discussion: Since this optimizer does not perform any partial result sharing, it is only useful in cases when sharing is not beneficial (when none of the slides have any similarities in their periodic features).

Weave To Lowest (W_{TL}). This optimizer builds on the G_{TL} algorithm and weaves all *ACQs* on a node into a single, shared tree.

Algorithm: After sorting *ACQs* by cost (as in G_{TL}), W_{TL} assigns each *ACQ* to a node with the current lowest total cost and weaves it into the shared tree on the node.

Discussion: The W_{TL} optimizer executes *Weavability* calculation only once per input which makes it more expensive to run than G_{TL}. Additionally, by limiting to a single shared tree and not considering the compatibility of existing *ACQs* with new ones, it produces plans with high *Total Cost*, and, consequently, high *Max Cost*, even though it performs rudimentary cost balancing.

Weave-Group To Lowest (WG_{TL}). This approach also builds on G_{TL}, but as opposed to W_{TL}, it allows both *selective weaving* and grouping *ACQs* together.

Algorithm: Similar to G_{TL} and W_{TL}, WG_{TL} first sorts the *ACQ* trees, then iteratively assigns each *ACQ* to the node with the current smallest cost. At a node, an *ACQ* is either *woven* with the smallest costing tree in the node or added as a separate tree, whichever leads to the minimum cost increase.

Discussion: The WG_{TL} has similar runtime cost as W_{TL} as both optimizers use the *Weavability* calculations only once per *ACQ*. Even though WG_{TL} attempts to take advantage of grouping, it does not produce much better execution plans than W_{TL}. By focusing only on the lowest cost tree on a node, it weaves together some poorly compatible *ACQs*, leading to comparatively low quality execution plans.

6.2 Category "To Nodes"

Optimizers in this category follow the "To Nodes" algorithm depicted in Algorithm 2.

Weave to Nodes (W_{TN}). This optimizer is directly based on the single node *WeaveShare* algorithms, thus it is targeted at minimizing the *Total Cost*.

Algorithm: W_{TN} starts its execution the same way as the single node *WeaveShare*. If it reaches the point where the current number of trees is less than or equal to the number of available nodes, W_{TN} stops and assigns each tree to a different node. If, however, *WeaveShare* finishes execution, and the current number of trees is still greater than the number of available nodes, the W_{TN} optimizer continues the *WeaveShare* algorithm (merging trees pairwise), even though it is no longer beneficial for total cost. The execution stops when the number of trees becomes equal to the number of available nodes.

Discussion: Since W_{TN} is a direct descendant of *WeaveShare*, it is optimized to produce the minimum *Total Cost*. However, since W_{TN} allows only one execution tree per node, in order to match the number of nodes to number of trees, W_{TN} forces *WeaveShare* to keep merging trees with less compatible *ACQs*. Hence, W_{TN} generates, in general, more expensive plans than the basic *WeaveShare*. Additionally, W_{TN} does not perform any load balancing, hence it can generate query plans with execution trees whose computational requirements exceed the capacity of the node with the most powerful CPU.

Weave-Group to Nodes (WG_{TN}). Like W_{TN}, this optimizer is also directly based on the single node *WeaveShare* algorithm and is targeted at minimizing the *Total Cost*.

Algorithm: The WG_{TN} optimizer starts by executing single core *WeaveShare* and, similarly to W_{TN}, stops execution if it reaches the point where the current number of trees is equal to or less than the number of available nodes. However, if *WeaveShare* finishes execution and the current number of trees produced is greater than the number of available nodes, WG_{TN} assigns them to the available nodes, without *weaving* them, in a balanced fashion by applying the G_{TL} optimizer. First, all trees are sorted by their costs, and, starting from the most expensive ones, the trees are assigned to the nodes with the smallest current total cost.

Discussion: Unlike W_{TN}, the WG_{TN} optimizer is designed to produce the minimum *Total Cost* and the minimum *Max Cost*. The latter is not always possible, since the execution trees produced by *WeaveShare* are sometimes of significantly different costs,

---

Algorithm 2. The *"To Nodes"* Algorithm

Input: A set of Q **Aggregate Continuous Queries,** N **computation nodes, and** *Category*
Output: Execution plan P
Create an execution tree $(t_1, t_2, \ldots, t_Q)$ for each query
$T \leftarrow Q$ ▷ T is the number of remaining trees
loop
    MaxReduction $\leftarrow -\infty$ ▷ maximum cost reduction is set to minimum
    for $i = 0$ *to* $T - 1$ **do**   ▷ iterate over all trees
      for $j = 1$ *to* T **do**   ▷ iterate over all trees again (to cover all pairs)
        CostRed $\leftarrow$ weave(t_i, t_j) ▷ cost reduction if weaving trees t_i and t_j
        if *CostRed* > *MaxReduction* **then**   ▷ find largest *CostRed*
          MaxReduction $\leftarrow$ *CostRed*   ▷ and save it to *MaxReduction*
          ToWeave $\leftarrow (t_i, t_j)$ ▷ trees t_i and t_j are saved to be weaved later
        end if
      end for
    end for
    if *MaxReduction* > 0 **then**   ▷ there is a benefit in weaving
      weave(*ToWeave*)   ▷ weave saved trees
    else
      switch *Category* **do**
      case *WeaveOnly*
        if $T \leq N$ **then**
          end (Return P)
        else
          weave(*ToWeave*)   ▷ weave saved trees
        end if
      case *WeaveAndGroup*
        $P \leftarrow G_{TL}(T)$ ▷ run *GroupToLowest* optimizer on remaining T trees
        end (Return P)
      end switch
    end if
    $T \leftarrow T - 1$
end loop

---

and the used load balancing technique cannot produce the desired output. WG_{TN} can achieve a better *Total Cost* than W_{TN} by not forcing trees that do not *weave* well together to merge, which would have increased the total cost of the plan. However, the penalty of grouping execution trees on nodes without merging them is that each tuple has to be processed as many times as the number of trees on a node. This effectively increases the *Total Cost* by a factor equal to the input rate multiplied by the number of the trees on each node. Clearly, the higher the input rate of a stream, the more costly it will be for the system to group trees without *weaving* them.

6.3 Category "Inserted"

Optimizers in this category follow the "Inserted" algorithm depicted in Algorithm 3.

Algorithm 3. The *"Inserted"* Algorithm

Input: A set of Q Aggregate Continuous Queries, N computation nodes, and *Category*
Output: Execution plan P
Assigning first N queries to N nodes $(n_1, n_2, \ldots, n_N)$ as separate trees
Calculate node costs for all N nodes
$Q \leftarrow Q - N$ $\triangleright$ Q is the number of remaining queries to be assigned
$WeaveCost \leftarrow \infty$ $\triangleright$ weave cost is set to maximum
for $i = 0$ *to* Q **do** $\triangleright$ iterate over the queries until all are grouped/weaved
 $MinNode \leftarrow findMinNode()$ $\triangleright$ determine the node with the current smallest cost
 for $j = 0$ *to* N **do** $\triangleright$ iterate over all nodes
  for $k = 0$ *to* NumTrees in n_j **do** $\triangleright$ iterate over all trees within a node
   $TempCost \leftarrow weave(q_i, t_k)$ $\triangleright$ determine plan cost if weaving query q_i into tree t_k
   if $TempCost < WeaveCost$ **then** $\triangleright$ find smallest $TempCost$
    $WeaveCost \leftarrow TempCost$ $\triangleright$ and save it to $WeaveCost$
    $ToWeave \leftarrow (q_i, t_k)$ $\triangleright$ query q_i is saved to be weaved to tree t_j later
   end if
   switch *Category* **do**
    case *WeaveOnly*
     $weave(ToWeave)$ $\triangleright$ weave saved trees
    case *WeaveAndGroup*
     $GroupCost \leftarrow group(q_i, MinNode)$ $\triangleright$ cost of $MinNode$ if q_i is grouped
     if $GroupCost < WeaveCost$ **then**
      $group(q_i, MinNode)$ $\triangleright$ group q_i to $MinNode$ as a separate tree
     else
      $weave(ToWeave)$ $\triangleright$ weave saved trees
     end if
   end switch
  end for
 end for
end for
end (Return P)

Weave Inserted (W_I). This approach is based on the *Insert-then-Weave* optimizer introduced in [12], in which every *ACQ* is either weaved in an existing tree or assigned to a new tree, whichever results in the smallest increase in the *Total Cost*. The difference of the W_I optimizer from the original *Insert-then-Weave* approach is that W_I keeps a fixed number of trees equal to the number of nodes in the distributed system.

Algorithm: W_I starts by randomly assigning an *ACQ* to each available node, then iterating through the remaining *ACQs*. For each node it computes the new cost if the *ACQ* under consideration is woven into the execution tree on the node and assigns the *ACQ* to the node that has the smallest new cost.

Discussion: W_I is attempting to optimize for the *Max Cost*, as well as the *Total Cost*, by taking into account both the *Weavability* of the inserted *ACQ* with every available node and performing cost-balancing of the computation nodes. The downside of W_I is that, since load balancing is the first priority of W_I, it sometimes assigns *ACQs* to nodes with underlying trees with which they do not *weave* well. This happens in cases where the tree that *weaves* poorly with the incoming *ACQ* currently has the smallest cost. Additionally, since W_I is limited to one execution tree per node, the *ACQs* that do not *weave* well with any of the available trees are still merged into one of these trees. This increases the *Total Costs* of the generated plans.

Weave-Group Inserted (WG_I). This optimizer is also a version of the *Insert-then-Weave* approach and similar to W_I. However, since the WG_I optimizer does not have to be limited to only one execution tree per node, it utilizes grouping to keep the *Total Cost* low while maintaining load balance between nodes.

Algorithm: WG_I starts by randomly assigning an *ACQ* to each available node, then iterating through the remaining *ACQs* similarly to W_I. By trying to weave each *ACQ* under consideration into every execution tree in every node, WG_I determines each node's minimum new cost and the most compatible underlying tree. Finally, the *ACQ* is either woven to the selected tree on the node with the minimum new cost or added as a separate tree to the tree with the minimum old cost, based on which option leads to the minimum *Total Cost* increase.

Discussion: WG_I is optimized for both *Max Cost* and *Total Cost*. However, even though WG_I allows grouping of execution trees, it does not always achieve a good *Total Cost*. This happens (similarly to W_I) in cases when the tree that *weaves* poorly with the *ACQ* under consideration has the smallest cost and is located in the node with the smallest current node cost, which forces WG_I to *weave* the non-compatible *ACQs*.

Note. A preprocessing step can be carried out for all optimizers by merging all *ACQs* with identical slides into the same trees, since such *ACQs weave* together perfectly. This reduces the workload down to a number of execution trees with multiple *ACQs* with the same slides. Note that this preprocessing is always beneficial in terms of the *Total Cost*, however, it is only beneficial in terms of the *Max Cost* if the distributed system has low number of nodes compared to the number of input *ACQs*. Otherwise, since the number of entities in the workload is decreased, it is more challenging to achieve balance among the high number of computating nodes.

7   Experimental Evaluation

In this section, we summarize the results of our experimental evaluation of all the optimizers for distributed processing environments listed in Table 1.

7.1   Experimental Testbed

In order to evaluate the quality of our proposed optimizers, we built an experimental platform and implemented all of the optimizers discussed above using Java. Our **workload** is composed of a number of *ACQs* with different characteristics. We are generating our workload synthetically in order to be able to fine-tune system parameters and perform a more detailed sensitivity analysis of our optimizers' performance. Moreover, it allows us to target many possible real-life scenarios and analyze them.

The **simulation parameters** utilized in our evaluation are:

- Number of *ACQs* (Q_{num}) that are installed on the same data stream and can share partial aggregations.
- Number of nodes in the target system (N_{num}).
- The input rate (λ), which describes how fast tuples arrive through the input stream.
- Maximum slide length (S_{max}), which provides an upper bound on the length of the slides of our *ACQs*. The minimum slide length allowed by the system equals one.
- Zipf distribution skew (Z_{skew}), which depicts the popularity of each slide length in the final set of *ACQs*. Zipf skew of zero produces uniform distribution, and Zipf skew of 1 is skewed towards large slides (for a more realistic example).
- Maximum overlap factor (Ω_{max}), which defines the upper bound for the overlap factor. The overlap factor of each *ACQ* is drawn from a uniform distribution between one and the maximum overlap factor.
- Generator type (*Gen*), which defines whether the workload is normal (*Nrm*), which includes any slides or diverse (*Div*), which includes only slides of a length that is a prime number. When the slides are prime, their *LCM* is equal to their product, which makes it more difficult to share partial aggregations.

We **measured the quality of plans** in terms of the cost of the plans as the number of aggregate operations per second (which also indicates the throughput). We chose this metric because it provides an accurate and fair measure of the performance, regardless of the platform used to conduct the experiments. Thus, our comparison does not include the actual execution of the plans on a distributed environment, which is part of our future work. All results are taken as averages of running each test three times. We ran all of our experiments on a single-node dual processor 8 core Intel(R) Xeon(R) CPU E5-2650 v2 @ 2.60 GHz server with 96 GB of RAM available.

7.2 Experimental Results

Experiment 1: Comprehensive Evaluation of Distributed Environment Optimizers

Configuration (Table 2). To compare the quality of produced plans by the distributed optimizers, we tried to cover as broad a range of different parameters as possible. Thus, we ran a set of 256 experiments, which correspond to all possible combinations of the parameters from Table 2 (i.e., our entire search space). For each one of these experiments, we generated a new workload according to the current parameters and executed all of the above mentioned optimizers on this workload.

Table 2. Experimental parameter values (total number of combinations = 256)

Parameter	Q_{num}	N_{num}	λ	S_{max}	Z_{skew}	Ω_{max}	Gen
Values	250, 500	4, 8, 16, 32	10, 100	25, 50	0, 1	10, 100	Nrm, Div
# options	2	4	2	2	2	2	2

Table 3. WG_I vs WG_{TN} breakdown (for 256 experiments)

Max Cost	Weave-Group Inserted (WG_I)	Weave-Group to Nodes (WG_{TN})	Total Cost	Weave-Group Inserted (WG_I)	Weave-Group to Nodes (WG_{TN})
Wins	Best in **80%** of cases	Best in **17%** of cases	**Wins**	Best in **5%** of cases	Best in **90%** of cases
Loses	Not best in 20% of cases, and within **3%** from the best on average	Not best in 83% of cases, and within **48%** from the best on average	**Loses**	Not best in 95% of cases, and within **9%** from the best on average	Not best in 10% of cases, and within **0.2%** from the best on average

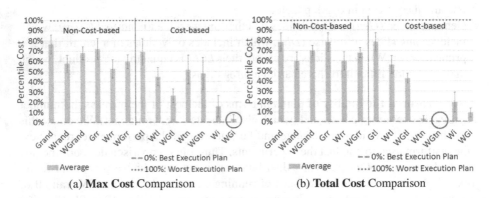

(a) **Max Cost** Comparison   (b) **Total Cost** Comparison

Fig. 2. *Average Plan Quality (from 256 experiments) where 0% and 100% are the average plan costs of all **best** and **worst** plans, respectively, across all optimizers. The error bars show the standard deviations Consistent with the definition of a standard deviation, about 68% of all plans produced by these optimizers lie in this margin.*

Results (Fig. 2 and Tables 3 and 4). Out of a very large number of results, we observed that the *Weave to Nodes* (W_{TN}) and *Weave-Group to Nodes* (WG_{TN}) produced good plans in terms of *Total Cost*, while *Weave Inserted* (W_I) and *Weave-Group Inserted* (WG_I) performed the best in terms of *Max Cost* (Fig. 2). However, we noticed that in the majority of the cases where the W_{TN} and W_I optimizers produced the best plans (in terms of *Total Cost* and *Max Cost*, respectively), their matching optimizers from the *Weave and Group* category (WG_{TN} and WG_I) produced output of either equal or very similar quality. In some other cases where W_{TN} and W_I performed poorly, the optimizer *Group to Lowest* (G_{TL}) performed better. In such cases, our optimizers WG_{TN} and WG_I were still able to match the best plans produced by G_{TL} with equal or better quality plans in most of the cases. Thus, we concluded that the WG_{TN} and WG_I optimizers were able

Table 4. Average plan generation runtime (for 256 experiments)

Optimizer	G_{Rand}	W_{Rand}	WG_{Rand}	G_{RR}	W_{RR}	WG_{RR}	G_{TL}	W_{TL}	WG_{TL}	W_{TN}	WG_{TN}	W_I	WG_I
Time (sec)	0.01	2.31	0.02	0.01	2.34	0.01	0.01	12.6	9.11	2.95	2.83	5.68	3.94

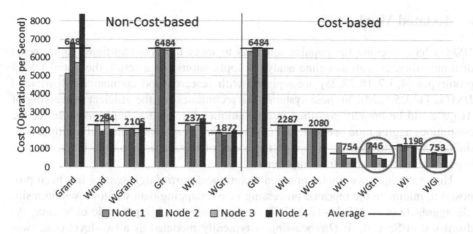

Fig. 3. Costs per node in a 4-node system

to successfully adapt to different environments and produce the best plans in terms of *Total Cost* and *Max Cost*, respectively.

To compare and contrast the two winning optimizers, we provide the breakdown of their performances in Table 3. From this table, we see that in terms of *Max Cost*, WG_{TN} significantly falls behind WG_I, since balancing is not the first priority of WG_{TN}. In terms of *Total Cost*, WG_{TN} always either wins or is within 0.2%, and WG_I falls behind, but not as significantly, since it is on average within 9% of the winning optimizer.

Additionally, we have recorded the runtimes of our optimizers (Table 4), and we see that plan generation time on average does not exceed 13 s per plan for all optimizers, which is fast considering that after an execution plan is generated and deployed to the *DSMS*, it is expected to run for a significantly longer time.

Take-away. WG_{TN} and WG_I produce the best execution plans in terms of *Total Cost* and *Max Cost*, respectively. WG_{TN} falls behind WG_I in terms of *Max Cost* more significantly than WG_I falls behind WG_{TN} in terms of *Total Cost*. All optimizers generate plans fast (<13 s).

Experiment 2: Load Balancing

Configuration. To show how all proposed algorithms compare in terms of balancing load and minimizing the total plan cost, we fix a few parameters ($Q_{num} = 250, N_{num} = 4, \lambda = 100, S_{max} = 25, Z_{skew} = 1, \Omega_{max} = 100, Gen = Nrm$) and run this experiment while recording the individual node costs of produced plans for all optimizers.

Results (Fig. 3). The results depict the typical behavior of the proposed algorithms in a 4-node environment. Since algorithms W_{TN} and WG_{TN} are optimized mostly for *Total Cost*, they produce plans with very imbalanced node loads. However, their *Total Costs* (as well as their *Average Costs*) are low. On the other hand, W_I and WG_I produce plans that are well balanced, and, at the same time, WG_I produces plans that also have a low *Total Cost* (practically as low as WG_{TN}).

Take-away. Algorithms that are producing execution plans with the lowest *Total Cost* typically perform poorly in terms of balancing load among the different nodes.

8   Related Work

DSMSs have become the popular solutions to meet the near-real-time requirements of monitoring, as well as online analytics applications. As a result, the initial *DSMS* prototypes [4,5,7,18,22,25] are replaced with research and commercial distributed *DSMSs* [1–3,5,6,24]. In these systems, the techniques for the efficient processing of *ACQs* could be broadly classified into techniques for: (1) the *implementation* of the continuous aggregation operator, and (2) the *multi-query optimization* of multiple continuous aggregate queries. Although the focus of this paper is on the latter, we first briefly review the former for completeness.

Under the operator implementation techniques, *partial aggregation* has been proposed to minimize the repeated processing of overlapping data windows within a single aggregate (e.g., [10,15–17,27,28]) by processing each input tuple only once. As discussed in Sect. 2, *ACQ* processing is typically modeled as a two-level (i.e., two-operator) query execution plan: in the first level, a *sub-aggregate* function is computed over the data stream generating a stream of partial aggregates, whereas in the second level, a *final-aggregate* function is computed over those partial aggregates. Recently, in order to minimize the cost of final aggregation, *TriOps* [11] uses an intermediate function between the sub-aggregation and final-aggregation levels to pipeline partial aggregate results to final-aggregate functions.

Under the multi-query optimization techniques, the general principle is to minimize (or eliminate) the repeated processing of overlapping operations across multiple aggregate queries. This repetition occurs as a result of processing the same data by different queries, which exhibit an overlap in at least one of the following specifications: (1) predicate conditions, (2) group-by attributes, or (3) window settings.

Techniques leveraging the overlaps in predicate conditions and group-by attributes across different *ACQs* are similar to classical multi-query optimization [21] that detects common subexpressions. Techniques leveraging shared processing of overlapping windows across different *ACQs* emerged with the paradigm shift for handling continuous queries. The *shared time slices* technique [15], for example, has been proposed to share the processing of multiple continuous aggregates with varying windows. It has also been extended into *shared data shards* in order to share the processing of varying predicates, in addition to varying windows. Orthogonally, [19] extends classical subsumption-based multi-query optimization techniques towards sharing the processing of multiple *ACQs* with varying group-by attributes and similar windows.

Like *shared time slices*, *WeaveShare* [12] addresses the problem of shared processing of aggregate queries with varying windows. *WeaveShare*, however, employs a novel *Weavability* metric that allows selective partitioning of the *ACQ* workload into multiple, disjoint execution trees resulting in a dramatic reduction in processing costs.

Weavability is also the underlying principle of our work in this paper, which we utilize to achieve scalability in distributed environments. Unlike our work, which is based on multiple query optimization, other work that addresses distributed processing of *ACQs* is based on MapReduce [9]. In [9], a demonstration of implementing event monitoring applications using the modified Hadoop framework was presented. Along the same lines are schemes for scaling operators/queries out when nodes get overloaded [13,14], but these do not focus on load balancing and combining *ACQs* as in this paper.

With respect to load balancing, the underlying principle of the cost-based *ACQ* assignment to nodes in our work is similar to the basic greedy approach in Operating System where a process is assigned to execute on the currently least loaded node [20].

9 Conclusions

In this paper, we explored how the sharing of partial aggregations can be done in the environment of distributed *DSMSs*. We formulated the problem as a distributed multi-*ACQs* optimization which combines sharing of partial aggregations and assignment to servers to produce high quality plans that keep the total cost of the execution low and balance the load among the computing nodes. We presented a classification of optimizers based on whether they are cost-based and how they utilize the concept of *Weavability*. We implemented and experimentally compared all of our proposed optimizers.

Our evaluation showed that the *Weave-Group Inserted* (*WG_I*) optimizer delivers the best quality in terms of load balancing, which makes it the most beneficial for *Cloud* service providers, since balancing helps conserve energy and prevents the need to over-provision systems hardware. At the same time, our evaluation showed that the *Weave-Group to Nodes* (*WG_{TN}*) optimizer best minimizes the total plan cost, which makes *WG_{TN}* the most beneficial for clients, since the monetary cost of *ACQ* computation in multi-tenant environments becomes lower.A closer look at the performance profiles of the two winning optimizers suggests that it might be more advantageous to choose the *WG_I* optimizer in the case where both service providers and clients should be satisfied "equally" – *WG_I* falls behind in terms of *Total Cost* less significantly (only 9% on average) than *WG_{TN}* does in terms of *Max Cost* (load balancing).

Currently, we are looking at extending our work in (1) heterogeneous environments, where nodes have different computational capacities, (2) dynamic environments, where *ACQs* and nodes can be added/removed on-the-fly, and (3) evolving workloads, where the input rate fluctuates as well as the background system utilization. In the future, we are planning to address *ACQ* optimization as part of general multi-query optimization of CQs with overlapping predicate conditions and group-by attributes.

Acknowledgments. We would like to thank Cory Thoma, Nikolaos Katsipoulakis, and the anonymous reviewers for the insightful feedback and Mark Silvis for his help with copyediting. This work was supported in part by NSF award CBET-1250171, a gift from EMC/Greenplum and an ACM SoCC 2015 Student Scholarship.

References

1. Apache samza. http://samza.apache.org
2. S4 distributed stream computing platform. http://incubator.apache.org/s4
3. Spark streaming. https://spark.apache.org/streaming
4. Abadi, D.J., et al.: Aurora: a new model and architecture for data stream management. VLDBJ **12**(2), 120–139 (2003)
5. Akidau, T., et al.: Millwheel: fault-tolerant stream processing at internet scale. PVLDB **6**(3), 1033–1044 (2013)

6. Ananthanarayanan, R., et al.: Photon: fault-tolerant and scalable joining of continuous data streams. In: ACM SIGMOD, pp. 577–588 (2013)
7. Chrysanthis, P.K.: AQSIOS - next generation data stream management system. CONET Newslett. **9**, 1–3 (2010)
8. Chung, C., Guirguis, S., Kurdia, A.: Competitive cost-savings in data stream management systems. In: Cai, Z., Zelikovsky, A., Bourgeois, A. (eds.) COCOON 2014. LNCS, vol. 8591, pp. 129–140. Springer, Cham (2014). https://doi.org/10.1007/978-3-319-08783-2_12
9. Condie, T.: Online aggregation and continuous query support in mapreduce. In: ACM SIGMOD, pp. 1115–1118 (2010)
10. Ghanem, T.M., Hammad, M.A., Mokbel, M.F., Aref, W.G., Elmagarmid, A.K.: Incremental evaluation of sliding-window queries over data streams. IEEE TKDE **19**(1), 57–72 (2007)
11. Guirguis, S., Sharaf, M., Chrysanthis, P.K., Labrinidis, A.: Three-level processing of multiple aggregate continuous queries. In: IEEE ICDE, pp. 929–940 (2012)
12. Guirguis, S., Sharaf, M.A., Chrysanthis, P.K., Labrinidis, A.: Optimized processing of multiple aggregate continuous queries. In: ACM CIKM, pp. 357–368 (2011)
13. Gulisano, V., Jimenez-Peris, R., Patino-Martinez, M., Soriente, C., Valduriez, P.: Streamcloud: an elastic and scalable data streaming system. IEEE TPDS **23**(12), 2351–2365 (2012)
14. Katsipoulakis, N.R., Thoma, C., Gratta, E.A., Labrinidis, A., Lee, A.J., Chrysanthis, P.K.: CE-Storm: confidential elastic processing of data streams. In: ACM SIGMOD, pp. 859–864 (2015)
15. Krishnamurthy, S., Wu, C., Franklin, M.: On-the-fly sharing for streamed aggregation. In: ACM SIGMOD, pp. 623–634 (2006)
16. Li, J., Maier, D., Tufte, K., Papadimos, V., Tucker, P.A.: No pane, no gain: efficient evaluation of sliding-window aggregates over data streams. ACM SIGMOD Rec. **34**, 39–44 (2005)
17. Li, J., Maier, D., Tufte, K., Papadimos, V., Tucker, P.A.: Semantics and evaluation techniques for window aggregates in data streams. In: ACM SIGMOD, pp. 311–322 (2005)
18. Motwani, R., et al.: Query processing, approximation, and resource management in a data stream management system. In: CIDR (2003)
19. Naidu, K., Rastogi, R., Satkin, S., Srinivasan, A.: Memory-constrained aggregate computation over data streams. In: IEEE ICDE, pp. 852–863 (2011)
20. Romeijn, H.E., Morales, D.R.: A class of greedy algorithms for the generalized assignment problem. Discrete Appl. Math. **103**, 209–235 (2000)
21. Roy, P., Seshadri, S., Sudarshan, S., Bhobe, S.: Efficient and extensible algorithms for multi query optimization. In: ACM SIGMOD, pp. 249–260 (2000)
22. Sharaf, M.A., Chrysanthis, P.K., Labrinidis, A., Pruhs, K.: Algorithms and metrics for processing multiple heterogeneous continuous queries. IEEE TODS **33**, 1–44 (2008)
23. Shein, A.U., Chrysanthis, P.K., Labrinidis, A.: F1: accelerating the optimization of aggregate continuous queries. In: ACM CIKM, pp. 1151–1160 (2015)
24. Toshniwal, A., et al.: Storm@ Twitter. In: ACM SIGMOD, pp. 147–156 (2014)
25. Xing, Y., Zdonik, S., Hwang, J.: Dynamic load distribution in the borealis stream processor. In: IEEE ICDE, pp. 791–802 (2005)
26. Yao, F., Demers, A., Shenker, S.: A scheduling model for reduced CPU energy. In: ACM FOCS, pp. 374–382 (1995)
27. Zhang, R., Koudas, N., Ooi, B.C., Srivastava, D.: Multiple aggregations over data streams. In: ACM SIGMOD, pp. 299–310 (2005)
28. Zhang, R., Koudas, N., Ooi, B.C., Srivastava, D., Zhou, P.: Streaming multiple aggregations using phantoms. VLDBJ **19**(4), 557–583 (2010)

High-Availability at Massive Scale: Building Google's Data Infrastructure for Ads

Ashish Gupta[✉] and Jeff Shute[✉]

Google Inc.,Mountain View, USA
{agupta,jshute}@google.com

Abstract. Google's Ads Data Infrastructure systems run the multi-billion dollar ads business at Google. High availability and strong consistency are critical for these systems. While most distributed systems handle machine-level failures well, handling datacenter-level failures is less common. In our experience, handling datacenter-level failures is critical for running true high availability systems. Most of our systems (e.g. Photon, F1, Mesa) now support multi-homing as a fundamental design property. Multi-homed systems run live in multiple datacenters all the time, adaptively moving load between datacenters, with the ability to handle outages of any scale completely transparently.

This paper focuses primarily on stream processing systems, and describes our general approaches for building high availability multi-homed systems, discusses common challenges and solutions, and shares what we have learned in building and running these large-scale systems for over ten years.

Keywords: Stream processing · Distributed systems · Multi-homing · Databases

1 Introduction

Google's Ads platform serves billions of advertisements every day to users around the globe, and generates a large volume of data capturing various user interactions, e.g., seeing an Ad, clicking on an Ad, etc. The Ads Data Infrastructure team is responsible for processing and managing all this data in near real-time, and delivering critical reports and insights to Google's Ad users and clients. This includes generating rich reports for our advertisers on how their Ad campaigns are performing, managing budget in the live serving system, etc. Reliable and timely delivery of this data is critical for Google and its partners, and for supporting Google's multi-billion dollar Ads Business. Consistency is also a strong requirement since the advertising data determines revenue and billing, and because inconsistent data is very confusing and hard to deal with, both for end users and for developers. In this paper we explore what it takes to build such mission-critical systems while ensuring consistency and providing high availability, particularly in the context of real-time streaming systems.

© Springer Nature Switzerland AG 2019
M. Castellanos et al. (Eds.): BIRTE 2015/2016/2017, LNBIP 337, pp. 63–81, 2019.
https://doi.org/10.1007/978-3-030-24124-7_5

Over several years and multiple generations, our strategies for high availability have evolved considerably. Our first generation systems focused primarily on handling machine-level failures automatically. Although datacenter failures are rare, they do happen, and can be very disruptive, and are especially difficult to recover from when data consistency is lost. Our next generation systems were designed to support datacenter failovers and recover state cleanly after failover. Furthermore, we implemented automated failure detection and failover, which reduced operational complexity and risk. Failover-based approaches, however, do not truly achieve high availability, and can have excessive cost due to the deployment of standby resources. Our current approach is to build natively multi-homed systems. Such systems run hot in multiple datacenters all the time, and adaptively move load between datacenters, with the ability to handle outages of any scale completely transparently. Additionally, planned datacenter outages and maintenance events are completely transparent, causing minimal disruption to the operational systems. In the past, such events required labor-intensive efforts to move operational systems from one datacenter to another.

We've recently published details of several of these large-scale systems (e.g. F1 [26], Mesa [21], and Photon [3]), all of which require large global state that needs to be replicated across multiple datacenters in real-time. F1 [26] is a distributed relational database system that combines high availability and the scalability of NoSQL systems like Bigtable [12], and the consistency and usability of traditional SQL databases. Photon [3] is a geographically distributed data processing pipeline for joining multiple continuously flowing streams of data in real-time with high scalability, low latency, strong consistency (exactly-once semantics), and high reliability. Finally, Mesa [21] is a petabyte-scale data warehousing system that allows real-time data ingestion and queryability, as well as high availability, reliability, fault tolerance, and scalability for large data and query volumes.

The rest of this paper is organized as follows. In Sect. 2, we state our assumptions and model, and what we mean by availability and consistency, particularly in the context of streaming systems. Section 3 provides the background about some of the common failure scenarios based on our experience with operating these systems. In Sect. 4, we describe the different availability tiers, followed by the challenges in building multi-homed systems in Sect. 5. Section 6 describes some of the multi-homed systems built for Google's Ads systems. Section 7 discusses related work and Sect. 8 summarizes our conclusions.

2   Availability and Consistency for Streaming Systems

2.1   Assumptions and Context

In any of our typical streaming system, the events being processed are based on user interactions, and logged by systems serving user traffic in many datacenters around the world. A log collection service gathers these logs globally and copies them to two or more specific logs datacenters. Each logs datacenter gets a complete copy of the logs, with the guarantee that all events copied to any one datacenter will (eventually) be copied to all logs datacenters. The stream processing systems run in one or more of the logs datacenters and processes all events. Output from the stream processing system is usually stored into some globally replicated system so that the output can be consumed reliably from anywhere.

In this paper, we use datacenter to mean a cluster of machines in the same region. As a simplification, we assume all datacenters are geographically distributed.

In these streaming systems, it is important to note that processing is often not deterministic and not idempotent. Many streaming pipelines have complex business logic with stateful processing, with order and timing dependencies. For example, identifying sessions and detecting spam events both require clustering events and are highly dependent on which events have been processed so far.

2.2 Availability for Streaming Systems

In most contexts, a system is available if it is alive and able to accept user requests. In a streaming system, availability has a different meaning. It is not critical that the system actually be responsive millisecond by millisecond. Instead, the system must stay alive over time and continue processing events. Typically, availability will be measured based on overall delay in the streaming system.

Availability targets are often expressed as a percentage availability over time. In a streaming system, a target could be that 99.9% of input events are fully processed in less than three minutes after arrival, and we consider the system available if this target is met for 99% of the time in a quarter. This system would not be meeting its availability goal if many events are delayed more than three minutes for long time intervals. Note that an availability target of 99% maps to 22 h of downtime every quarter, which is too high for mission critical systems. Our systems often target 4 to 5 nines of availability.

2.3 Consistency for Streaming Systems

Consistency in streaming systems is analogous to consistency in databases. The ACID properties are the fundamental consistency expectations in a database. In a streaming system, the core consistency requirement is exactly once processing, i.e., each input event must be processed *exactly once*. Both systems have some additional consistency properties about visibility of outcomes. In a database, a user that commits a transaction and then does a query should see the result of the previous write. In a streaming system, a user observing state repeatedly should see the state moving forward, i.e., if a state at time t includes an event e then any future state at time $t' \geq t$ must also include event e. In both cases, where there are multiple stored outcomes, an observer should see consistent outcomes. For example, on any screen with multiple reports or multiple graphs, users expect the totals to match.

It is possible to view a streaming system as a database processing micro-transactions, one per event, with the same expectations of transactional consistency that would be expected in a database. The key difference is that a streaming system is optimized to run these micro-transactions at extreme scale, using techniques like *batching* to optimize for throughput rather than latency.

Streaming systems can be used to solve many problems, only some of which require consistency. Many streaming systems are used to scan a stream of events and compute some approximate summary [16, 17, 20, 24, 25], based on a transient time window, with the summary used primarily for display, or as a coarse input signal to another system. A common example in many streaming systems is an application that extracts user sentiment from recent tweets in the Twitter stream. Consistency is not critical in such systems. If events are lost or inconsistent at some point, it won't matter once the output moves past that point and shows current data.

In other cases, streaming systems are required to process each event exactly once, and generate some exact and permanent record of the set of events observed. The system may make automated decisions based on the observed stream, which may have permanent side-effects. For example, an advertising system may be tracking user clicks on an ad, making decisions about which events are spam, deciding how much to charge for each click, accumulating an invoice and then charging an advertiser's credit card. In these cases, all decisions must be permanent, and side-effects cannot be lost.

In this paper, we are considering streaming systems where consistency is paramount.

3   Failure Models

3.1   Typical Failure Scenarios

There are many classes of failures in a distributed system:

Machines. In a large datacenter, individual machine failure occurs frequently, and can be caused by hardware or software issues. Multi-machine failures like power failures can also happen at the rack or datacenter level, but are much rarer.

Network Connectivity. Network connectivity issues also happen, within a datacenter and between datacenters. In rare circumstances, network partitions can happen that separate some datacenters completely from the rest of the wide area network. Partial failures are more common, with effects like reduced bandwidth, increased latency, unreliable connections, asymmetric connectivity, and unexplained flakiness. These failures can be triggered by hardware issues or by software issues, like throttling caused by network bandwidth over-subscription.

Underlying Infrastructure. Complex distributed systems are often built in layers, where the user-facing system has several underlying infrastructure components like distributed filesystems, databases, and communications services. Building on top of existing infrastructure allows reuse and simplifies systems, but it also means systems are exposed to failures in underlying infrastructure. In particular, with shared services, isolation between users can be very challenging, and if a shared system is over-subscribed, some users will see compromised performance.

3.2   Planned vs Unplanned Failures

Failures can be either *planned* or *unplanned*. Planned outages happen when machines, networks, datacenters, or software systems are taken offline for hardware changes, kernel upgrades, reconfiguration, software releases, etc. Before a planned outage, systems have the opportunity to gracefully shut down, drain any in-flight work, generate checkpoints, and resume in an alternate datacenter. Unplanned failures provide no opportunity for clean shutdown, and no general mechanism to discover the state of a system before it failed.

3.3   Partial vs Full Failures

Complete unplanned failure of a datacenter is a rare occurrence that may happen only once every several years. *Partial failures* affecting some significant fraction of resources in a datacenter are much more common. During a partial failure, a system may have fewer working machines, may have less bandwidth and higher latency, and components may have reduced reliability. In general, systems will run slower and have less capacity, and may see elevated failure rates and more timeouts. Streaming system may not be able to keep up with the input stream, and may fall behind.

While partial failures are more common than total failure, they are also harder to detect, diagnose and recover from. The problem often cannot be detected until after a system has already fallen behind, and then an engineer must try to diagnose which component is slow and why. In a complex system with many feedback loops, this can be very difficult because the component with the visible backlog may not be source of the problem.

Once a problem is diagnosed, it is often unclear how long a fix will take. An operations team may provide estimates of when a networking problem can be repaired or an infrastructure issue can be mitigated, but fixes may take longer, or may not work on the first try.

Uncertainty about fixes can put teams in a difficult position. For example, in a common scenario, the primary datacenter for a system is compromised, a fix is estimated to take one hour, and failover to a secondary (less desirable) datacenter is possible but will take 90 min, and requires a complex procedure which includes some risk. In this situation, the team must make a difficult decision about whether to wait out the outage or trigger a failover, with incomplete information about the outcome of either option.

4   Availability Tiers

To ensure high-availability in the case of a datacenter level outage, there are several possible approaches. Each approach has different trade-offs in availability SLAs, consistency guarantees, resource usage, etc. We categorize these approaches into different availability tiers.

4.1   Singly-Homed Systems

Singly homed systems are designed to primarily run in a single datacenter. In case of an intermittent datacenter outage, processing gets delayed. If the datacenter is unavailable for an extended period, the system must be restarted from some arbitrary point in another datacenter. This results in extended unavailability, as well as potential loss of data and consistency.

Singly-homed systems are relatively simple to build and are a good solution when inconsistencies or data losses are acceptable. One simple technique used to achieve high availability is to run a singly-homed system in parallel in multiple datacenters, and either allow user queries to go to any datacenter, or designate one datacenter as the primary that receives all user traffic, with alternate datacenters available as hot standbys that can be made into the new primary quickly. This approach does not require inter-datacenter coordination, but this simplification comes at the expense of consistency guarantees between datacenters.

4.2   Failover-Based Systems

In failover-based systems, processing still happens in a single primary datacenter, but the critical system state capturing what has been processed is replicated as a *checkpoint* in an alternate datacenter. In case of a primary datacenter outage, processing can be moved to the alternate datacenter and restarted from the latest checkpoint.

Checkpoints can be used in two ways. In the simple case, a checkpoint is taken asynchronously and periodically, expressing what work has already been completed. This checkpoint provides an approximate restart point that will ensure all events still get processed at least once, without excessive reprocessing of already-completed events. These asynchronous checkpoints are sufficient to preserve exactly once processing during planned outages; in-progress work can be drained before taking a checkpoint, and the checkpoint can be used to restart the pipeline in an alternate datacenter from exactly where it left off.

More advanced systems can be built where checkpoints are taken synchronously and describe exactly what has been processed. At some point during processing, the pipeline generates a checkpoint and blocks until the checkpoint is replicated before proceeding. Synchronous checkpoints can exactly capture the processing state, even for unplanned failovers, but the systems are typically much more complex since checkpoints must be tied directly into the processing and recovery pipelines.

With large complex systems, failover procedures (with synchronous or asynchronous checkpoints) tend to be very complex and risky. Complex systems have many components and many dependencies, all of which need to restarted and potentially reconfigured. Manual failovers means handling each component individually, which is time consuming and error-prone.

Our teams have had several bad experiences dealing with failover-based systems in the past. Since unplanned outages are rare, failover procedures were often added as an afterthought, not automated and not well tested. On multiple occasions, teams spent days recovering from an outage, bringing systems back online component by component, recovering state with ad hoc tools like custom MapReduces, and gradually tuning the system as it tried to catch up processing the backlog starting from the initial outage. These situations not only cause extended unavailability, but are also extremely stressful for the teams running complex mission-critical systems.

It is usually clear that failover should be automated to make it faster and safer, but automation has its own challenges. In complex systems, failover processes are also complex and have many steps. Furthermore, as systems evolve, failover scripts must be updated with every change. Keeping scripts up to date can be challenging, and real-life failovers are often not well tested because the full process cannot be exercised without causing an outage.

With effort, failovers can be successfully automated and made to run relatively quickly, but there are still inherent problems. First, during an outage, a team has to make difficult decisions with incomplete information about the nature of an outage and the time until it will be resolved (See Sect. 3.3). Second, failover procedures are still complicated, and must still be maintained with every change and regularly tested on live systems. This imposes a significant burden on a team's development bandwidth, and makes failover-based systems inherently high-maintenance.

4.3   Multi-homed Systems

Many of the problems with failover-based systems stem from the fact that failover is usually built as an add-on feature on top of an inherently singly-homed design, adding complex new behavior that is not part of the primary execution path.

In contrast, multi-homed systems are designed to run in multiple datacenters as a core design property, so there is no on-the-side failover concept. A multi-homed system runs live in multiple datacenters all the time. Each datacenter processes work all the time, and work is dynamically shared between datacenters to balance load. When one datacenter is slow, some fraction of work automatically moves to faster datacenters. When a datacenter is completely unavailable, all its work is automatically distributed to other datacenters. There is no failover process other than the continuous dynamic load balancing.

Multi-homed systems coordinate work across datacenters using shared global state that must be updated synchronously. All critical system state is replicated so that any work can be restarted in an alternate datacenter at any point, while still guaranteeing exactly once semantics. Multi-homed systems are uniquely able to provide high availability and full consistency in the presence of datacenter-level failures. Building multi-homed systems, however, poses novel challenges, which we explore in the next section.

5   Challenges in Building Multi-homed Systems

5.1   Synchronous Global State

In order to process each work unit exactly once, and support unplanned failover to an alternate datacenter, the state of work units must be stored globally. If work has been completed in one datacenter, the system must not lose that state after a failover because that could lead to double-processing.

Maintaining global state consistently and reliably introduces significant latency. In general, processing datacenters are geographically distributed to avoid correlated outages such as power failures, network failures, or natural disasters. Typically, round trip network latency between geo-distributed datacenters is at least tens of milliseconds. Thus updating global state synchronously takes at least that long. We use Paxos-based commit to update metadata synchronously [22]. In most cases, this means storing metadata in Spanner [15], which acts as a globally replicated database with synchronous commit.

The latency involved in synchronous commits makes it necessary to design systems for maximal throughput despite high latency of individual operations. Systems must support high parallelism, and typically use some form of batching to reduce round trips to global state. Serial operations using global state must be avoided as much as possible. In many cases, pipelines can be arranged so several operations can be clustered together and applied as a group locally, with global state updates only at the boundaries between operation clusters.

Global metadata commits also require wide area network bandwidth, which is more expensive than local bandwidth. The size of global state should be minimized to limit this bandwidth usage as much as possible. Global state should usually be used for metadata only, and not the data itself. Additionally, work should be batched, and batches of work should be represented with small state when possible. For example, when input comes from files, describing a batch with a byte range of an input file is much more compact than storing a list of event IDs included in the batch (as long as the same input file will be reproducible in alternate datacenters).

5.2   What to Checkpoint

A complex processing pipeline may have multiple inputs, multiple outputs, and many internal nodes. As data flows through the pipeline, each node has some state (i.e. data), and some metadata (e.g. queues of pending and completed work). Some nodes may produce deterministic output based on their input, but some nodes may be non-deterministic. For example, a node may do lookups into a mutable database, or may perform some time-sensitive or order-sensitive computation (e.g. clustering events into sessions, identifying the first unique occurrence of an event, etc.).

As discussed earlier, checkpointing to global state has high cost in latency and bandwidth, so it is desirable to minimize the number and size of checkpoints. Checkpointing can be minimized by clustering processing nodes together and only checkpointing at the endpoints of the cluster. Within the cluster, all state should be kept local within a datacenter.

Clustering checkpoints requires understanding what state exists at each point, and determining what state can be regenerated after a failure. Any deterministic state can be trivially recomputed, but non-deterministic state can also be regenerated (possibly with different results) as long as no output was produced and no observable side-effects have happened.

In the best case, a system may be able to run with no checkpoints at all, up to the point of final output, where the global state is used to determine whether some particular output has already happened. More typically, systems do initial checkpointing at the input stage of the pipeline to record what events were batched together, so later state can be recorded per-batch, and so failover and re-processing can happen efficiently at the batch level. In complex pipelines with multiple outputs and side-effects, it is often necessary to checkpoint state at intermediate nodes where the output of some node will be used as input to multiple downstream nodes leading to multiple different final outputs.

5.3 Repeatable Input

Storing small checkpoints selectively at particular nodes is a significant optimization, as discussed above. One key property that makes that optimization possible is repeatability of input. If the same input data will be available in multiple datacenters, then a checkpoint can describe input using a pointer to the input data (e.g. an event ID or an offset in a file) rather than storing a copy of the input itself. If the input data is not itself multi-homed, then a checkpoint in global state will not be useful unless it contains a full copy of the input data, which could be very expensive. In many of our systems, the input comes from event logs, which are collected by a logging system that ensures that all log events are (eventually) copied to two separate datacenters.

Many processing pipelines also have secondary inputs, where data from other sources is joined with the event data from the primary source. For example, database lookups are common. Logged events typically include object IDs but not the full state of the object. The business logic computed in the pipeline often references other attributes of the referenced objects, which requires a database lookup. If these lookups are not inherently deterministic, additional checkpointing is more complicated.

Some database lookups are inherently repeatable. For example, looking up the country name where an event occurred should be deterministic because the set of countries and their attributes is immutable in the database. Any lookups of objects that are insert-only and immutable and guaranteed to exist can also be treated as deterministic.

Any database lookup for a mutable object will not be repeatable. For example, a currency rate will change frequently. Most data objects store their current state only, which can be updated (or deleted) at any time by a user or by other business logic, changing the results of future lookups. To reduce checkpoint cost, sometimes it is possible to make these lookups repeatable. For example, a database may support snapshot reads as of a timestamp, or the schema may be designed to record history of changes. In either case, if each event has a timestamp, database lookups can retrieve the state as of that timestamp.

Where a lookup cannot be made repeatable, the result of the lookup must be stored as part of any checkpoint stored post-lookup so that if the pipeline resumes from the checkpoint, it will have the same starting point. To avoid storing this state, it may be beneficial to push non-deterministic lookups near the end of the pipeline, when possible.

5.4   Exactly Once Output

As mentioned earlier, a key semantic property is that each input event should be processed exactly once. This can be challenging to guarantee in a multi-homed system because pipelines may fail at any point while producing output, and multiple datacenters may try to process the same events concurrently. Distributed systems typically employ backup workers [18] attempting duplicate work to reduce tail latency, which means that even without any failures, multiple machines may try to process the same data concurrently. All outcomes from that processing must be observable exactly once in the visible output.

Ideally, updating global state should be atomic with the actual output operation of the pipeline. This is possible when the stream metadata and final output are stored in a shared storage system that supports transactions across entities, making clean handoff from the streaming pipeline to the output system easy, and providing exactly-once trivially. Shared transactions like this are often not possible, however, since the pipeline and output systems do not usually share the same infrastructure or the same databases. There are two possible solutions to ensure exactly-once processing in such cases.

Idempotent Output. When possible, idempotence can provide exactly-once guarantees. The processing system writes output first, and then commits global state to record completion. If another datacenter processes the same work, it will repeat the same writes, which will have no effect. It is critical that all input and all processing be deterministic so that duplicate processing actually produces duplicate output that can be elided by idempotence.

Some outcomes are naturally idempotent. For example, some systems generate notification events where duplicate notifications have no side-effect in the receiver. When output is written into an insert-only storage system, where each record has a key and there are no deletions or mutations, writes can be made idempotent by ignoring or overwriting on key collisions. Note that if another system consumes records from this output and then updates or deletes the record, the writes will be no longer idempotent.

Some outcomes are not inherently idempotent but can be made idempotent. For example, applying an arbitrary transaction to a database will not be idempotent, but if each transaction can be assigned a deterministic ID, and the processed IDs can be inserted transactionally in a separate table in the same output database, then checking presence of the target ID will make the transaction idempotent.

Two-Phase Commit. When a system's output cannot be made idempotent, it is often necessary to use some form of two-phase commit to atomically move output from the streaming system into the output system. The general protocol commonly looks like

1. Record decision to commit a batch of work in the source system.
2. Write final output into the target system and commit. (It must be possible to inspect whether this has happened.)
3. Record completion of the commit in the source system.

The streaming system drives commit with a state machine, and after a restart or any operation with indeterminate output, the current state can be retrieved by inspection and the state machine can resume cleanly and still provide exactly-once handoff.

5.5   Resource Cost

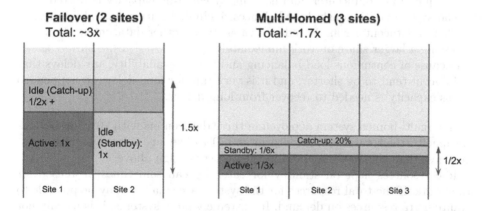

Fig. 1. Resource Cost for failover-based and multi-homed systems

Running a multi-homed pipeline means having processing capacity in multiple datacenters (Fig. 1). Perhaps surprisingly, the resource requirements can actually be significantly less than would be required to run singly homed pipelines with failovers.

Consider a failover-based system running with two datacenters - one live and one on standby. The live datacenter needs capacity to process 100% of the traffic, and the idle datacenter must have equal potential capacity so it could take over after failover. It is not sufficient to have exactly 100% of required steady state capacity, however. There must be sufficient capacity to handle load spikes, and there must be sufficient capacity to catch up after delays or failures. Because partial failures are common and can be hard to diagnose, a datacenter may run with reduced performance for some time before the datacenter recovers or failover happens, which will lead to large delays. A system then needs to be able to process data faster than real-time in order to catch back up, which requires proportional extra capacity. For example, if a system has only 10% extra capacity, a one-hour delay would take ten hours to catch up, and recovering from multi-hour delays would take multiple days.

Deploying our systems with at least 50% extra capacity for catch-up and recovery is typical, which means the total resource footprint is 300% of steady state, because extra capacity needs to be available in whichever datacenter is live at the time.

In a multi-homed system, all datacenters are live and processing all the time. Deploying three datacenters is typical. In steady state, each of the three datacenters process 33% of the traffic. After a failure where one datacenter is lost, the two remaining datacenters each process 50% of the traffic. As before, additional capacity is needed to handle spikes and to catch up after any delay. The catch-up capacity requirement is lower, for several reasons:

- During catch-up, all remaining datacenters can contribute work, so less work is required per datacenter, and no standby catch-up capacity is wasted.
- The system continuously load balances, including during partial failures, so when a datacenter runs at reduced capacity, all other datacenters start processing a larger share of work immediately.
- Because of continuous load balancing and higher availability, any delays that do occur tend to be shorter, and it is very rare for long delays to happen, so less capacity is needed to recover from long delays.

In a multi-homed system deployed in three datacenters with 20% total catch-up capacity, the total resource footprint is 170% of steady state. This is dramatically less than the 300% required in the failover design above.

Idle resources kept on standby for catch-up can sometimes be reused for other work. If the total resources for the system are small, it may be possible to acquire extra resources on demand. In extremely large systems, it is usually not possible to acquire resources on-demand because it is expensive and wasteful to run datacenters with low utilization. Additionally, in a disaster scenario, after one datacenter has been lost, many independent systems may be competing to acquire any available idle resources in alternate datacenters. If a system wants to guarantee that it will have spare capacity when it needs it, those resources must be pre-allocated.

6 Multi-homed Systems at Google

At Google, we have built several multi-homed systems to guarantee high availability and consistency even in the presence of datacenter level outages. This section summarizes how we solve some of the multi-homing challenges discussed in the previous section for these systems. The conference papers [3,21,26] have more details.

6.1 F1/Spanner: Relational Database

F1 [26] is a fault-tolerant globally-distributed relational database built at Google to serve as the primary storage system for transactional data in AdWords and other advertising and commerce related applications. F1 is built on top of Spanner [15], which provides extremely scalable data storage, synchronous replication, and strong consistency and ordering properties. F1's core storage and transactional features are provided by Spanner. F1 adds a distributed SQL query engine, and additional database features for indexing, change recording and publishing, schema management, etc.

One of Spanner's primary purposes is to manage cross-datacenter replicated data. Data in a Spanner database is partitioned into *groups*, and each group typically has one replica *tablet* per datacenter, each storing the same data. Transactions within one group update a majority of replica tablets synchronously using the Paxos [23] algorithm. Multi-group transactions are supported using an additional two-phase commit protocol on top of Paxos.

Spanner has very strong consistency and timestamp semantics. Every transaction is assigned a commit timestamp, and these timestamps provide a global total ordering for commits. Spanner uses a novel mechanism to pick globally ordered timestamps in a scalable way using hardware clocks deployed in Google datacenters. Spanner uses these timestamps to provide multi-versioned consistent reads, including snapshot reads of current data. Spanner also provides a global safe timestamp, below which no future transaction can possibly commit. Reads at the global safe timestamp can normally run on any replica without blocking behind running transactions.

Spanner is a fully multi-homed system. For each group, one tablet is elected as the Paxos leader, and acts as the entry-point for all transactional activity for the group. A group is available for transactions if its leader and a majority quorum of replicas are available. If a leader tablet becomes unavailable or overloaded, an alternate tablet will automatically be elected as leader. During a full datacenter outage, all leaders will immediately move to alternate datacenters. During a partial outage, as machine capacity or performance degrades, leaders will gradually move to alternate datacenters. We commonly deploy Spanner instances with five replicas, so we can lose up to two datacenters and can still from a quorum of replicas and elect a leader tablet. (Five replicas is considered the minimum for high availability because during a full outage of one datacenter, availability must still be maintained during machine-level failures or transient failures in any remaining datacenter.)

The F1 system uses servers in front of Spanner that receive all F1 user traffic. The F1 servers are deployed in multiple datacenters and are mostly stateless. For writes, the F1 server must communicate with a Spanner leader replica. For reads, the F1 server can often communicate with a local Spanner replica. As an optimization, the system tries to shape traffic so that requests from a client, to F1, and to the Spanner leader replica all happen in one datacenter as often as possible. This is not required however, and after a failure anywhere in this stack, traffic will be transparently redirected to alternate datacenters to maintain high availability.

Transactions in F1 and Spanner require communication between replicas in multiple datacenters. We typically choose to distribute replicas widely across the US, which leads to commit latency of at least 50 ms. Users coming from typical singly-homed databases are used to much lower latency. F1 users follow a set of best practices for application and interface design, emphasizing high throughput, parallelism and data clustering, to mitigate the effects of high transaction latency. We have found that by following these recommendations, applications on F1 can achieve similar performance to predecessor applications, and often have better long-tail performance because these approaches are inherently more scalable.

While F1 and Spanner are not stream processing systems, they provide good examples of the same multi-homing principles, and are often used as components inside other systems. Most of our stream processing systems require some form of global state for metadata, and sometimes for data, and this is usually stored in a Spanner or F1 database. These systems provide high availability reads and writes, with full durability and consistency, even during or after datacenter failure.

6.2   Photon: Joining Continuous Data Streams

Photon [3] is a geographically distributed system for joining multiple continuously flowing streams of data in real-time with high scalability and low latency. One of the key applications of Photon within Google's Advertising System is to join data streams such as web search queries and user clicks on ads. When a user issues a search query at google.com, Google serves ads to the user along with search results. The web server that serves the ad also sends information about this event to multiple logs-datacenters, where the data is stored persistently. The logged data includes information such as advertiser identifier, ad text, and online ad auction parameters. After receiving the results of the search query, the user may click on one of the ads. The click event is also logged and copied to multiple logs datacenters. Due to technical limitations on the size of the click URL, the click logs do not contain all the rich information in the original query log. Photon is responsible to join these streams of data arriving in multiple datacenters, and producing a joined log, which can then be consumed by other systems at Google to derive key business metrics, including billing and reporting for advertisers.

Given the business critical nature of the output joined logs, Photon is designed to tolerate infrastructure degradation and datacenter-level outages without any manual intervention. With the input logs available in multiple datacenters, Photon workers are able to run independently in each of these datacenters to join the same input event, but workers coordinate their output to guarantee that each input event is joined and outputted at-most-once. The critical state shared between the workers consists of the set of event_ids that have already been joined. This system state is stored in the *IdRegistry* (as illustrated in Fig. 2), which is built using Paxos [23] and guarantees synchronous replication of the joined event_ids across the majority of its replicas. With this, Photon guarantees that there will be no duplicates in the joined output (at-most-once semantics) at any point in time, that most joinable events will be present in the output in real-time (near-exact semantics), and that exactly-once semantics are provided eventually.

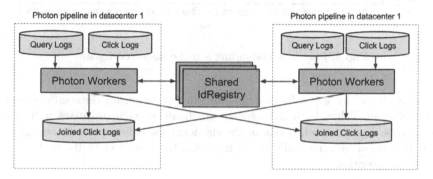

Fig. 2. Photon pipeline running independently in two datacenters with the IdRegistry storing the global state synchronously in multiple datacenters.

To ensure that an outage of one relatively large geographical region does not affect the IdRegistry, Photon places IdRegistry replicas in different geographical regions such that replicas from multiple geographical regions must agree before a transaction can be committed. The downside of requiring such isolation zones is that the throughput of the IdRegistry will be limited by network latency. Based on typical network statistics, the round-trip-time between different geographical regions (such as east and west coasts of the United States) can be over 100 ms. This would limit the throughput of Paxos to less than 10 transactions per second, which is orders of magnitude fewer than our requirements—we need to process (both read and write) tens of thousands of events (i.e., key commits) per second. This was one of the biggest challenges with Photon, and by effectively using client and server side batching, and sharding of the IdRegistry (more details in the Photon [3] paper), Photon was able to scale to our needs.

Photon has been deployed in production at Google for several years, and it has proven to be significantly more reliable than our previous singly-homed and failover-based systems, handing all datacenter-level outages automatically, without loss in availability. For example, Fig. 3 shows the numbers of joined

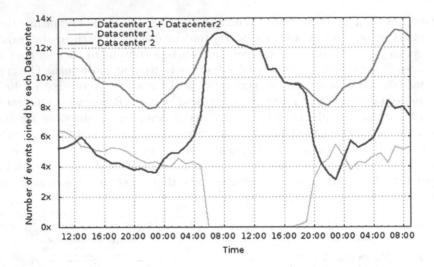

Fig. 3. Photon withstanding a real datacenter disaster

events produced by a production pipeline in two separate datacenters over a period of time. When both datacenters are healthy, each processes half of the total events. However, when one of the datacenters suffers from an outage, the other datacenter automatically starts handling the complete traffic without any manual intervention.

6.3   Mesa: Data Warehousing

Mesa [21] is a highly scalable analytic data warehousing system that stores petabytes of data, processes millions of row updates per second, and serves billions of queries per day. At Google, Mesa is used to store detailed information associated with each served ad, such as the targeting criteria, number of impressions and clicks, etc., which are recorded and processed in real time. This data is used extensively for different use cases, including reporting, internal auditing, analysis, billing, and forecasting.

Mesa is commonly used as the output storage system for stream processing systems. The streaming system consumes raw log events as input, applies business logic compute updates, and then aggregates these updates into multiple tables in the Mesa data warehouse. These Mesa tables store aggregates broken down by various metrics, so exactly-once event processing is necessary to provide accurate totals. Each input event can update aggregates in many tables, and end-users look at reports and graphs from multiple tables, expecting to see consistent totals.

Mesa is designed to provide consistent transactional updates in petabyte-scale tables with millions of updates per second, and uses multi-homing to provide high availability. This is possible because of Mesa's novel batch-update data model and transaction protocol. Mesa tables use multi-versioning, and each applied update batch gets a new version number. Update batches are written as deltas, and deltas are merged into the base in the background and as necessary at query time. A query at a particular version always sees consistent data at that version.

The large update volume in mesa makes it impractical to apply updates transactionally through Paxos-style commits. Instead, each update batch is copied asynchronously to multiple datacenters. A committer job waits until an update is copied to a quorum of datacenters, and then commits the update globally using a metadata-only Paxos commit. The version that is committed and queryable is always determined based on state in the central Paxos metadata database. This protocol scales to very large updates while providing full consistency and transparent handling of full or partial datacenter failures.

We use similar techniques in many of our streaming systems; Metadata indicating the state of work batches is synchronously committed in a global database, while the data is processed outside that transaction. For streaming systems, we often do most processing locally, then asynchronously replicate the results, and then commit. Like in Mesa, this technique minimizes synchronous global writes, enabling processing at very high scale and throughput, while still supporting multi-homing and consistent failover.

7 Related Work

There is a large body of early research on managing consistency for replicated data [10,27]. The context since then has changed via the introduction of geo-replication. The wide-area latency in a geo-replicated environment introduces challenges not considered by the traditional approaches. Early geo-replication solutions experimented with weakening consistency guarantees to ensure high performance [4,9,14,19]. More recently, however, there is wider interest in providing transactional guarantees to geo-replicated data. Spanner [15] is the first system to provide consistent geo-replicated transactions at scale.

Many stream processing systems have been built, but we are unaware of any published systems other than Photon [3] using geo-replication and multi-homing to provide high availability even in the presence of datacenter failures, and full consistency. Many systems have been built using relaxed consistency models that do not provide exactly-once semantics (Storm [7], Samza [6], Pulsar [8]). Systems that do provide exactly-once semantics either do not run at scale with fault tolerance (Aurora [1], TelegraphCQ [11], Niagara [13]) or do so within a single datacenter only (Dataflow [2], Spark streaming [28], Flink [5]).

8 Conclusion

As part of Google's advertising infrastructure, we have built and run several large-scale streaming systems, through multiple generations of system design, over many years. We have found that clients consider both consistency (exactly-once processing) and high availability to be critical properties. We have tried various approaches in various systems over time, and have learned that building natively multi-homed systems is the best solution in most cases.

Most of our systems began as singly-homed systems, and then some kind of multi-datacenter design was added on. When consistency requirements are low, running two singly homed pipelines is a simple solution that works well. When consistency is required, it becomes necessary to design failover procedures, which add significant complexity and cost.

Our experience has been that bolting failover onto previously singly-homed systems has not worked well. These systems end up being complex to build, have high maintenance overhead to run, and expose complexity to users. Instead, we started building systems with multi-homing designed in from the start, and found that to be a much better solution. Multi-homed systems run with better availability and lower cost, and result in a much simpler system overall.

The simplicity of a multi-homed system is particularly valuable for users. Without multi-homing, failover, recovery, and dealing with inconsistency are all application problems. With multi-homing, these hard problems are solved by the infrastructure, so the application developer gets high availability and consistency for free and can focus instead on building their application.

Based on our experiences, we now expect all of our systems, and any future systems we build, to have native multi-homing support as a key part of the design.

Acknowledgements. We would like to thank the teams inside Google who built and ran the systems we have described, and the earlier generations of systems that informed our current designs. We would like to thank Divyakant Agrawal for his help preparing this paper.

References

1. Abadi, D.J., et al.: Aurora: a new model and architecture for data stream management. VLDB J. **12**(2), 120–139 (2003)
2. Akidau, T., et al.: The dataflow model: a practical approach to balancing correctness, latency, and cost in massive-scale, unbounded, out-of-order data processing. Proc. VLDB Endow. **8**(12), 1792–1803 (2015)
3. Ananthanarayanan, R., et al.: Photon: fault-tolerant and scalable joining of continuous data streams. In: Proceedings of the ACM SIGMOD International Conference on Management of Data, (SIGMOD 2013), New York, NY, USA (2013)
4. Apache Cassandra (2011). Accessed 5 Oct 2011
5. Apache Flink (2014). http://flink.apache.org
6. Apache Samza (2014). http://samza.apache.org
7. Apache Storm (2013). http://storm.apache.org
8. Astley, M., et al.: Pulsar: a resource-control architecture for time-critical service-oriented applications. IBM Syst. J. **47**(2), 265–280 (2008)
9. Bailis, P., Ghodsi, A.: Eventual consistency today: limitations, extensions, and beyond. ACM Queue **11**(3), 20:20–20:32 (2013)
10. Bernstein, P.A., Hadzilacos, V., Goodman, N.: Concurrency Control and Recovery in Database Systems. Addison-Wesley, Boston (1987)

11. Chandrasekaran, S., et al.: TelegraphCQ: continuous dataflow processing. In: Proceedings of the 2003 ACM SIGMOD International Conference on Management of Data, SIGMOD 2003, pp. 668–668. ACM, New York (2003)
12. Chang, F., et al.: Bigtable: a distributed storage system for structured data. In: 7th Symposium on Operating Systems Design and Implementation (OSDI 2006), 6–8 November, Seattle, WA, USA, pp. 205–218 (2006)
13. Chen, J., et al.: NiagaraCQ: a scalable continuous query system for internet databases. In: Proceedings of the 2000 ACM SIGMOD International Conference on Management of Data, SIGMOD 2000. ACM, New York (2000)
14. Cooper, B.F., et al.: Pnuts: Yahoo!'s hosted data serving platform. Proc. VLDB Endow. 1(2), 1277–1288 (2008)
15. Corbett, J.C., et al.: Spanner: Google's globally-distributed database. In: 10th USENIX Symposium on Operating Systems Design and Implementation, (OSDI 2012), 8–10 October 2012, Hollywood, CA, USA, pp. 261–264 (2012)
16. Cormode, G., Garofalakis, M.N.: Approximate continuous querying over distributed streams. ACM Trans. Database Syst. 33(2), 9 (2008)
17. Cormode, G., Muthukrishnan, S., Yi, K., Zhang, Q.: Continuous sampling from distributed streams. J. ACM 59(2), 10 (2012)
18. Dean, J., Ghemawat, S.: MapReduce: simplified data processing on large clusters. In 6th USENIX Symposium on Operating System Design and Implementation (OSDI 2004), San Francisco, California, USA, pp. 137–150 (2004)
19. DeCandia, G., et al.: Dynamo: Amazon's highly available key-value store. In: Proceedings of 21st ACM Symposium Operating Systems Principles, pp. 205–220 (2007)
20. Flajolet, P., Martin, G.N.: Probabilistic counting algorithms for data base applications. J. Comput. Syst. Sci. 31(2), 182–209 (1985)
21. Gupta, A., et al.: Mesa: geo-replicated, near real-time scalable data warehousing. PVLDB 7(12), 1259–1270 (2014)
22. Lamport, L.: Time, clocks, and the ordering of events in a distributed system. Commun. ACM 21(7), 558–565 (1978)
23. Lamport, L.: The part-time parliament. ACM Trans. Comput. Syst. 16(2), 133–169 (1998)
24. Metwally, A., Agrawal, D., El Abbadi, A.: An integrated efficient solution for computing frequent and top-k elements in data streams. ACM Trans. Database Syst. 31(3), 1095–1133 (2006)
25. Shrivastava, N., et al.: Medians and beyond: new aggregation techniques for sensor networks. In: Proceedings of the 2nd International Conference on Embedded Networked Sensor Systems, SenSys 2004, Baltimore, MD, USA (2004)
26. Shute, J., et al.: F1: a distributed SQL database that scales. PVLDB 6(11), 1068–1079 (2013)
27. Weikum, G., Vossen, G.: Transactional Information Systems: Theory, Algorithms, and the Practice of Concurrency Control and Recovery. Morgan-Kaufman Publishers, Burlington (2002)
28. Zaharia, M., et al.: Discretized streams: fault-tolerant streaming computation at scale. In: Proceedings of the Twenty-Fourth ACM Symposium on Operating Systems Principles, pp. 423–438. ACM (2013)

BIRTE 2016

Past and Future Steps for Adaptive Storage Data Systems: From Shallow to Deep Adaptivity

Stratos Idreos$^{(\boxtimes)}$, Manos Athanassoulis, Niv Dayan, Demi Guo,
Mike S. Kester, Lukas Maas, and Kostas Zoumpatianos

Harvard University, Cambridge, USA
stratos@seas.harvard.edu

Abstract. Data systems with adaptive storage can autonomously change their behavior by altering how data is stored and accessed. Such systems have been studied primarily for the case of adaptive indexing to automatically create the right indexes at the right granularity. More recently work on adaptive loading and adaptive data layouts brought even more flexibility. We survey this work and describe the need for even deeper adaptivity that goes beyond adjusting knobs in a single architecture; instead it can adapt the fundamental architecture of a data system to drastically alter its behavior.

Keywords: Adaptive data systems · Adaptive indexing · Adaptive storage

1 Adaptive Data Systems

Data systems design is a massive collection of small decisions that collectively make the architecture of a data system [1,8,19]. Typically data systems come with several tuning knobs that allow adjusting the system for different workloads and even for different hardware. As data systems have grown more complex over the years, the same is true for their tuning knobs. As a result, this task is offloaded to human experts, database administrators, that understand very well both the internals of the data system at hand and the specifics of the target application and environment.

One of the most important tuning knobs that dramatically affects performance is the selection of secondary and primary indexes that should be materialized to support a given application. This choice has attracted a lot of attention over the years given its drastic effect on performance and the complexity of making the right decisions. The main solution that helped scale such tuning choices is the introduction of auto-tuning tools. These tools automate the discovery of good candidate indexes and propose a possible configuration to the database administrator. In turn, the administrator may approve or edit the final tuning

© Springer Nature Switzerland AG 2019
M. Castellanos et al. (Eds.): BIRTE 2015/2016/2017, LNBIP 337, pp. 85–94, 2019.
https://doi.org/10.1007/978-3-030-24124-7_6

options [11]. Such tools rely primarily on what-if analysis and interaction with the optimizer to obtain estimated query costs should a candidate index set be materialized. There has been significant progress over the years including work that periodically reconsiders the tuning choices [9,10].

A big part of why the choice of indexes is such a critical factor is that it truly affects the architecture of a data system as it changes how data is stored and accessed. With the continuing trend of CPUs improving at a faster pace than memory, having the right data layout is one of the biggest deciding factors in performance of data systems as it allows us to minimize data movement. Having the correct index, i.e., the one that contains just enough relevant data (attributes) and in the best layout for the given query, means that all appropriate queries will use this optimal storage layout to access data while otherwise they would use a plain scan or a less appropriate index resulting in the need to move around many more data (pages).

While the work on auto-tuning tools has provided significant advances, it has limitations when it comes to varying workloads and data exploration scenarios [26]. In such cases, the workload cannot always be predicted up front. This means that auto-tuning tools cannot rely on a known workload to perform what-if analysis. Similarly, if the workload is changing unpredictably and often, a tool that only periodically triggers auto-tuning cannot always capture such changes.

Another disadvantage of this process is that it relies on expensive actions that materialize complete indexes. This is not a design problem of auto-tuning tools; it is rather an inherent feature of how indexing is performed, i.e., fully generating a candidate index. With bigger data sets, though, index generation actions can take a significant amount of time (e.g., it can be in the order of several hours). By the time indexing is done, the workload might have already changed and any indexing action is now irrelevant. If anything, it can even be a bottleneck because now the system must maintain unneeded indexes during updates.

Finally, another fundamental bottleneck with the indexing process is the involvement of a human in the loop. Auto-tuning tools helped minimize this involvement and scale the process but the fact that a human database administrator is still needed means that the cost of ownership of a data system is high and it slows down the process.

Adaptive indexing, adaptive partitioning, and adaptive layouts came to address the above issues by promising data systems that can automatically generate the right indexes and layouts without a human in the loop and without the requirement to know the workload up front, quickly adapting to the workload changes with small incremental actions [2–7,13–15,17,20–25,27–38]. The main innovation in these works comes from the fundamental feature of integrating physical data reorganization actions to query processing and triggering lightweight reorganization purely based on query requests.

In this paper, we briefly survey recent advances on adaptive storage work in modern data systems, highlight common principles, open problems and challenges. We term this line of work as shallow adaptivity in data systems, i.e., work that while it changes crucial knobs in the data system architecture it does not fundamentally affect the system's primary design. We then motivate the need for a new class of systems that can (automatically) perform changes at a deeper architectural level which results in system instances that would typically be considered different systems (not just differently tuned instances of the same system). We term this direction as deep adaptivity and we highlight some examples of capabilities that such deep adaptive systems should have.

There have been numerous other efforts in the general area of adaptivity. Most prominently work on adaptive query processing allows systems to change their query processing strategy by adapting to data and query properties [12, 18]. While this is one more extremely important direction with equally exciting past work and future opportunities (including possible synergy between all above directions), in this paper we focus solely on adaptive storage work that primarily changes the way data is stored and uses this as a way to modify the system behavior and properties.

2   Shallow Adaptivity

In this section, we briefly survey work on adaptive storage. We first highlight common principles and motivation. Towards the end, we discuss several open research challenges.

Principle 1: Lazy Tuning. The primary principle behind adaptive storage works is that critical tuning decisions that typically happen as part of the tuning and initialization phase of a data system, can happen during query processing time instead. The motivation for this step is twofold. First, it allows users and applications to minimize data to query time. That is, minimize the time taken for all steps required to set-up the system and ingest data from the moment that data becomes available to the moment one can issue a query. Typical steps in modern systems, include loading data into the system, choosing indexes and materialized views, and setting up several knobs. The second reason why this is a good idea is that it enables us to delay tuning decisions that may otherwise lock the system into a suboptimal state. Instead, if we take tuning decisions after we have seen the actual workload, tuning decisions can better match the desired state.

Principle 2: Continuous Layout Adaptation. Expanding from above, the second principle of adaptive storage works is that every request from the outside world (e.g, a read or write query), is treated as advice on how to store the data. This property means that the system can adapt its access patterns exactly to what the workload needs and as the workload evolves. In this way, even if the properties of the workload are not known up front, or even if they change over time, adaptive storage can capture such changes and react by physically reorganizing the data towards what would be the optimal for the running workload.

Principle 3: On-the-Fly Adaptation. Third, adaptation actions happen as part of query processing. This property is important to minimize the cost of adaptation. Adaptive storage relies on physical data reorganization which implies read and write actions to transform data between different formats. Performing the adaptation actions during query processing, means that adaptation algorithms can piggy back on I/O actions that would happen anyway for the active queries. Most typically, we may read data just once to answer a query and to perform adaptation on the relevant data. In all advanced adaptive storage works query processing and physical reorganization happen as part of the same algorithm and as part of the same pass over the data. This is key to achieve good performance.

Principle 4: Incremental Adaptation. Fourth, adaptation actions are lightweight actions that incrementally improve the state of the system. This is important to maintain low overhead for active queries that run in parallel with adaptation actions. This results in systems that are always in a transient state in terms of their storage layout. The exact state, and thus the exact data layout, at a given time depends on the types of queries the system has processed in the (recent) past. Small incremental actions have the added benefit of allowing to balance (read/write) trade-offs at a fine granularity.

Adaptive Storage. Work on adaptive storage for modern systems began with the idea of adaptive indexing in column-stores with dense and contiguous columns [22]. The idea is that instead of having to fully sort columns to create a good index, database cracking incrementally and continuously partitions columns using query predicates as pivots. This happens during query processing and effectively cracking builds a new select operator that handles both a read request and physical reorganization at the same time. As more queries are processed, columns are further partitioned; every read query needs to touch at most two pieces of a column and given that for the same column, pieces become smaller and smaller as we get more queries, performance quickly improves. Effectively the result is similar to what we would get from a fully sorted column and a binary search access path, i.e., the result of every select operator is a contiguous area in the partitioned column.

Later work on cracking pushed this idea deeper in the db kernel to be able to handle more complex queries and to mitigate any side-effects of physical reorganization. For example, work on sideways cracking showed how to process queries over more than one attributes (columns) by adaptively propagating physical reorganization across columns [24]. Work on cracking updates shows how to update such columns while maintaining the side-effects of past adaptive actions by lazy merging of updates [23]. Work on partial cracking demonstrates that the storage overhead of auxiliary indexes can be managed by both vertical and horizontal partitioning based on the workload [24]. Subsequently, work on transactional processing revealed that while indeed adaptive storage turns read queries into write queries (due to on-line adaptation), the fact that adaptive storage only affects data structure and not contents provides significant flexibility to mitigate transactional concerns [13,14]. In addition, to work around the fact that certain query sequences may provide bad partitioning schedules for columns, stochastic cracking introduced the idea that queries should indeed be treated as advice on how to store the data but they should be complemented by random reorganization actions that help balance off any bad patterns [17].

Other algorithmic efforts have focused on understanding the trade-off of how much reorganization effort should go into every query and how this affects the pace of adaptation [25,36]. Finally work on utilizing multi-core enables adaptation and full utilization of modern hardware by taking advantage of the inherent partitioned nature [6,31,36]. More recent proposals also utilize idle CPU cycles in multi-core environments to keep improving the state of the system in no peak workload periods [30].

Other than work on columnar systems, adaptive storage has also been studied for more traditional B-tree settings which triggered the work for balancing initialization costs with adaptation pace (more important when data needs to be persistent to disk) [16] as well as for more operation such as joins [28] and lightweight indexes [32].

Furthermore, work on distributed environments has utilized adaptive storage locally in each node to gain local improvements in the performance of each node [34] or even across nodes for complex operations by carefully selecting and adapting where data resides [29].

In addition, adaptive storage has been studied for the case of hybrid storage systems that provide a balance between row-stores and column-stores. Static solutions to this problem decide upfront which hybrid layout should be materialized based on the expected workload. This is exactly the same as the index tuning problem. Adaptive storage in this case can decide the right layout on-the-fly based on the access patterns required by the queries [5,7]. A new design point here is that in order to utilize the different data layouts such as an adaptive system also needs to generate code that matches the right layout. This allows to minimize both cache misses and instruction misses and branches in the code [5].

Adaptive storage is not only about physically reorganizing existing data; it is also about how we ingest data to form the desired layout. Adaptive approaches in this direction choose to wait until queries arrive to decide which data to bring into the system and in what form [2,4,21]. This removes even more overhead from the initialization phase of a data system as now we can skip the data loading step completely. The additional design point here is that touching raw data repeatedly as more queries arrive can be expensive and so adaptive works in this area are primarily concerned with minimizing this cost, e.g., by creating indexes on top of raw files.

Other than the relational model, adaptive storage has also been studied in time-series scenarios for nearest neighbor queries [37,38]. While the concepts remain the same there are some interesting differences with time-series. More importantly given that there is no strict global order across time-series there is no notion of performing small adaptation actions that refine an index. Instead, what the adaptive storage works do in this case is that they incrementally build the index by lazily indexing time-series as queries arrive. The adaptive time-series index builds initially a basic tree index but without populating it with any time series (using only high level representations) and then it actually inserts time-series in the index only when a relevant query arrives. This amortizes the cost of building the index across numerous queries in the same way as adaptive storage works do in the relational model.

Benchmarking. Benchmarking adaptive storage work requires a different approach than in traditional works. Here, the performance of the system evolves as we process more queries. Thus, each adaptive storage approach has to be evaluated over a window of time and expose properties about how the performance changes over time [15]. There are three main metrics: (1) How much slower is the very first query of adaptive storage compared to the default performance of a system (e.g., the standard one assuming no optimization has been applied via tunning)? (2) How fast the adaptive storage becomes faster than the standard approach (e.g., what is the crossover point)? (3) Does adaptive storage become as good as the optimal approach that we would get after tunning and how fast does this happen?

Open Topics. Overall there has been significant progress in adaptive storage both in terms of individual techniques and in terms of developing the concepts and principles. There are numerous open topics. Some of the most prominent open challenges include using machine learning to make tuning decisions when it is not easy to create a precise model that describes the effect of certain choices. A typical example in this direction is the choice of which column or sets of columns to optimize in a column-store. Another important open topic is studying the trade-offs of persistence vs. query response time and updates. This creates a triangle of choices that are mutually exclusive, i.e., any action taken to optimize one of them, hurts one or both of the other two. Finally, another important direction is merging adaptive indexing with traditional auto-tuning tools such that we can utilize both known workload knowledge if available and adapt to tight time budgets and workload changes. For example, while existing auto-tuning tools work only when there is enough workload knowledge and idle time to go through the tuning phases, an approach that merges both auto-tunning and adaptive indexing properties has the potential to be able to utilize (1) any workload knowledge even if it is not complete and (2) any idle time even if it is not enough to create all indexes we know we should create.

3   Deep Adaptivity

While the premise of the above work, termed as shallow adaptivity, is promising, it still has a fundamental limitation. It only works within a given architecture design. That is, it takes critical tuning steps that primarily have to do with data layout and devises adaptive/lazy approaches to adjust the layout to the workload. However, the options supported are within the design space of the original architecture. For example, in the case of generating the right indexes for a column-store system, adaptive storage decides which indexes to generate, when and how fine-grained the indexes should be. At all states, though, the fundamental architecture of the system does not change; it is still a column-store and behaves well only for the set of properties for which we can tune a column-store.

We term as deep adaptivity, a future class of data systems that would be able to cross architecture designs, i.e., designs that are typically considered fundamentally different systems today. A fundamentally different architecture is one that has significant design differences which typically stems from focusing to specific workloads, functionalities and hardware.

There are numerous reasons why such a path would lead to desirable systems. The primary one is similar to the need for adaptivity but at an even higher level. With ever more complex and diverse workloads today, industry and sciences need support from different kinds of systems which in turn increases the complexity of managing and tuning these systems as well as the cost of ownership. Having a single system that can change its behavior drastically would decrease costs and make access to data generally easier to manage instead of needing a new tailored system for every different scenario we need to support within a business. One of the most typical examples is the ability to support drastically different or even varying read/write ratios.

Perhaps even more importantly, a system that can change its shape drastically can better adapt to evolving hardware. As it stands today, new hardware appears faster than the pace at which software can follow. Having systems that are inherently flexible to adapt their design in more fundamental ways than the knobs exposed today would allow for easier adaptation.

As an example of possible deep design changes, consider changes that are fundamentally shifting the shape of underlying access methods in data systems. Given that access methods define the read/write performance of systems such a step does affect the overall performance. However, introducing new access methods or drastically changing existing ones in most systems that are older than a few years quickly becomes increasingly hard and is only worthwhile if we are close 100% sure about the final performance impact (which is a huge problem by itself). This restricts innovation and system adaptation to change. In this way, even the ability to manually adapt and test the design of systems in a low-overhead way would be a significant step even if it does not happen completely automatically.

Deep adaptivity requires several steps such as high level languages to express design (and change), methods to quickly test the impact of possible changes, allowing for semi-automatic human in the loop design, and most importantly fully mapping the possible design space. Similarly to shallow adaptivity, deep adaptivity needs to be evaluated against new metrics that capture the ability to change and adapt quickly.

4   Summary

This paper briefly surveys past work on adaptive storage and introduces the need to go beyond shallow adaptivity, to enable deeper architectural changes either automatically or semi-automatically. Having the ability to easily change the shape of a data system in a drastic way means that we can easily test possible alternative designs and quickly adapt to new application features or hardware, a process that typically may take several months or even years for mature systems with accumulated complexity.

References

1. Abadi, D.J., Boncz, P., Harizopoulos, S., Idreos, S., Madden, S.: The design and implementation of modern column-oriented database systems. Found. Trends Databases **5**(3), 197–280 (2013)
2. Alagiannis, I., Borovica, R., Branco, M., Idreos, S., Ailamaki, A.: NoDB: efficient query execution on raw data files. In: Proceedings of the ACM SIGMOD International Conference on Management of Data, pp. 241–252 (2012)
3. Alagiannis, I., Borovica, R., Branco, M., Idreos, S., Ailamaki, A.: NoDB in action: adaptive query processing on raw data. Proc. VLDB Endow. **5**(12), 1942–1945 (2012)
4. Alagiannis, I., Borovica-Gajic, R., Branco, M., Idreos, S., Ailamaki, A.: NoDB: efficient query execution on raw data files. Commun. ACM **58**(12), 112–121 (2015)
5. Alagiannis, I., Idreos, S., Ailamaki, A.: H2O: a hands-free adaptive store. In: Proceedings of the ACM SIGMOD International Conference on Management of Data, pp. 1103–1114 (2014)
6. Alvarez, V., Schuhknecht, F.M., Dittrich, J., Richter, S.: Main memory adaptive indexing for multi-core systems. In: Tenth International Workshop on Data Management on New Hardware, DaMoN 2014, 23 June 2014, Snowbird, UT, USA, pp. 3:1–3:10 (2014)
7. Arulraj, J., Pavlo, A., Menon, P.: Bridging the archipelago between row-stores and column-stores for hybrid workloads. In: Proceedings of the ACM SIGMOD International Conference on Management of Data (2016)
8. Athanassoulis, M., Idreos, S.: Design tradeoffs of data access methods. In: Proceedings of the ACM SIGMOD International Conference on Management of Data, Tutorial (2016)
9. Bruno, N., Chaudhuri, S.: To tune or not to tune?: a lightweight physical design alerter. In: Proceedings of the International Conference on Very Large Data Bases (VLDB), pp. 499–510 (2006)
10. Bruno, N., Chaudhuri, S.: An online approach to physical design tuning. In: Proceedings of the IEEE International Conference on Data Engineering (ICDE), pp. 826–835 (2007)
11. Chaudhuri, S., Narasayya, V.R.: An efficient cost-driven index selection tool for Microsoft SQL server. In: Proceedings of the International Conference on Very Large Data Bases (VLDB), pp. 146–155 (1997)
12. Deshpande, A., Hellerstein, J.M., Raman, V.: Adaptive query processing: why, how, when, what next. In: Proceedings of the ACM SIGMOD International Conference on Management of Data, 27–29 June 2006, Chicago, Illinois, USA, pp. 806–807 (2006)
13. Graefe, G., Halim, F., Idreos, S., Kuno, H., Manegold, S.: Concurrency control for adaptive indexing. Proc. VLDB Endow. **5**(7), 656–667 (2012)
14. Graefe, G., Halim, F., Idreos, S., Kuno, H.A., Manegold, S., Seeger, B.: Transactional support for adaptive indexing. VLDB J. **23**(2), 303–328 (2014)
15. Graefe, G., Idreos, S., Kuno, H., Manegold, S.: Benchmarking adaptive indexing. In: Nambiar, R., Poess, M. (eds.) TPCTC 2010. LNCS, vol. 6417, pp. 169–184. Springer, Heidelberg (2011). https://doi.org/10.1007/978-3-642-18206-8_13
16. Graefe, G., Kuno, H.: Self-selecting, self-tuning, incrementally optimized indexes. In: Proceedings of the International Conference on Extending Database Technology (EDBT), pp. 371–381 (2010)

17. Halim, F., Idreos, S., Karras, P., Yap, R.H.C.: Stochastic database cracking: towards robust adaptive indexing in main-memory column-stores. Proc. VLDB Endow. **5**(6), 502–513 (2012)
18. Hellerstein, J.M., et al.: Adaptive query processing: technology in evolution. IEEE Data Eng. Bull. **23**(2), 7–18 (2000)
19. Hellerstein, J.M., Stonebraker, M., Hamilton, J.R.: Architecture of a database system. Found. Trends Databases **1**(2), 141–259 (2007)
20. Idreos, S.: Database cracking: towards auto-tuning database kernels. Ph.D. thesis, University of Amsterdam (2010)
21. Idreos, S., Alagiannis, I., Johnson, R., Ailamaki, A.: Here are my data files. Here are my queries. Where are my results? In: Proceedings of the Biennial Conference on Innovative Data Systems Research (CIDR), pp. 57–68 (2011)
22. Idreos, S., Kersten, M.L., Manegold, S.: Database cracking. In: Proceedings of the Biennial Conference on Innovative Data Systems Research (CIDR) (2007)
23. Idreos, S., Kersten, M.L., Manegold, S.: Updating a cracked database. In: Proceedings of the ACM SIGMOD International Conference on Management of Data, pp. 413–424 (2007)
24. Idreos, S., Kersten, M.L., Manegold, S.: Self-organizing tuple reconstruction in column-stores. In: Proceedings of the ACM SIGMOD International Conference on Management of Data, pp. 297–308 (2009)
25. Idreos, S., Manegold, S., Kuno, H., Graefe, G.: Merging what's cracked, cracking what's merged: adaptive indexing in main-memory column-stores. Proc. VLDB Endow. **4**(9), 586–597 (2011)
26. Idreos, S., Papaemmanouil, O., Chaudhuri, S.: Overview of data exploration techniques. In: Proceedings of the ACM SIGMOD International Conference on Management of Data, Tutorial, pp. 277–281 (2015)
27. Karras, P., Nikitin, A., Saad, M., Bhatt, R., Antyukhov, D., Idreos, S.: Adaptive indexing over encrypted numeric data. In: Proceedings of the ACM SIGMOD International Conference on Management of Data, pp. 171–183 (2016)
28. Liu, Z., Idreos, S.: Main memory adaptive denormalization. In: Proceedings of the ACM SIGMOD International Conference on Management of Data, pp. 2253–2254 (2016)
29. Lu, Y., Shanbhag, A., Jindal, A., Madden, S.: AdaptDB: adaptive partitioning for distributed joins. PVLDB **10**(5), 589–600 (2017)
30. Petraki, E., Idreos, S., Manegold, S.: Holistic indexing in main-memory column-stores. In: Proceedings of the ACM SIGMOD International Conference on Management of Data (2015)
31. Pirk, H., Petraki, E., Idreos, S., Manegold, S., Kersten, M.L.: Database cracking: fancy scan, not poor man's sort! In: Proceedings of the International Workshop on Data Management on New Hardware (DAMON), pp. 1–8 (2014)
32. Qin, W., Idreos, S.: Adaptive data skipping in main-memory systems. In: Proceedings of the ACM SIGMOD International Conference on Management of Data, pp. 2255–2256 (2016)
33. Richter, S., Quiané-Ruiz, J.-A., Schuh, S., Dittrich, J.: Towards zero-overhead static and adaptive indexing in Hadoop. VLDB J. **23**(3), 469–494 (2013)
34. Schuh, S., Dittrich, J.: AIR: adaptive index replacement in Hadoop. In: 31st IEEE International Conference on Data Engineering Workshops, ICDE Workshops 2015, 13–17 April 2015, Seoul, South Korea, pp. 22–29 (2015)
35. Schuhknecht, F.M., Jindal, A., Dittrich, J.: The uncracked pieces in database cracking. Proc. VLDB Endow. **7**(2), 97–108 (2013)

36. Schuhknecht, F.M., Jindal, A., Dittrich, J.: An experimental evaluation and analysis of database cracking. Very Large Database J. VLDBJ **25**(1), 27–52 (2016)
37. Zoumpatianos, K., Idreos, S., Palpanas, T.: Indexing for interactive exploration of big data series. In: Proceedings of the ACM SIGMOD International Conference on Management of Data, pp. 1555–1566 (2014)
38. Zoumpatianos, K., Idreos, S., Palpanas, T.: ADS: the adaptive data series index. Very Large Database J. VLDBJ **25**(6), 843–866 (2016)

PolyRecs: Improving Page–View Rates Using Real-Time Data Analysis

Mihalis Papakonstantinou[✉] and Alex Delis[✉]

University of Athens, 15703 Athens, Greece
{mihalispapak,ad}@di.uoa.gr

Abstract. In this paper, we outline our effort to enhance the page-view rates of *e*-content that online customers read on a popular portal in Greece. The portal, `athensvoice.gr`, provides continuous coverage on news, politics, science, the arts, and opinion columns and its customers generate approximately 6 million unique visits per month. Gains both in terms of advertisement and further e-content market penetration were the objectives of our effort which yielded the `PolyRecs` system, in production for more than a year now. In designing `PolyRecs`, we were primarily concerned with the use of pages in real-time and to this end, we elected to utilize five key criteria to achieve the aforementioned goals. We selected criteria for which we were able to obtain pertinent statistics without compromising performance and offered a real-time exploitation of the user page-views on the go. In addition, we were keen in realizing not only effective on-the-fly calculations of what might be interesting to the browsing individuals at specific points in time but also produce accurate results capable of improving the user-experience. The key factors exploited by `PolyRecs` entail features from both collaboration and content-based systems. Once operational, `PolyRecs` helped the news portal attain an average increase of 6.3% of the overall page-views in its traffic. To ascertain the `PolyRecs` utility, we provide a brief economic analysis in terms of measured performance indicators and identify the degree of contribution each of the key factors offers. Last but not least, we have developed `PolyRecs` as a domain-agnostic hybrid-recommendation system for we wanted it to successfully function regardless of the underlying data and/or content infrastructure.

Keywords: Timely delivery of news articles · Content-based furnishing of news · Hybrid recommendation systems · Real-time content analysis

1 Introduction

Serving just-on-time pertinent news items has become a key requirement for a broad range of web portals, online publications and news agencies [1,2]. Appropriately recommending content in real-time has become the enabler for conducting successful business in both online dissemination and e-publishing. By being

© Springer Nature Switzerland AG 2019
M. Castellanos et al. (Eds.): BIRTE 2015/2016/2017, LNBIP 337, pp. 95–112, 2019.
https://doi.org/10.1007/978-3-030-24124-7_7

proactive and by furnishing more accurate suggestions providers undoubtedly benefit as users expend longer periods of time online, click-through-rates are increased and ultimately, revenue grows either directly from advertisements or indirectly from ratings [3,4].

Until recently, suggestions for further reading for no-global content providers have been mostly served using either one or a combination of the following criteria: *(a)* time that an article appeared, *(b)* selection of articles from a single subject category, *(c)* choosing items either with semi- or manual manner, and *(d)* picking items written by the same author, source, etc. In this paper, we outline an effort to *enhance* the existing recommendation system of `athensvoice.gr`, a popular news portal in the country that offers news, articles on politics, arts, local affairs, opinion columns and user comments; the portal has been operational for a number of years now and has seen its market share to increase. We seek to accomplish the aforementioned objective by offering a novel combined approach of content-based and collaborative filtering [5] along with real-time analysis for newly arriving news items and improved user-experience through more effective suggestions of items. To this end, we have improved the operation of the *e-magazine* by offering a truly hybrid system for recommendations. To the best of our knowledge, this is the first system in its kind that is both hybrid in nature and deploys multiple selection criteria that get to be evaluated in real-time.

An exploratory effort to better understand the specific constraints based on *JavaScript*-functions used to provide workbench measurements for `PolyRecs`'s key functionalities showed that the slack for the time window within which recommendation can be compiled is approximately 1 s before the user actually sees the corresponding portion of the display. This is clearly a very tight period within which both computation and displaying have to occur. We should indicate that `athensvoice.gr` receives approximately 6 million visitors from unique IPs every month, with an average of 2.3 pages served per user.

The developed system, termed `PolyRecs`, has both real-time and off–line components. It serves recommendations produced dynamically as a visitor scrolls within a web-page in a pre-specified portion of the page; the form of latter differs across devices used to access content from the portal. Our prime objective has been two-pronged as we seek to: *(1)* maintain strict requirements for the system's responsiveness by having 97% of suggestions appearing in less than 1 s; displaying suggestions does call for computing overheads that include elimination of news items already seen, incorporation of just-arrived-pieces in the display, and implications due to specific profiling users may elect to adopt, *(2)* divide the computational work as effective as possible between the off–line (initial) component of the portal and the introduced on-line part of `PolyRecs`. The off–line work gets done mostly through `cron` script jobs and they mostly involve computations that have to do with the re-computation of correlation among subject categories. In particular the tasks at hand entail computing cosine similarities among new and old articles, backing up data and purging obsolete ones no longer required for the engine, and finally, clearing up data from the database table that are considered noise [6,7]. This task is a CPU-hog [8] but in short time intervals required by the average portal user, it contributes to the requisite overhead only incrementally.

We present the specific multiple criteria that collectively contribute towards recommendations presented to unique users and outline the `PolyRecs` functional elements that place special emphasis on new posts. Clearly, the corpus of diversified content items for `athensvoice.gr` does continuously change and/or gets updated. It is worth mentioning that we have designed and developed both the underlying database and content delivery system in a way that is agnostic to the particular characteristics of the portal for which we sought out to increase pageviews. In this regard, the salient features of `PolyRecs` recommendation engine could be readily incorporated into news and dissemination portals.

`PolyRecs` has been operational for more than an year now and this has given us the opportunity to carry out extensive experimentation and evaluation of all its key aspects. To gauge the yield in terms of economic benefit to the site, we introduce a metric to quantify possible gains; over time, the metric has helped us ascertain the effectiveness of our overall recommendation strategy in conjunction with the data we obtain from the *Google Analytics Service*. The proposed metric uses a visitor's clicks as its main factor that helps track the criteria which triggered the produced recommendations.

Our approach has assisted `athensvoice.gr` to increase on the average the time visitors stay on the portal by approximately 6% as well as it has yielded improved rates for content retrieval. To the best of our knowledge, this is the first such production system, that is both hybrid and uses multiple criteria, deployed and evaluated on an operational *e*-content portal. Our paper is organized as follows: Sect. 2 offers related work and Sect. 3 outlines key requirements for the proposed system. Section 4 presents all key aspects of our recommendation approach. Finally, Sects. 5 and 6 presents key findings and concluding remarks respectively.

2   Related Work

The emergence of digital forums, e-shops, and modern electronic marketing ecosystems has ushered in a flurry of activity in developing recommending systems [1,3,5,9,10]. Moreover, a range of metrics have been proposed to help ascertain the corresponding value of such prototypes and/or production systems in specific areas of application [4–6,11–14].

Efforts in [1,5] have focused on recommendations for search engines using machine learning algorithms for predicting news on the wire [15,16], expanded vertical search [17] and crowd-sourcing to better evaluate the learned approaches deployed [1]. In [3] the deployment of a hybrid recommending engine for the Google-News, a news aggregator, and its comparison with a collaborative filtering approach [9] is carried out; if only logged–in users are considered, a noteworthy performance improvement is reported with respect to plain filtering approaches. In [18], the imprecision of the click-through rates is examined in the context of the *Plista* news-recommender on hourly and weekly bases; *Plista* functions as an aggregator and delivers suggestions to multiple web portals. Our approach combines characteristics from both collaborative [2] and item/user-based content-based filtering [3,5]. In this respect, our approach resembles in part prior efforts [3,5,11] when it comes to combining techniques for yielding recommendations. However, we use diverse criteria that can be dynamically introduced during the calibration of our system. More importantly, we combine real-time and off–line characteristics for we strive to comply with short timing requirements to produce quality suggestions for users.

In [1,6,19], a number of metrics were introduced using predominantly click-rates to derive recommendations; the effectiveness of such metrics is also compared with that of prior approaches [1,6,19]. PolyRecs markedly differs from the above efforts as we not only exploit clicks users perform but more importantly, we keep track of the degree by which the used criteria are affected by the dwelling of unique users. This does lead to a more sophisticated calibration of the overall recommendation engine used by athensvoice.gr. Moreover, PolyRecs provides a framework for introducing specialized machine learning approaches in recommending items from the continually changing content of the portal.

3   PolyRecs Approach

As we wanted to improve PolyRecs page-views and increase unique visits to the production portal, we actively avoided during the design of the engine to provide recommendations based on widely used heuristics such as articles written by same (or similar) authors, content in the same category and/or just popular items within the portal. These techniques although effective at times, fail to consider a reader's own interests at the time of browsing. In addition, prior stated-preferences may be discarded and possible correlations among categories might be overlooked.

In PolyRecs, we combine a number of techniques so that we can present visitors with suggestions that not only fall within the realm of their interests but they also are "fresh"; the notion of being "fresh" pertains to pages that either have not been read so far or may have appeared on the portal data infrastructure recently. In this context, a key factor that we had to take into consideration was the very large amount of data collected within a matter of minutes in user activity. Effectively managing the inflow of information as well as the outflow of the portal data constitutes a challenge. In an exploratory phase, we instrumented athensvoice.gr and measured the average dwelling time for a visitor: we found it consistently to be around 1 s using JavaScript events. It is within this window of time that recommendations have to be compiled and be timely shown to the reader so as to increase page-view rates and consequently time spent on athensvoice.gr. This timing benchmark also indicated that regardless of the sophistication of the recommendation algorithm, if we take longer times to generate suggestions this will render the engine ineffective. In this case, the majority of visitors will fail to receive both personalized and accurate recommendations within the designated real-time slack. To accommodate the above requirement, PolyRecs's design follows a *hybrid* approach exploiting a variety of key operational aspects by:

1. predominantly focusing on the responsiveness of such an engine,
2. being able to process important data flows and events real-time,
3. profiling both users and incoming pieces of content in a timely manner,
4. deploying effective features from traditional techniques used in the athensvoice.gr engine to this date,
5. training on–the–fly as much as possible while relegating off–line work for resource-intensive tasks only,
6. designing a system that can work in a plug-and-play fashion, regardless of the underlying infrastructure (i.e., database and content management systems used).

All the above features influenced the design of PolyRecs and led us to deploy an engine that embeds multi-criteria in its core operation with the time slack for all jobs taken continuously into account. In addition, we deploy a fail-over mechanism that addresses issues introduced due to new content, users, content category re-alignment, and classification re-adjustment.

A number of factors influence the way PolyRecs yields its suggestions and include:

– the visitor's unique profile based on user-id and IP number,
– articles whose categories are strongly related to content currently in browsing,
– the time of day the visitor is browsing the portal,
– articles that share a high textual–similarity to the one currently being accessed,
– articles that are popular on this content–category today.

By default, each of the above criteria may equally contribute –in terms of weight– to the outcomes computed by PolyRecs. In this regard, we seek to ensure the objectiveness of the evaluation while we offer the capability to appropriately gauge the weighting scheme so as to provide content of timely interest. Moreover, we want to offer warranties that PolyRecs regardless of the nature of the visitor and/or the item currently in browsing, we can locate suggestions even if one or more of the contributing criteria fail to produce suggestions. In this case, the rest of the criteria will kick in and help fill in the required quota for compiling the list of the suggestions.

We aspire to carry the necessary functionalities in real-time and compute all required aspects on-the-fly in a way that the user has the time to view recommendations, evaluate their worthiness and likely proceed to read one of those suggestions. If so, a new batch of recommendations is computed while user clicks generate valuable input in term of the navigation provided for our engine.

4   PolyRecs Architecture

This section outlines the overall functional architecture of PolyRecs in a way that mostly focuses in the flow of data as well as both user-input/output generated.

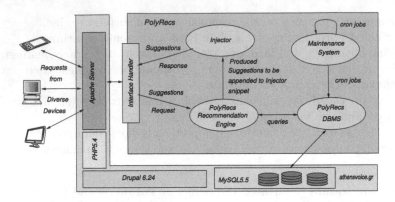

Fig. 1. PolyRecs functional overview in the context of *athensvoice.gr*

Figure 1 depicts the overall organization in terms of constituent components of PolyRecs as well as the data/control interactions with the other major components of the athensvoice.gr. We realize the PolyRecs engine by weaving five key elements together:

1. the database system (*DBMS*) responsible for storing and querying user traffic events and requisite (meta-)data,
2. the recommendation engine (*RE*) responsible for processing the data and executing our recommendation algorithm,
3. the interface handler (*IH*) which appropriately displays results based on the devices users interact with,
4. the maintenance system (*MSys*) that performs all necessary off-line computation work and maintenance operations such as cleaning, staging and archiving,
5. the injector (*Inj*) that helps quantify the (financial) benefits of integrating PolyRecs to the athensvoice.gr by code-instrumenting the suggestions made.

Although PolyRecs is embedded in the athensvoice.gr portal and essentially interacts with the respective *Apache* web-server and *Drupal* CMS, we have followed a highly modular design so that it can function with any other portal layout. In what follows, we discuss the operation of the key PolyRecs components and indicate their interactions.

4.1   The Database (*DBMS*)

MySQL is deployed to help store data and realize queries in PolyRecs while using two schemas: the *main* schema that essentially hosts all real-time data and a *backup* schema in which we stage data deemed stale yet potentially useful for forthcoming retrieval(s). The more critical of the tables existing in the PolyRecs database main schema manages all data that are generated by data flows incurred by the user activity. The table stores facts such as user-ids involved in accessing portal content, time-stamps and URLs visited. Once acquired through the click-through activity of users, these data have to be further processed and passed along to other database tables holding respective information. In this context, every URL gets analyzed to its ingredients that are: the article-id (information shared between the DBMSs of both portal and PolyRecs), category classification, as well as time-stamp of the click. The main table termed *init_data*, rapidly builds volume due to all recorded input/output operations performed on the portal's *Apache*-server on a daily basis. Apparently, the way we handle this table may affect the performance of our engine and is deemed an enabler for furnishing timely responses to user queries.

Overall, the main schema of our *MySQL* database features tables that predominantly store processed information accumulated over time, and statistics that are fed to PolyRecs's recommendation engine to assist in creating suggestions. Among others, these tables include: (1) the users profile table, (2) the categories profile table, (3) day time profile table, (4) article to article similarity table, (5) popular articles per day table. We should point out that the information maintained by the above tables has to do mostly with meta-data of articles and items whose actual content resides in the portal's database. The design of the backup schema is identical to that of the main for its hosts dated, less useful or occasionally obsolete information and gets to be occasionally purged.

4.2 PolyRecs Recommendation Engine (*RE*)

The engine undertakes the task to produce within the time slack permitted, suggestions for a specific visitor. Its function highly depends on the database and essentially works as a go-between the interface and *MySQL*. Given as input the unique identifier for a visitor in conjunction with the current URL he/she is viewing (from which the article-id and category are derived), the engine returns a predefined number of suggestions. The input in discussion is used by the *RE* as follows: *(a)* the visitor's id is utilized to fetch and enrich his/hers profile in terms of favorable categories, pieces of content already read, preferences, etc, *(b)* the URL currently being viewed is marked as seen and is used to "select" a category of items so that similar items are suggested, and *(c)* PolyRecs by design imposes an upper-limit on the number of suggestions displayed to its user interface; this can lighten the work carried out by the database in its effort to produce *top-k* items for queries on suggestions.

After a lengthy empirical evaluation and detailed study of user-cases, we set this $k=15$ for predominantly two reasons: (i) the portion of the web-page reserved for these suggestions could not exceed this limit for this would not effectively facilitate the user view of the results, and (ii) as we mainly derive recommendation using 5 criteria in our *RE* (see below), we wanted to adopt a viable yet proportional representation of these criteria when it came to their respective contributions into the list of suggestions. By and large, this limit for k may be highly dependent on the choices made by the portal and so, it can be reconfigurable.

The 5 distinct and likely weighted categories `PolyRecs` depends on to create its recommendations are the following:

1. A visitor's favorite categories (weight w_1),
2. Articles whose categories appear to be "strongly related" to the current category being read (w_2)
3. The time of day a visitor browses a specific piece of content on the portal (w_3),
4. Articles that share a high *cosine*–similarity value to the one currently in access (w_4), and finally,
5. Articles that are popular today (w_5).

`PolyRecs` stores aggregated data associating each visitor with the number of times she has accessed a specific category. Using such counters, pieces of content are fetched that are tagged with categories present on the top 85% of her most frequent reads. The above percentage was set after observing that the lowest 15% of the categories a visitor views, usually have very low counters indicating negligible impact.

A category's strong or weak relation to one another, is generated based on the number of times one has been read after the other. Tracking each visitor's behavior throughout `athensvoice.gr`, `PolyRecs` is able to create this correlation between categories of the portal and return pieces of content from pertinent categories. Each visitor's click in the portal is also associated with the time at which it occurred. This allows `PolyRecs` to associate categories frequently accessed at specific times of day (e.g., articles that describe recipes, or restaurants are more frequently read during midday). In `PolyRecs` *DBMS* data concerning the popularity of each piece of content is stored. This allows the *RE* to suggest articles that show a high popularity today. The criterion utilizing the similarity between articles is based on the *cosine* similarity value. Having this value available for each piece of content present on `athensvoice.gr`, `PolyRecs` can recommend articles that share a high value to the one a visitor is currently reading.

In the above 5 categories, we should have that $\Sigma(w_i) = k$ holds true at all times. Although we could use an equal-weighted approach for these w_i, in the context of `athensvoice.gr`, we empirically found that a slightly different weight vector does work more effectively in our applications setting; this vector is $w =< 4, 3, 3, 3, 2 >$.

We should also point out that content that has been already browsed by the user at any point in her dwelling on the portal is explicitly excluded from the suggestions. In the final compilation of recommendation, we also do carry out duplicate elimination and if needed our engine brings in additional results to appropriately fill in the list of suggestions. As items are continually introduced to the portal through the *Drupal* CMS, their meta-data pass on to the `PolyRecs` database and so they immediately become available for the computations performed by *RE*.

4.3 PolyRecs Interface Handler (*IH*)

IH is responsible for the presentation of the recommendations coming from the core of PolyRecs and helps with the rendering of this result set on specific devices. Initially, the interface handler receives the triplet of data generated during the browsing of an article and passes this information as input to PolyRecs. With its turn, the engine sends out the recommendation list for the article in question and the *IH* manages the generation of the required HTML snippet; the snippet also contains style-sheet rules as well as automatically generated *JavaScript* event-functions. The snippet is then transported to the consuming *Apache* web-server for final dispatching to the user device (Fig. 1).

Figure 2 depicts how the result-sets for recommendations appear to either a desktop or mobile device. Evidently, when the outcome of a presentation may have multiple forms which are generated with the intervention of the *IH*. The specifics of the rendering involved here are exclusively an assignment taken over

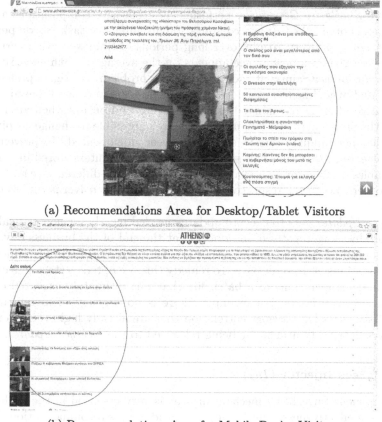

(a) Recommendations Area for Desktop/Tablet Visitors

(b) Recommendations Area for Mobile Device Visitors

Fig. 2. Recommendation areas for various devices

by the interface handler. In addition to the suggestions, each specific recommendation on the user-device is escorted by a specific *JavaScript* event function whose goal is to inform the `PolyRecs` database if and where a user elects to click and go further. This *JavaScript* mechanism provides the capability for `PolyRecs` to very accurately account for clicks induced from the lists of provided recommendations.

4.4 `PolyRecs` Maintenance System (*Msys*)

The maintenance component consists of a number of php–scripts that get executed within `PolyRecs` and are mostly *cron*-jobs. Among those tasks, the most important are:

- *User Profile Reset* cleanses a user's profile from data that are at some point considered noise. These data are about category reads that rank significantly low to make it into the output. To this end, they have essentially ceased to characterize a visitor's active preferences.
- *Content Similarity Generation* performs the respective computations among pieces of content. As this is a computationally intensive task [8], we perform it as a *cron*-job every 20 min; over long periods of time we have ascertained that every 20 min a new article appears on the average on `athensvoice.gr`.
- *Plasticity Solver* aims at addressing the problem of rigid preferences attributed over time to a user. The problem appears in content–based or collaborative filtering recommendation algorithms and occurs when after some time, the preferences of a user are practically impossible to change despite the fact that her unique visits to article has been documented. To prevent this phenomenon, *MSys* runs this solver to reduce the counters stored in cumulative tables by 25% for those values that display a big difference (e.g., >80%) with other rows in the respective tables. Typically, the solver is run every few days.
- *Delayed Updater* gets to execute updates needed mostly for non-critical data and produces aggregates of information at the end of the business day. Over time, we observed that during peak-periods, `PolyRecs` used to produce recommendations at a slower pace. To remedy this, we opted to stage less critical data update operations to a batch file that was ultimately executed once a day in off-peak hours. For example, there is no urgency to increment values of statistics for category correlation that are already high; this operation receives delayed treatment by being relegated to the *Delayed Updater*.

4.5 `PolyRecs` Injector (*Inj*)

This component furnishes a mechanism that is very essential in the evaluation of `PolyRecs` effectiveness. The *RE* module produces its recommendations based on the 5 earlier-stated criteria. It is however crucial that a feedback mechanism be established so that `PolyRecs` ultimately becomes aware of which suggestions

```
<a href="/article/design-home/article/open-house-athens-2015"
onclick="clicked(123,109891,2)">Open House Athens 2015</a>
```

Fig. 3. PolyRecs *Injector* snippet addition

as well as the corresponding criteria were ultimately used out of the recommendation list. In this respect, *Inj* maintains statistics in terms of counters and instruments the list of recommendations bound for the *IH* by automatically adding *JavaScript* code for every item on this list. A *JavaScript* event function is generated on-the-fly and gets attached to every recommendation produced.

Figure 3 shows the result of *Inj*'s instrumentation of the recommendations; this outcome will finally make it through the *IH* and *Apache* web-server to the user's browser. As Fig. 3 indicates, this function takes as input 3 parameters: *(1)* the *visitor-id* for whom the recommendations were created, *(2)* the *id* of the article being recommended, and *(3)* the *criterion-id* (i.e., numbers 1..5) by which the suggestion was generated. If a browsing user clicks a recommendation, the accompanied *JavaScript* code-snippet is executed. As a consequence, the aforementioned 3 pieces of information along with the time-stamp of the click are inserted into PolyRecs's *DBMS* to be evaluated at a later stage. The evaluation is performed to measure the performance of each criterion integrated into PolyRecs.

We have found that this method of providing instrumentation for evaluation does offer two clear advantages:

1. By tracking the clicks of each visitor, we can more effectively evaluate the PolyRecs performance and analyze the possible benefits in terms of *CTR* (click-through-rate).
2. By keeping track of the criterion by which every click was produced, we can better quantify the effect each criterion has on PolyRecs.

In addition, this approach does offer opportunities for extensions by for instance being able to integrate seamlessly in the future more sophisticated techniques (such as machine-learning) to help automatically compute the weights for each criterion over time.

5   Evaluation

In evaluating the PolyRecs prototype, we aim at establishing the effectiveness of our overall approach, in pointing out the benefits of our hybrid proposal and in assessing PolyRecs's contribution to the overall running of the athensvoice.gr portal. Using Google's Analytics and having access to both PolyRecs-enabled and stand-alone versions of the production portal, we are able to present page-view rates over lengthy periods of observation. Google's Analytics is an independent service commonly used by web-based systems to gain insight on operational trade-offs and evaluate performance. In this section, we also gauge the merit of integrating PolyRecs into the production portal through a succinct cost/benefit analysis.

Table 1. Increasing page-views/session through `PolyRecs`(month period)

Page-Views/Session with `PolyRecs` enabled	Desktops & Tablets	Mobile Devices
Page-Views/Session Increase	+73.81%	+17.81%

5.1   Analysis with Google's Analytics

We commence by examining the number of page-views the portal received over a 1-month period while using the `PolyRecs` engine and compare these page-views with their counterparts that occurred a year before. In this, we investigate the traffic generated by both desktop/tablet and mobile devices. We are interested in this grouping for two reasons: firstly, the web-page lay out is different for these two types of machinery and secondly, user-behavior has been shown to differ when hand-held devices are used for browsing [20].

The reported time periods are those of *24/07/2015-24/08/2015* and *24/07/2014-24/08/2014*. We selected this specific day-span so as to remain as much as possible unaffected by user behavior; by and large, this period coincides with the summer vacations in the country.

Table 1 depicts the increase observed in page-views per session for the two classes of devices used for access. We should note here that we have managed to augment the rates despite a 9.58% experienced drop in the unique number of visitors over the 2015 period. On average, `PolyRecs` manages to deliver an increase of 45.81% in combined page-views per session.

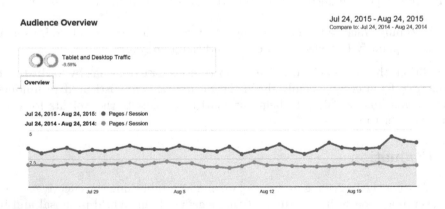

Fig. 4. Chart for average daily page-view/session for desktop/tablet users

Figure 4 shows how the page-views/sessions fared for each day of the observation period when only desktop and tablet traffic was taken into consideration. Clearly, there exists an indisputable positive effect from the deployment of `PolyRecs` as the curve from the 2015 remains consistently higher at all times

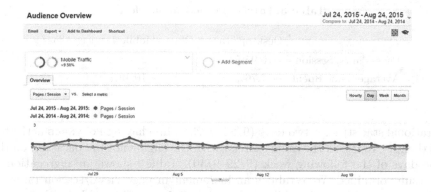

Fig. 5. Chart for average daily page-views/session for mobile devices visitors

Table 2. Page-views/session and unique visitors

	Desktop/Tablet without PolyRecs 9/29–9/30	Desktop/Tablet with PolyRecs enabled 9/22–9/23	Mobile Devices without PolyRecs 9/29–9/30	Mobile Devices with PolyRecs enabled 9/22–9/23
Page-Views/Sess.	2.83	3.18	1.42	1.46
Unique Visitors	167,240	148,921	117,003	128,784

from that of 2014. Similar results can be seen in Fig. 5 that depicts the respective curves when we analyze activity generated only by mobile devices. The PolyRecs-enabled curve invariably produces improved page-views per session rates throughout the month.

In an effort called "4-day experiment", we seek to ascertain the value of PolyRecs within a short and recent period of time. Hence, we collected

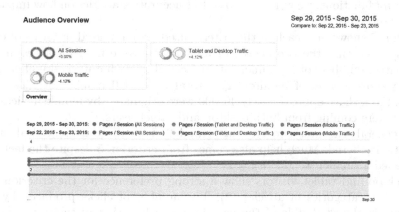

Fig. 6. Google's Analytics-chart comparing page-views/session for the 4-day exper.

Table 3. PolyRecs deactivation effect

	Desktop/Tablet Class	Mobile Devices Class
Page-Views/Session	−10.95%	−2.85%
Average Time Spent	−17.76%	−10.49%

operational statistics for two days (9/22–9/23) while having PolyRecs activated and then, we repeated the same exercise with the engine not in operation. on the same days of the following week (9/29–9/30). Table 2 shows an aggregation of the results obtained. We establish an increment in page-views/session rates for both desktop/tablet and mobile classes when PolyRecs is enabled although the gain in the mobile devices is limited. Overall, PolyRecs demonstrates its value by offering a higher by 6.3% average page-views per session. Figure 6 depicts an overview of the change in terms of the page-views/session metric for all portal users in the above 4-day experiment. The metric does remain higher during the period that the engine is on. It is also worth pointing out that during the period of 9/22–9/23 all rates are higher for both user groups than those attained in 9/29–9/30.

Table 3 outlines the "deactivation effect" in terms of percentages for both page-view/session as well as average dwell time on the portal (delivered by Google's Analytics). By in-activating the recommendation engine, the page-view/session rates do fall but more importantly, visitors spent less time reading content from the portal.

5.2   Assessing the Impact of the Recommendation Criteria

In this section, we analyze the impact the 5 criteria used by the engine in the compilation of recommendation lists. For this endeavor, we use data harnessed by the portal in a 12-day period of 10/10/2015–10/22/2015. Through the use of *JavaScript* functions, we were able to collect accurate statistics on how impactful the 5 criteria are.

Figure 7 shows how each of the criteria used (x-axis) fared in terms of clicks (y-axis) given that the two classes of user-devices were used for accessing. As anticipated, numbers of recommendations served by each criteria do differ. During the above period of monitoring, a total of $74,030$ number of clicks were logged. From those approximately $40,000$ were originated by mobile devices and the rest were coming from both desktop and tablet users.

In general, the first two criteria (1 and 2) contribute a great deal in the suggestions offered. Much help also comes from criterion 5 despite the fact that is assigned a smaller weight ($w_5 = 2$).

Desktop and tablet visitors show a strong preference for the criterion that profiles the categories of articles (2). The number of clicks produced by this criterion, is almost double of the next best which is that of the most popular content (5). For the mobile device group of visitors, the user profile criterion

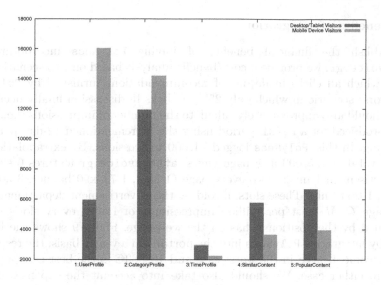

Fig. 7. PolyRecs criteria impact

(1) ranks first in for the number of clicks generated; also, criterion 2 comes a close second whereas the remaining three come in close with each other with an average of approximately 3, 300 clicks a piece. It is worth noting that in for the "user profile" category (i.e., 1), there is an impressive difference between the clicks of mobile and desktop users; while desktop/tables contribute 5, 956 clicks, the mobile devices generate 16, 040 clicks.

The pie-chart of Fig. 8 depicts how the criteria used in the engine fared regardless of the class of user devices. Approximately 35% of the user clicks to PolyRecs recommendations were attributed to the "category criterion" (e.g., 2) with another 30% coming off the "user profile" criterion (1); all other three criteria scored below 15%.

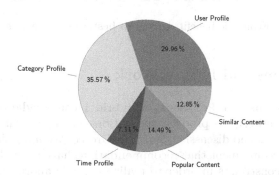

Fig. 8. Percentages of user clicks due to 5 recommendation criteria

5.3   Benefits of Integration

To establish the financial benefits of having `PolyRecs` incorporated in `athensvoice.gr`, we provide a cost/benefit analysis based on two scenarios: the best in which all clicks made out of recommendations furnished by `PolyRecs` and a worst scenario in which only 25% of clicks in discussion finally occurred.

We should also approximately calculate the number of impressions (i.e., page-views) produced for a month period using the aforementioned 12-day period of monitoring. In this, `PolyRecs` logged 74,000 impressions. By extrapolation, we derive a total of 185,000 new page views. `athensvoice.gr` features 6 slots for for advertisement banners into every page (1 skin, 1 728x90 banner, 3 300x250 banners, 1 text link). These slots, if sold by the advertisement department, have an average *CPM* (cost per million impressions) of 1.50€; every slot's cost is determined by the position it has on the web-page. Figure 9 shows the benefit reaped by integrating `PolyRecs` into the portal. On a yearly basis, the respective values become 4,994€ in the worst case and 19,980€ in the best case–a sizable benefit in either case. We should also take into account the expenses needed for `PolyRecs`'s hosting, which is at 69€ on a monthly basis; approximately the revenue from one advertising banner in the worst case scenario.

The above projected benefits are highly dependent of the following factors: *(a)* should `PolyRecs` be integrated with a portal enjoying a higher traffic, it would bring in higher income, *(b)* the limited number of recommendations served by the *RE* and their style/format, *(c)* the placement of `PolyRecs`'s recommendation on the page rendered. Without doubt, the slot within which the suggestion appears, plays a key role in the viewing and the likely clicking by the users, and *(d)* the total number of advertisement slots on web page and the average expected *CPM*.

Revenue Per Month	Worst Case (46,250 impr.)	Best Case (185,000 impr.)
1 banner	69.38€	277.50€
6 banners	416.30€	1,665.00€

Fig. 9. Economic benefit derived in best/worst case scenarios

6   Conclusions and Future Work

In this paper, we present `PolyRecs`, a hybrid recommendation system that deploys multiple criteria to produce suggestions for a popular news, politics, arts, opinion articles and discussion portal in Greece. We have placed particular emphasis on the requirement that recommendations have to be delivered within very strict time constraints in order to realize a viable approach for improving pages-views and traffic for the `athensvoice.gr` publication. We have developed `PolyRecs` in a way that it can be successfully integrated with any contemporary data infrastructure consists of modern `CMS` and database systems. We have deployed the prototype and have used the resulting production system to collect statistics and ascertain the utility of our proposal. While observing the behavior of the prototype, we have established that the use of PolyRecs in the *AthensVoice* portal has led to average in increase of 6.3% in the page-views consumed by visitors. In terms of numbers, there was a total of almost 74, 000 clicks increase in a period of 12 days.

In the future, we would like to extend PolyRecs in a number of ways. More specifically, we plan to: *(a)* embed social media features and so become able to access demographic characteristics for visitors; this can clearly offer a wealth of personalized information for creating more effective suggestions, *(b)* exploit user location and use geographically-pertinent articles to furnish more focused recommendation criteria, *(c)* experiment with spots for listing recommendations to further enhance *CTR*-rates, and *(d)* use machine learning approaches on the accumulated statistics to drive the weighting scheme in a more sophisticated and likely more effective way.

Acknowledgements. we are grateful for the reviewer comments received; partial support for this work has been provided by the *GALENA EU* Project and *Google*.

References

1. McCreadie, R., Macdonald, C., Ounis, I.: News vertical search: when and what to display to users. In: Proceedings of 36th International ACM SIGIR Conference, Dublin, Ireland (2013)
2. Wang, J., de Vries, A.P., Reinders, M.J.T.: Unifying user-based and item-based collaborative filtering approaches by similarity fusion. In Proceedings of 29th International ACM SIGIR Conference, Seattle, WA, August 2006
3. Liu, J., Dolan, P., Pedersen, E.R.: Personalized news recommendation based on click behavior. In: Proceedings of 15th International Conference on Intelligent User Interfaces (IUI), Hong Kong, PR China (2010)
4. Maksai, A., Garcin, F., Faltings, B.: Predicting online performance of news recommender systems through richer evaluation metrics. In: Proceedings of 9th ACM RecSys Conference, New York, NY (2015)
5. Lu, Z., Dou, Z., Lian, J., Xie, X., Yang, Q.: Content-based collaborative filtering for news topic recommendation. In: AAAI Conference, February 2015
6. Yi, X., Hong, L., Zhong, E., Liu, N.-N., Rajan, S.: Beyond Clicks: dwell time for personalization. In: Proceedings of 8th ACM RecSys Conference, Foster City, CA (2014)
7. Weinsberg, U., Bhagat, S., Ioannidis, S., Taft, N.: Inferring and obfuscating user gender based on ratings. In: Proceedings of 6th ACM RecSys Conference, Barcelona, Spain, September 2012
8. Schmidt, K., Bächle, S., Scholl, P., Nold, G.: Big scale text analytics and smart content navigation. In: Castellanos, M., Dayal, U., Pedersen, T.B., Tatbul, N. (eds.) BIRTE 2013-2014. LNBIP, vol. 206, pp. 167–170. Springer, Heidelberg (2015). https://doi.org/10.1007/978-3-662-46839-5_12
9. Das, A.S., Datar, M., Garg, A., Rajaram, S.: Google news personalization: scalable online collaborative filtering. In Proceedings of the 16th International Conference on World Wide Web, Banff, Canada (2007)

10. Garcin, F., Faltings, B., Donatsch, O., Alazzawi, A., Bruttin, C., Huber, A.: Offline and online evaluation of news recommender systems at `swissinfo.ch`. In: Proceedings of 8th ACM Conference on RecSys, Foster City, CA (2014)
11. Zhang, W., Wang, J., Chen, B., Zhao, X.: To personalize or not: a risk management perspective. In: Proceedings of 7th ACM RecSys Conference, Hong Kong, China (2013)
12. Wu, X., et al.: Personalized next-song recommendation in online karaokes. In: Proceedings of 7th ACM RecSys Conference, Hong Kong, PR China, October 2013
13. Vargas, S., Castells, P.: Rank and relevance in novelty and diversity metrics for recommender systems. In: Proceedings of 5th ACM RecSys Conference, Chicago, IL (2011)
14. Garcin, F., Dimitrakakis, C., Faltings, B.: Personalized news recommendation with context trees. In: Proceedings of 7th ACM RecSys Conference, Hong Kong, China (2013)
15. Diaz, F.: Integration of news content into web results. In: Proceedings of 2nd ACM International Conference on WSDM, Barcelona, Spain, pp. 182–191 (2009)
16. König, A.C., Gamon, M., Wu, Q.: Click-through prediction for news queries. In: Proceedings of the 32nd International ACM SIGIR Conference, Boston, MA, pp. 347–354 (2009)
17. Arguello, J., Diaz, F., Callan, J., Crespo, J.-F.: Sources of evidence for vertical selection. In: Proceedings of 32nd International ACM SIGIR Conference, pp. 315–322, Boston, MA (2009)
18. Said, A., Bellogin, A., Lin, J., de Vries, A.: Do recommendations matter?: news recommendation in real life. In: Computing of 17th ACM Conference on CSCW on Social Computing, Baltimore, MD, pp. 237–240 (2014)
19. Gebremeskel, G., de Vries, A.P.: The degree of randomness in a live recommender systems evaluation. In: Working Notes, Conference and Labs of the Evaluation Forum (CLEF), Toulouse, France, September 2015
20. Song, Y., Ma, H., Wang, H., Wang, K.: Exploring and exploiting user search behavior on mobile and tablet devices to improve search relevance. In: Proceedings of 22nd International WWW Conference, Rio de Janeiro, Brazil, pp. 1201–1212. ACM (2013)

Enabling Real Time Analytics
over Raw XML Data

Manoj K. Agarwal[1]($\boxtimes$), Krithi Ramamritham[2], and Prashant Agarwal[3]

[1] Microsoft Bing (Search Technology Center - India), Hyderabad 500032, India
agarwalm@microsoft.com
[2] Department of Computer Science and Engineering, IIT-Bombay, Powai,
Mumbai 400076, India
krithi@cse.ittb.ac.in
[3] Flipkart, Bangalore, India
agprashant.mnnit@gmail.com

Abstract. The data generated by many applications is in semi structured format, such as XML. This data can be used for analytics only after shredding and storing it in structured format. This process is known as Extract-Transform-Load or ETL. However, ETL process is often time consuming due to which crucial time-sensitive insights can be lost or they may become un-actionable. Hence, this paper poses the following question: How do we expose analytical insights in the raw XML data? We address this novel problem by discovering additional information from the raw semi-structured data repository, called complementary information (CI), for a given user query. Experiments with real as well as synthetic data show that the discovered CI is relevant in the context of the given user query, nontrivial, and has high precision. The recall is also found to be high for most queries. Crowd-sourced feedback on the discovered CI corroborates these findings, showing that our system is able to discover highly relevant and potentially useful CI in real-world XML data repositories. Concepts behind our technique are generic and can be used for other semi-structured data formats as well.

Keywords: XML · Real time · Analytics · Information retrieval

1 Introduction

Example 1: Consider a web based business application, managing stock information for its customers. Suppose a portfolio manager invokes a continuous query on this application data to find those customers who have a turnover of more than $10000 *since morning*. For such applications, often the raw data to answer the query is in XML format. The application data is shown in Fig. 1. The corresponding XQuery would be *doc("example.xml")/ApplicationData/TradeData[Date = $CurrentDate]/customers/ customer[TurnOver $\geq$ 10000]/custID*. Suppose, along with the queried information, the response also includes that all of these customers have traded in a few common stocks (i.e., "IBM" and "Microsoft" as shown in Fig. 1(c)) and that these customers have either "Charles Schwab" or "Fidelity" (Fig. 1(d)) as their brokerage firm and that these firms have issued a *Buy* or *Sell* advisory about these stocks in their morning briefing.

© Springer Nature Switzerland AG 2019
M. Castellanos et al. (Eds.): BIRTE 2015/2016/2017, LNBIP 337, pp. 113–132, 2019.
https://doi.org/10.1007/978-3-030-24124-7_8

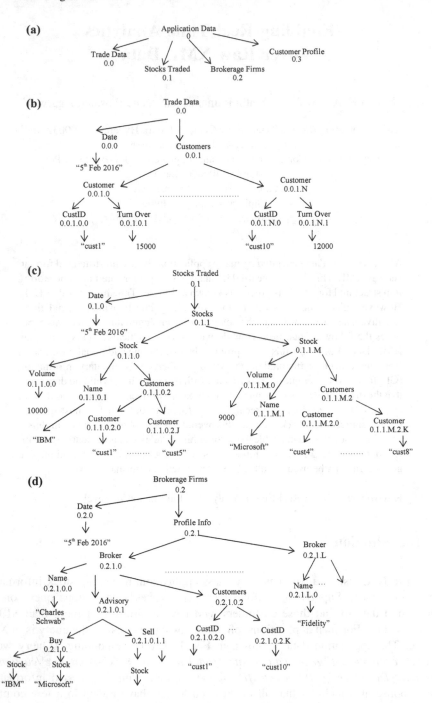

Fig. 1. (a) An example XML document (b) XML Structure in 'Trade Data' Node Tree (c) XML Structure in 'Stocks Traded' Node Tree (d) XML Structure in 'Brokerage Firms' Node Tree

With this *insight,* the overall perspective for the portfolio manager is significantly improved. The timely insight can improve the quality of their services. For instance, the portfolio manager can now provide a customized real time briefing to her customers as a value added service.

This example illustrates the following points: (1) if useful analytical insights are discovered in the context of a user query, at query run time, they can significantly enrich the query response; and (2) enabling discovery of such insights over raw XML data helps expose the actionable insights in real time. Such insights may provide useful business intelligence for applications such as in Example 1. In this paper, we present a novel system to identify the most relevant analytical insights in the raw XML data in the context of a user query at query run time. We call these analytical insights *complementary information (CI).* CI – discovered in the context of the user query – enhances users' ability to better comprehend the original query response. CI highlights the hidden patterns in the underlying XML data.

Our system takes into account the query response and the structure of the XML data to discover the *CI.* With semi-structured data such as XML and JSON being the default format for web applications to exchange data, a natural application of our system is to discover insight over raw semi-structured data, significantly improving the turn around time. Timely discovery of these insights may make them actionable for many applications. Our system is *capable of discovering non-trivial CI seamlessly without any further input from the users beyon their original query.* To the best of our knowledge, ours is the first system to expose analytical insights over raw XML data, in the context of a user XQuery. *CI* is retrieved in addition to the response to the original user query. With changes in the underlying data, just as with query results, a different *CI* may be found for the same user query.

1.1   Challenges in Discovering CI

Typically, data warehouse tools such as IBM Cognos, SAS (www.sas.com) or SPSS (www.spss.com) are used to store and analyze semi-structured data. XML data is parsed, shredded in structured format and normalized [17] before being stored in the data warehouse. This process is known as Extract-Transform-Load or ETL process [17]. On this aggregated data, ad-hoc queries are run offline to identify analytical insights. However, the current approach results in the following shortcomings: (1) while shredding, semantic relationship between the data elements embedded in the schema may be lost; (2) the analytical information can only be used for post-hoc analysis. Many a times, crucial information may become un-actionable due to inherent delay involved in such ETL processing and most importantly; (3) existing ETL systems, for processing semi-structured data, do not have the capacity to analyze the XML data in the context of a given user query.

A major challenge in discovering *CI* from raw XML data arises due to the absence of foreign key-primary key links in the XML data. Foreign key-primary key links have been exploited in the literature to expose analytical insights, similar to *CI,* over relational data [13, 16]. Conceptually foreign keys may exist in XML schema, for instance through *keyref,* but we encounter the following shortcomings: (1) XML data is typically used to exchange information by web applications. Therefore seldom does a unified data model exist across applications and in most cases *keyref* is not usable; (2) there is no way to enforce schema constraints on individual files if XML data is distributed across multiple files. Though one can merge all the files and create a unified schema on top of it, this is not practical in most cases; (3) unlike relational models, existence of such foreign keys is not mandatory in XML data repositories – one cannot assume the existence of such foreign key-primary key links.

1.2   Solution Ingredients and Research Contributions

XML data is represented as an ordered and labelled tree as shown in Fig. 1. To discover the *CI*, we exploit the node categorization model proposed in [10]. We present this model in Sect. 3.1. In the model in [10], a subset of XML nodes in the XML tree are termed *entity nodes* [cf. Def. 3.1.3]. The basic idea behind discovering *CI* is as follows: An *entity* node captures the context for the collection of repeating nodes in its sub-tree with the aid of its attributes. For example, in Fig. 1(b), node <Stock> (with node-id 0.1.1.0) is an entity node and it captures the fact that all the <customer> nodes in its sub-tree has traded the 'IBM' stock with the aid of XPath/StocksTraded/Stocks/ Stock/. <Customer> nodes are repeating nodes (cf. Def. 3.1.2). The <Name> node (node-id 0.1.1.0.1) is an attribute node (cf. Def. 3.1.1) in the sub-tree of entity node < Stock>$_{0.1.1.0}$. We exploit this observation to discover *CI*. Following are the steps:

(i)   We parse the response of a user XQuery and prepare a set of keywords by identifying the *important* text keywords embedded in the query response.

(ii) We look at the distribution of these keywords in the rest of the XML data repository. The entity nodes (other than the entity nodes containing the original query response) that contain a large enough subset of these keywords are the candidate nodes for discovering *CI*.

(iii) We introduce a novel ranking function that ranks each candidate entity nodes by taking into account its tree structure and the distribution of the query response keywords in its sub-tree. The rank of a candidate entity node helps our system identify the entity nodes to discover the most relevant *CI* for a given user XQuery. At the same time, our system ensures that the *CI* is meaningful and does not overwhelm the user.

The contributions of our work are as follows. In this paper,

1. We introduce a novel problem of exposing as *CI*, interesting analytical insights in the raw XML data, in the context of a given user XQuery. Our technique enables discovery of actionable insights in the XML data in a timely manner.
2. Our technique is able to identify interesting *CI* in the absence of *any* schema information about the data.
3. We show that identifying optimal *CI* is NP-complete. We propose an algorithm with good approximation bounds for discovering relevant *CI*.
4. We propose a novel ranking function that helps discover the most relevant *CI* for a given user query in an efficient manner.

5. Crowd-sourced feedback on the CI discovered by our system shows that it is able to discover useful *CI* in real-world XML data repositories with high precision and recall.

This paper is organized as follows. In Sect. 2, we position our system in the context of related work. In Sect. 3, introduce the XML node types. In Sect. 4, we define *CI* formally. In Sect. 5, we present the methodology to infer CI and our technique to rank the candidate entity nodes based on the underlying XML data structure. In Sect. 6, the problem of discovering optimal *CI* for a given user query is shown to be NP-complete. We present an approximation algorithm to find *CI* for a given user query and our method to find *CI* recursively. In Sect. 7, we present our evaluation results on real and synthetic datasets. We present our conclusion and future work in Sect. 8.

2 Related Work

It is difficult for users to understand complex XML schema, hence XML Keyword Search (XKS) is an active area of research [2, 4–6, 10]. XKS enables users to search XML data without writing complex XQueries. Users provide the keywords and the underlying algorithm interprets the user's intent and tries to identify the return nodes [2, 3].

Another related area is query expansion [4, 9]. Users provide queries with whatever schema they know along with query keywords [4]. The system interprets in a best effort manner and expands the queries automatically [4] or with the aid of users' feedback [9].

Keyword based search over XML data does not yield precise answers as the semantic relationship between keywords, embedded in the XML structure, is lost. However, since knowing the XML schema and writing XQueries is considered a tedious task, a large body of work exists to improve answers to the keyword search based queries on XML data.

In XSeek [3], authors propose a technique to find the relevant return nodes for a given keyword query. The keywords in the query are understood as the 'where' clause whereas 'return' nodes are inferred based on the semantics of 'input keywords'.

Even though the problem of identifying return nodes for a given keyword search query has some similarity with our problem, the problem being addressed in this paper and the XML keyword search have different input data and are expected to provide different results. In XML keyword search algorithms, the challenge is to understand the most relevant return nodes, for the given set of keywords. On the other hand, for our system, users provide a well formed query. The objective is to find the analytical insights in the context of the query.

Top-K Keyword Search in XML databases [6] is another area, where the objective is to efficiently list the top-K results for a given keyword search query on an XML database. XRank [7], XSearch [8] are techniques to rank the keyword query search results. In [12], authors propose techniques that limit the keyword search to a given context, i.e., within a sub-tree of the entire document structure.

3 Background

In Fig. 1. an XML tree is shown. The nodes in the tree are labelled with Dewey id [1]. Dewey id is a unique id assigned to a node in the XML tree and it describes its position in the document. A node with Dewey id 0.1.1 is the second child of its parent node 0.1. In [10], authors presented a novel node categorization model. We present this node categorization model below. As shown in Sect. 5, this model can be exploited to discover the analytical insights from XML data, in the context of a user query.

3.1 Node Categorization Model

3.1.1. Attribute Node (AN): A node which contains only one child that is its value. For instance, in Fig. 1(c) node <Date> (0.1.0) and <Name> (0.1.1.0.1) are attribute nodes. Attribute nodes are also represented as 'text nodes' in XML data.

3.1.2. Repeating Node (RN): A node that repeats multiple times, i.e., has sibling nodes with the same name. For instance, nodes with label <Customer> in Fig. 1(b) and < Stock> in Fig. 1(c) are repeating nodes. In a normalized XML schema [18], repeating nodes correspond to a physical world object which can be a concrete or an abstract object [3]. A node that directly contains its value *and* also has siblings with the same name is considered a repeating node (and not an attribute node).

3.1.3 Entity Node (EN): The lowest common ancestor of *attribute nodes* and *repeating nodes* is termed the entity node. *Entity node* need not have repeating nodes as its direct children. In Fig. 1 <Dept> is an *entity node* but the repeating node < Course> in its sub-tree is not its direct child.

3.1.4. Connecting Node (CN): Nodes which are in none of the above categories. Node <Courses> in Fig. 1 is a *CN*.

XML documents follow in-order arrival of nodes. Hence, different node types are identified in a single pass over the data [10].

A node can be an *entity node* as well as a *repeating node* for another *entity node* higher up in the hierarchy. However, it does not impact the computation of *CI* for the query as each relevant entity node is identified and ranked independently (Sect. 5.2).

3.2 Set of Keywords

For the XML document shown in Fig. 1, if the query is *doc ("example.xml")/ ApplicationData/BrokerageFirms/ProfileInfo/Broker [Name = "Charles   Schwab"]/ Advisory Buy/Stock*, it will yield the following output:

    <Stock>IBM</Stock>
    <Stock>Microsoft</Stock>

We *convert* this output to a set of keywords {"IBM", "Microsoft"}. For *CI* discovery, given a query response, first we prepare a keyword set $R(Q) = \{k_1 \ldots k_n\}$ containing the text keywords embedded in its attribute nodes with the aid of a function

$R(.)$. Function $R(.)$ parses the query response and removes all XML tags from the XML chunk and converts the text of attribute nodes into a set of keywords after stop-word removal and stemming.

3.3 Least Common Entity (LCE) Node

Least Common Ancestor (LCA) node is the lowest ancestor in the XML tree T for a given set of keywords. Similarly, we define the *Lowest Common Entity* node. An *Entity node* is the common parent of repeating nodes and attribute nodes [10]. Thus it defines the local context for the nodes in its sub-tree. To find the *CI* for a given query, we discover a set of lowest entity nodes that contains at least c keywords present in set R (Q) or we identify the Least Common Entity (LCE) nodes as defined below.

Let Q be a user XQuery and $R(Q) = \{k_1 \ldots k_n\}$ be the text keywords in the query response ($|R(Q)| = n$). Let e be an entity node that contains $S \subseteq R(Q)$ keywords in its sub-tree such that $|S| \geq c$; c is an integer constant. Let $e \prec_a e_i$ denote that entity node e is an ancestor of entity node e_i. Let $S \in e$ denote that e contains keyword(s) in S in its subtree. We define the *Least Common Entity* (LCE) node as follows:

Def. 3.3.1 LCE Nodes: Given set $S \subseteq R(Q)$ ($\|S\| \geq c$) for a query Q and entity node e such that $S \in e$, e is the least common entity node w.r.t. $R(Q) \exists k \subset S | k \subset e \wedge \forall e_i | e \prec_a e_i, k \notin e_i$.

Hence, for a node e to be least common entity (*LCE*) node, there exists at least one keyword in the sub-tree of e, belonging to query response $R(Q)$, which is *not* contained in any other entity node within the sub-tree of e. Only those entity nodes which contain at least c keywords from set $R(Q)$ are considered.

4 Complementary Information

In this section, we define the *complementary information* (*CI*) formally and also describe how deeper insights are found in the data by recursive *CI* discovery.

Example 2: Suppose we have an XML data repository containing information about Nobel prize winners. A user queries this data for the list of Nobel winning scientists in 2009 (query Q_1). Let's say, along with the list of winners, our system also returns the information that '8 out of 9 of them are US citizens' (assuming this information is present in the data). Next, say the user asks for the list of 2010 Nobel winning scientists (total 6) (query Q_2). For this query the CI could be 'most of them are UK (3) and US (2) citizens'. Similarly, for 2011 (Q_3), the list contains 7 scientists from 4 different countries.

Though users may find the *CI* for Q_1 interesting, will they find the *CI* for Q_2 or Q_3 interesting enough? Thus, the natural question is: What constitutes an interesting *CI*? A user can define the interesting-ness of *CI* with the aid of α and β, defined below.

Let $|R(Q)| = n$. We define a set of LCE nodes U as follows:

$$U = \{e | (S \in e, S \subseteq R(Q) \wedge |S| \geq c\}$$

U is the set of all the LCE nodes such that each $e \in U$ contain at least c keywords from set $R(Q)$ in its sub-tree. Let P be a subset of U, $P \subseteq U$ containing a β fraction of the keywords in $R(Q)$, i.e., at least $\beta.n$ keywords from set $R(Q)$ appear in the subtrees of LCE nodes in set of LCE nodes P. Set P is called the *Complementary Information* (*CI*). Formally:

Def. 4.1.1 Complementary Information (CI): For given α, β, $(0 < \alpha < \beta \leq 1)$ and $R(Q)$, $|R(Q)| = n$, let P be a set of LCE nodes containing $\beta.n$ keywords from set $R(Q)$. If $|P| \leq \alpha.n$, then P is *CI*.

The attributes nodes of LCE nodes in set P, along with their XPaths, represent the complementary information (cf. Sect. 4). $|P|$ represents the number of LCE nodes which contain this *CI*. Thus, if there are small enough number of LCE *nodes* that contain β fraction of keywords in $R(Q)$, then these LCE nodes expose a pattern, enabling the discovery of interesting and actionable insights.

Coverage Threshold (β): For a given $\beta; 0 < \beta \leq 1$; nodes in *CI* must cover β fraction of the keywords from the original query. $\beta > 0.5$ as a thumb rule.

Convergence Ratio (α): α defines the number of LCE nodes that must be part of the *CI*.

Users express their interest in *CI* by specifying non-zero values for α and β. β must be greater than α ($\beta/\alpha \geq c$ and $c > 1$). In Example 1 in Sect. 1, let $|R(Q)| = n = 10$. Let $\beta = 0.8$ and $\alpha = 0.2$. According to Def. 4.1.1, there must exist no more than α. $n = 2$ entity nodes that cover at least $\beta.n = 8$ keywords in set $R(Q)$. Let there exist two entity nodes, say corresponding to stock nodes "IBM" and "Microsoft", which together contain 8 of the 10 customer ids in set $R(Q)$ in their sub-trees. Let's say no other combination of two <stock> nodes contain at least eight customer ids in their sub-trees. We call this information *CI* for the given α and β and these nodes the *CI nodes*, since they expose a 'meaningful' pattern.

Def. 4.1.2 Minimal CI: If minimal *CI* contains k LCE nodes to cover β fraction of nodes in $R(Q)$, there exists no smaller *CI*.

For a given β, our goal is to find the *minimal CI*. When $\beta = 1$, *minimal CI* is *optimal CI* (Def. 6.1). It is possible that in some cases no *CI* is found which satisfies given α, β thresholds for a given query. In that case, no *CI* is returned. In Sect. 6 we show that for a given query, the problem of finding optimal *CI (defined as CI-Discovery or CID)* for hierarchical data is NP-complete.

Users specify their information needs by tuning α and β. α defines how many LCE nodes can be returned as *CI*. β defines how many keywords from the original query response must be present in the XML sub-trees of these nodes. α and β are defined as fraction of keywords in the original query response $R(Q)$; $0 < \alpha < \beta \leq 1$. For Q_2, with $\alpha = 1/3$, $\beta = 5/6$ and $n = 6$, CI may consist of two LCE nodes (both UK, US as *CI*). If we reduce α, no CI can be returned, as no single LCE node covers 5/6 fraction of names. Thus, by tuning α and β, users can control what constitutes interesting analytical insights for them.

β/α is the average number of query response keywords in a LCE node in *CI*. Tuning of α, β is dependent on underlying data. To increase the precision, users can increase β or reduce α or both. To increase recall, they can reduce β or increase α or both. By judiciously choosing α and β, users can find the relevant CI for a given XML data while ensuring good precision and recall.

4.1 Recursive CI Discovery

In Example 1, suppose we do not find a small enough number of <Stock> nodes that expose any CI for a given α and β. For example, there exist no two <stock> nodes that contain at least eight customer ids for $\beta = 0.8$, $\alpha = 0.2$ and $|R(Q)| = 10$. However, when we examine the stocks bought or sold by customers, we may still find that most of these stocks are indeed recommended by "Fidelity" and "Charles Schwab", and thus this information may qualify as CI for given α and β. This information could be exposed as CI as follows: Let $P \subseteq U$ represent the smallest set of entity nodes containing β fraction of keywords in $R(Q)$. Also, $|P| > \alpha.n$ (else P itself would be CI). If we replace the keywords in set $R(Q)$ (customer ids) with keywords in the text nodes in entity nodes $\in P$ (names of the stock), we can identify the CI described above. This example highlights that interesting CI, hidden deeper in the data, may be found in a recursive manner. Our system identifies such deeper insights in the XML data completely seamlessly. Automatic discovery of such insights, in the absence of any foreign key-primary key relationship in the XML data, is the key contribution of our system.

The discovery of CI depends on the underlying XML schema and may change for differently structured XML data even though the information present in the different instances may be the same. Although CI depends on the underlying XML structure, the *CI discovery process does not need the schema information.*

5 Complementary Information

In this section, we describe our methodology to infer CI from a given LCE node and also how to rank the LCE nodes to find most relevant CI.

5.1 Inferring CI

For a normalized XML schema [18], the attribute node(s) of an entity node represent the information applicable to the repeating nodes in its sub-tree. For instance, node $<Stock>_{0.1.1.0}$, in Fig. 1(c), has an attribute node (0.1.1.0.1) with value "IBM", representing that the customers within its sub-tree have all traded in "IBM" stock. For a given query, if a significant fraction of customers are appearing in the sub-tree of a <Stock> node, its attribute node(s) expose a 'pattern'. This 'pattern' is regarded as CI. The XPath to the entity node describes the context. For instance, for entity node <Stock> containing the 'customers' ids from the original user query, the XPath *doc ("example.xml")/ApplicationData/StocksTraded/Stocks/Stock* provides the context that these customers have traded in the corresponding stock.

For a normalized XML schema [18], the attribute node(s) of an entity node represent the information applicable to the repeating children of that node. This principle is exploited to infer the CI and the attribute nodes of node e are considered the CI. The XML chunk representing the CI contains the complete XPath from the root till the

LCE node *e* along with its attribute nodes and the keywords in set *S* present in the sub-tree of node *e*. XPath to the node *e* defines the context of the keywords in its sub-tree. The LCE node constitutes the local context for the keywords in its sub-tree and its attribute nodes and XPath to the entity node *e* help explain this context.

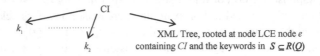

Fig. 2. CI node attached with the query response

If keywords in set *S* are distributed over attribute nodes, remaining attribute nodes are inferred as *CI*. If *all* the attribute nodes of an entity node *e* are in set *S*, we ignore that *e*.

The discovered *CI* is attached with the original query response as shown in Fig. 2. <CI> XML tag is created which contains the keywords ($k_i \in S$) from original query response on which *CI* is applicable and relevant XML structure from the LCE node. The semantic of *CI* is understood with the aid of this XML structure. For instance, for query in Example 1, the keywords are the customer ids and its XML tree contains the tree rooted at node <Stock>$_{0.1.1.0}$ along with its attribute node with value "IBM"./*Stock/Name/"IBM"* explains that "IBM" is the name of a stock traded by the customers in its sub-tree.

For a given query response, function *FindCITerms* takes as input an XML chunk, containing the sub-tree in an LCE node. It infers the *CI* as explained above and produces an XML chunk containing the *CI* as shown in Fig. 2. This function invokes function *R* (.) to infer the keywords which represent the *CI*.

5.2   Ranking the LCE Nodes

For a given keyword set $R(Q)$, the distinguishing features a candidate LCE node *e* has, are: (i) number of keywords from set $R(Q)$ appearing in its sub-tree; (ii) structure of its sub-tree. We introduce a novel ranking function that computes the rank of a node by exploiting these features. Our ranking method is different from the statistical methods to rank the XML nodes [8, 11]. Node rank helps identify more relevant LCE nodes for a given user query. Node Rank is computed using two scores, Coverage score and Structure score.

5.2.1   Coverage Score (*cScore*)

LCE nodes containing a higher number of keywords in query response $R(Q)$ are better candidates to infer *CI*. Hence, for a given LCE node *e,* its *cScore* is equal to the number of *unique* query keywords appearing in its sub-tree.

$$cScore_e = |S|; S \subseteq R(Q) \land contains(e, S); R(Q) = \{k_1, \ldots, k_n\}$$

$cScore_e$ just accounts for the presence of a keyword in the LCE node tree e. If a keyword is present multiple times, only its highest occurrence in that LCE node is considered. In Fig. 3(f), for node L_6, only the first occurrence of A will be considered. Our objective is to discover CI applicable on maximum number of keywords in $R(Q)$. Hence, counting the same keyword multiple times does not improve the quality of CI.

5.2.2 Structure Score (*sScore*)

sScore takes the tree structure of XML nodes into account. Let us look at the LCE nodes in Fig. 3. Let us assume set $R(Q) = \{A, B\}$ for a given user query. Hence, for Fig. 3(a) and (d) $Attr_1$ and $Attr_4$ represents the CI respectively (Sect. 5.1). However, node L_4 (Fig. 3(d)) contains a larger number of sibling nodes besides keywords in R (Q) whereas L_1 contains keywords belonging to set $R(Q)$ only. Therefore, $Attr_1$ contains a CI, which is more specific to keywords in set $R(Q)$ compared to $Attr_4$. Hence, L_1 must be ranked above L_4. Thus, the *sScore* of an LCE node is inversely proportional to the total number of children it has.

Further, for a given LCE node e, closer the query keywords are to the root of node e, the more relevant the corresponding CI is. For instance, for two LCE nodes L_1 and L_3 (Fig. 3(a) and (c)), L_1 must be ranked higher than L_3 due to its more compact tree structure. Therefore, the LCE nodes with lesser average distance from the root of the tree to the query keywords are ranked higher compared to the LCE nodes with greater average distance. Similarly, node L_5 should be ranked below nodes L_1 and L_3 as it has a large number of sibling nodes at level 2, thereby making the corresponding CI (L_5/ $Attr_5$) less specific. Therefore, the desired ranking order for the LCE nodes shown in Fig. 3 is, $L_1 > L_3 > L_4 > L_5$. Node L_2 is not an LCE node (Node/L_2/C could be if it has repeating nodes in its sub-tree).

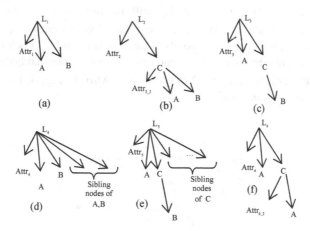

Fig. 3. Various LCE nodes containing keywords in set $R(Q) = \{A,B\}$

Let D_q represent the set of XML elements lying on the path from the LCE node root till the lowest keyword in its sub-tree belonging to set $S \subseteq R(Q)$, both these nodes included. Thus, $|D_q|$ is called the *CI-depth* of this sub-tree. For example, in Fig. 3(c), $D_q = \{L_3, C\}$ for set S = R(Q) = {A, B} and $|D_q| = 2$.

Thus, the *sScore* of an LCE node *e* is computed based on (i) *CI–depth* $|D_q|$; and (ii) total number of nodes at each level till level $|D_q|$. For keywords belonging to set $S \subseteq R(Q)$ appearing at level $i \leq |D_q|$, the inverse of *sScore* at level *i* is computed as follows:

$$1/sScore_i = (\sum_{l=1}^{i} \log_2(1 + l)^{f_l});$$

where f_l is the number of nodes at level *l* in the sub-tree of an LCE node *e*. *l* is the level w.r.t. the root of LCE node. f_l is 1 if the node at level *l* is just a connecting node. Therefore, *sScore* captures the structure of the LCE node tree.

The overall ranking for an LCE node is computed as the weighted sum of Structure scores at each level *i* as follows:

$$Rank = \sum_{i \in \{1..|D_q|\}} cScore_i \times sScore_i$$

$cScore_i$ is the number of distinct keywords $k_i s \in R(Q)$ at level *i and* $sScore_i$ is corresponding Structure score.

Example 4: Consider the XML tree shown in Fig. 4. Suppose $R(Q) = \{k_1, k_2...k_n\}$. Let there be an LCE node with a subset of these keywords distributed in its sub-tree as follows: L_1 (level 0) has 100 repeating nodes L_2s (at level 1). One of these nodes (node no. L_{2_97}) contains k_3 and k_4 as its children. Keywords k_1 and k_2 occur at level 3. The *Rank* for the sub-tree rooted at L_1 will be $Rank = 2 \times 1/(\log(1+1)^{100}) + 2 \times 1/(\log(1+1)^{100} + \log(1+3)^2)$. The first term of *Rank* corresponds to keywords k_3 and k_4 and the second term corresponds to keywords k_1 and k_2. Each of these terms is multiplied by the respective *cScore* (2 each in this case). Note that node L_{2_31} is also an LCE node. Its rank score is $2 \times 1/\log(1+2)^2$. Also, in Fig. 4, L_{2_31} is an *entity node* as well as a *repeating node*.

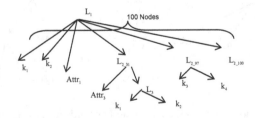

Fig. 4. An example LCE node used for computing rank

The weight of an LCE node e is defined as:

$$weight(e) = \frac{1}{Rank_e}$$

LCE nodes with low weight (high rank) are good candidates to be included in CI.

6   Discovering Optimal CI

To discover the most relevant analytical insights, CI, we find the smallest weighted set of LCE nodes containing β fraction of keywords in set $R(Q)$. For a query Q and set R (Q) $(|R(Q)| = n)$, suppose there is a set P of m LCE nodes, each containing a subset $S \subseteq R(Q)$ of keywords. Each LCE node is assigned a weight, as per its rank score.

Def. 6.1 Optimal CI: If optimal CI contains k LCE nodes, containing all the keywords in set $R(Q)$ in their sub-trees, there exists no smaller set of LCE nodes that contain all the keywords in set $R(Q)$.

$\beta = 1$ for optimal CI. We show that finding optimal CI is NP-complete. We define the problem of discovering optimal *Complementary Information Discovery (CID)*.

Def. 6.2 Complementary-Information Discovery (CID): Find the least weight collection C of LCE nodes, $C \subseteq P$, of size at most k ($|C| \le k$), such that the nodes in C contain all the keywords in $R(Q)$. C is called *CI-cover*.

Lemma 1: CID is in NP
Given a set of LCE nodes it is easy to verify that the set contains at most k nodes and check if the union of these nodes contains all the keywords in set $R(Q)$.

Theorem 1: CID is NP-Complete
The weighted set cover problem is NP-complete [14]. It is defined as follows: Given a set of elements $V = \{v_1, v_2, ... v_n\}$ and a set of m subsets of $V, S = \{S_1, S_2, ... S_m\}$, each having a cost c_i, find a least cost collection C of size at most j such that C covers all the elements in V. That is: $\cup_{S_i \in C} S_i = V; |C| \le j$.

Weighted set cover is polynomial time reducible to CID, Weighted $SetCover \le_P CID$. Let $R(Q) = V$; each element v_i in V is mapped to a keyword k_i in $R(Q)$. We define m subsets of CID as follows: Each subset of V is mapped to an entity node. One can construct an XML document in polynomial time where each entity node contains exactly the same keywords corresponding to set $S_i \subseteq V$. We also set $k = j$ and weight of each LCE node is set to be the cost of the corresponding subset in V. The instance of set cover is covered by a cover of size j if and only if the CID instance is also covered by size k. CI-cover is true *iff* SetCover is true.

6.1   A Greedy Algorithm for Finding CI

The CID is NP-complete. We present a greedy approach for identifying the LCE nodes in CI. It is shown in [15] that no improvement is possible on the approximation bounds of a greedy algorithm for the weighted set cover problem. In algorithm $CIDGreedy$, the entity node containing the minimum weight for keyword set $S \subseteq R(Q)$ is identified first in the CI-cover. We continue adding LCE nodes in CI-cover till the algorithm covers $\beta.|R(Q)|$ nodes. Let P be set of all the LCE nodes for query Q. We use the method in

[10] to discover U. Let *weight (e)* be the weight of LCE node e and $S_e \subseteq R(Q)$ be the set of keywords from $R(Q)$ in its sub-tree. The node with least cost is picked in *CI*-cover, to cover a yet uncovered keyword.

```
Algorithm CIDGreedy (Set R(Q) , List LCENodes)
    CI ← φ      /*Set containing CI nodes*/
    Kc ← φ      /*Set containing keywords covered*/
    N ← 0            /*CI node counter*/
    While (|Kc|< β.|R(Q)|)
```
$$e \leftarrow \arg\min_{e \in U} \frac{weight(e)}{|(S_e \mid R(Q)) - K_c|}$$
```
        Kc← Kc U(Se | R(Q));
        CI ← CI U e; FindCITerm(e, R(Q))
        N++;
        if (N / |R(Q)| > α)
                return null
    return CI.
```

FindCITerms(Node e, set R(Q)) finds the CI terms as per the method presented in Sect. 5.1. The running time complexity of *CIDGreedy* is $O(\alpha.|R(Q)|.|U|)$.

For algorithm *CIDGreedy*, the number of LCE nodes $|CI|$ in *CI-cover* and β are related as follows: $|CI| \leq \left\lceil \log(\frac{1}{1-\beta+(1/n)}).OPT \right\rceil$ where *OPT* is number of nodes in optimal *CI-cover* when $\beta = 1$ and $|R(Q)| = n$ (proof omitted).

6.2   Recursive CI Discovery

As explained in Sect. 4.1, the deeper insights in the XML data can be discovered by discovering *CI* recursively. Below is the algorithm for recursive *CI* discovery:

```
Algorithm RecursiveCIDGreedy (Set R(Q) , List LCENodes)
    CI ← φ      /*Set containing CI nodes*/
    Kc ← φ      /*Set containing keywords covered*/
    N ← 0            /*CI node counter*/
    While |Kc|< β.|R(Q)|
```
$$e \leftarrow \arg\min_{u \in U} \frac{weight(e)}{|S_e \mid R(Q) - K_c|} ;$$
```
        Kc ← Kc Y(Se I R(Q));
        CI ← CI Y e; FindCITerm(e, R(Q));
        N++
                If (N/|SQ|> α & |Kc|≥ β.|SQ|)
                        RecursiveCIDGreedy(R(CI), FindLCENodes(R(CI)));
    return CI.
```

FindLCENodes (Set R(Q)) finds all the LCE nodes corresponding to keywords in the argument set. Users can also limit the level of recursion easily.

7   Experimental Results

In this section, we describe the experimental results over various XML data sets: Mondial[1] (worldwide geographical data), Shakespeare's plays[2] (distributed over multiple files), SIGMOD Record (See footnote 1), DBLP (See footnote 1), Protein Sequence database and a synthetic dataset mimicking New York Stock Exchange data. The experiments were carried out on a Core2 Duo 2.4 GHz, 4 GB RAM machine running Windows 8.1. Java is used as programming language.

7.1   Discovered *CI* and Its Perceived Usefulness

Table 1 shows the queries over different datasets. Nominal value of β is 0.7 and α is always set to less than β/c ($c = 2$ for most experiments). In the table, we also show the *CI* discovered by our system for these queries. *CI* is returned as an XML chunk, as shown in Fig. 2. Since we do not expect readers to be aware of the schema of the datasets, and due to space constraints, we present the queries and results in English, instead of XML chunks.

The *CI* for some queries expands when we increase α, more LCE nodes qualify as *CI*. For some queries, larger α may not have any impact if existing LCE nodes already cover β fraction of nodes. Interesting *CI* is found in a recursive manner for queries QM4 and QD1.

Table 1. Data sets and queries

ID	Query	CI
SIGMOD/DBLP Records		
QS1	Who are the authors of a given article?	1. Volume, number of the issue in which article was published 2. Other articles by a subset of authors (when α is increased)
QS2	Who are the co-authors of a given author?	1. Title of the articles written by a subset of authors 2. Volume number in which a subset of authors have published (when α is increased)
QS3	What is the starting page of a given article? (SIGMOD)	1. Article and the last page of the article
QS4	Authors name, starting page of a given article (SIGMOD)	1. Volume and number of the issue to which the article belongs 2. Volume and number of another issue in which a subset of authors have published (when α is increased)

(continued)

---

[1] http://www.cs.washington.edu/research/xmldatasets/www/repository.htm.

[2] http://xml.coverpages.org/bosakShakespeare200.html.

Table 1. (*continued*)

ID	Query	CI
Synthetic Data Set		
QN1	Which stocks are owned by a given customer?	1. All of them are large cap stocks 2. Most of the companies belong to a particular industry 3. Most of them belong to particular subsector
QN2	Name the companies in a given subsector	1. Forestry and Paper is the sector. Basic Resources is the super-sector. Basic Materials is the industry 2. Most of the companies are based in United States of America
QN3	Name the companies in a given country	1. Belongs to a particular sub-sector, sector, super-sector industry
Shakespeare's Plays		
QP1	Name of the speaker of a given line	1. Name of the act 2. Title of the play, scene description, etc 3. Other lines from the same speech (when α is increased)
Mondial (Geographic Data set)		
QM1	Which are the provinces crossed by a given river?	1. Depth of the river and other attributes of the river 2. Details of provinces and country in which most of these provinces are present
QM2	Name the religious and ethnic groups in a given country	1. Other details of the country and details of other countries that have similar religions and ethnic groups
QM3	Who are the neighbors of a given country?	1. Details of the country and that most of these countries are members of a particular organization
QM4	What are the ethnic groups in a given country?	1. Other countries that have similar ethnic groups **2. Recursively**, these countries are found to belong to a particular organization
Protein Sequence Database		
QD1	What are the references for a given protein type?	1. Most of these articles are published in a given journal 2. Most of these articles are written by some particular authors (for some instances, when α is increased) **Recursively,** list of other protein types where these authors are appearing again in the reference lists

7.2   Crowd-Sourced Feedback: Discovered *CI* and Its Perceived Usefulness

In this experiment, we asked 40 expert users to rate if the *CI* is useful. Users rate the *CI* for a query on a scale of 1–4;1 being 'Very Useful' and 4 being 'Not Useful'. The results are shown in Table 2. We found, except query QS3, the *CI* is found to be either very useful (1) or moderately useful (2). If we categorize the response as either 'useful' (rating 1 or 2) or 'less/not useful' (rating 3 or 4), 435 out of 520 responses found the *CI* useful (i.e., 83.7%). Only 3.85% responses gave rating 4 for the discovered *CI*.

7.3 Precision and Recall

As is evident from the definitions of α and β in Sect. 4, β/α is the average number of keywords covered by an LCE node in CI cover. Since users themselves specify α and β, any node that has at least $\lceil \beta/\alpha \rceil$ keywords in its sub-tree is considered to be a relevant LCE node for that query and is included in set *Rel*. Thus, for a user query Q, *Rel* is defined as: $Rel = \{e | (R(e) \cap R(Q)) \geq \lceil \beta/\alpha \rceil \}$. Minimum number of keywords in an LCE node is set to 2 ($c = 2$). Set *Ret* contains all the LCE nodes returned to the user in *CI*. *Precision* and *recall* are computed as follows [3]:

Table 2. User response to discovered CI

Query	1	2	3	4
QS1	24	16	0	0
QS2	16	23	1	0
QS3	7	13	15	5
QS4	8	21	7	4
QN1	24	15	1	0
QN2	17	15	6	2
QN3	20	18	1	1
QP1	24	12	4	0
QM1	13	20	6	1
QM2	13	17	8	2
QM3	12	16	7	5
QM4	15	21	4	0
QD1	22	14	4	0

$$\text{Precision} = \frac{|Rel \cap Ret|}{|Ret|} \text{ and Recall} = \frac{|Rel \cap Ret|}{|Rel|}$$

We ran 5–7 instances for each of the queries shown in Table 1. These instances are run for different values of α and β. We have varied the β from 0.4 to 1.0 and α from 0.1 to 0.5. Since at least c keywords must occur in an LCE node, $\alpha \leq \beta/c$.

Table 3. Average precision and recall

Query	Average precision	Average recall
QS1	0.98	1.0
QS2	0.85	0.1
QS3	1.0	1.0
QS4	0.90	1.0
QN1	1.0	1.0
QN2	1.0	0.81
QN3	0.92	1.0
QP1	1.0	0.96
QM1	0.94	0.36
QM2	0.8	0.9
QM3	0.97	0.15
QM4 (1)	1.0	0.96
QM4 (Rec)	1.0	1.0
QD1 (Rec)	1.0	0.42

The results for precision and recall for the queries are shown in Table 3. We see that (a) for most queries average precision and recall are high; (b) for few queries, precision is high but recall is low. The reason for (a) is that there exist *only* a small number of highly relevant LCE nodes which are always included in *Ret*. Therefore, size of *Rel* and *Ret* is similar. Due to this reason, we have tabulated the *average* of precision and recall since for most instances, precision and recall were found to be consistent. There are four queries in category (b) namely QS2, QM1, QM3 and QD1. The query response keywords for these queries were relatively more popular in the datasets. Hence many LCE nodes qualify for *CI*. α limits the *CI* to a few high ranked LCE nodes, improving the users' ability to consume the *CI*.

7.4   Effect of CI Thresholds on Precision and Recall

In Figs. 5 and 6, we plot average precision and recall on the Mondial data set for queries shown in Table 1. X-axis in Figs. 5 and 6 is β and α respectively. For each value of β (α), we take average over multiple runs with different values of α (β). From the graph we see that (1) If α is too low, the recall suffers (as relevant LCE nodes may not be part of discovered CI); (2) If α and β both are too high, the precision suffers (as few LCE nodes that are part of CI may not be relevant). With high β and low α, recall suffers. We see from these results that $\beta = 0.6$-0.7 is a good thumb rule with $\alpha \leq \beta/c$. When we applied α, β based on these rules on SIGMOD dataset, the average precision and recall are found to be 0.96 and 0.82 respectively.

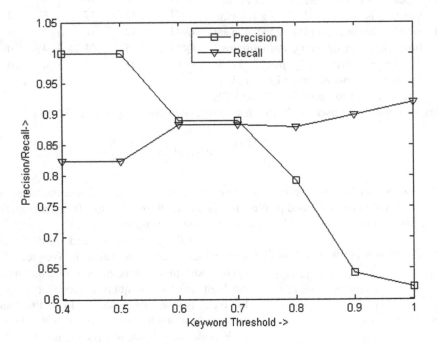

Fig. 5. Effect of β on precision and recall

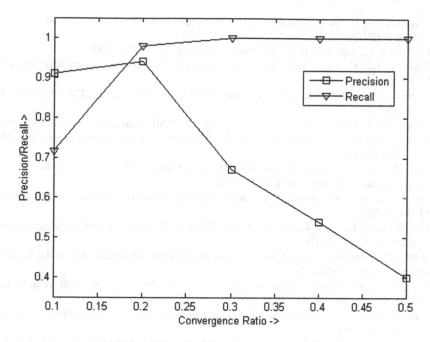

Fig. 6. Effect of α on precision and recall

8 Conclusion

In this paper, we presented a novel system that finds useful insights from raw XML corpus seamlessly, in the context of a given user query. To the best of our knowledge, ours is the first system to enable analytics over raw XML data for given user queries. The capability of our system to expose interesting insights on raw XML data improves the state-of-the art for advanced analytics on such data. As XML and JSON are the default format for exchanging data, our system can enable discovery of actionable business and analytical insights in real time. The crowd-sourced feedback for the *CI* discovered over real XML data sets show that *CI* is found to be highly useful.

Making our technique work with streaming XML data is part of our future research. Another interesting research direction is to optimize the *CI* discovery process by caching *CI* results. For streaming data, given a query which partially or fully overlaps with a previous query and whose results are cached, we may optimize the performance by serving them from the cache.

References

1. Tatarinov, I., et al.: Storing and querying ordered XML using a relational database system. In: SIGMOD (2002)
2. Xu, Y., Papakonstantinou, Y.: Efficient keyword search for smallest LCAs in XML databases. In: EDBT (2008)

3. Liu, Z., Chen, Y.: Identifying meaningful return information for XML keyword search. In: SIGMOD (2007)
4. Li, Y., Yu, C., Jagadish, H.V.: Schema-free XQuery. In: VLDB (2004)
5. Zhou, R., Liu, C., Li, J.: Fast ELCA computation for keyword queries on XML Data. In: EDBT (2010)
6. Chen, L., Papakonstantinou, Y.: Supporting top-k keyword search in XML databases. In: ICDE (2010)
7. Guo, L., et al.: XRANK: ranked keyword search over XML documents. In: SIGMOD (2003)
8. Cohen, S., Mamou, J., Kanza, Y., Sagiv, Y.: XSEarch: a semantic search engine for XML. In: VLDB (2003)
9. Cao, H., et al.: Feedback-driven result ranking and query refinement for exploring semi-structured data collections. In: EDBT (2010)
10. Agarwal, M.K., Ramamritham, K., Agarwal, P.: Generic keyword search over xml data. In: EDBT (2016)
11. Bao, Z., Ling, T., Chen, B., Lu, J.: Effective XML keyword search with relevance oriented ranking. In: ICDE (2009)
12. Botev, C., Shanmugasundaram, J.: Context-sensitive keyword search and ranking for XML documents. In: WebDB (2005)
13. Roy, P., et al.: Towards automatic association of relevant unstructured content with structured query results. In: CIKM (2005)
14. Vazirani, V.: Approximation Algorithms. Springer, Berlin (2001). https://doi.org/10.1007/978-3-662-04565-7
15. Feige, U.: A threshold of ln n for approximating set cover. J. ACM (JACM) **45**(4), 634–652 (1998)
16. Bhalotia, G., et al.: Keyword searching and browsing in databases using BANKS. In: ICDE (2002)
17. Hui, J., Knoop, S., Schwarz, P.: HIWAS: enabling technology for analysis of clinical data in XML documents. In: VLDB (2011)
18. Arenas, M.: Normalization theory for XML. In: SIGMOD Record, vol. 35, no. 4, December 2006

Multi-engine Analytics with IReS

Katerina Doka[1(✉)], Ioannis Mytilinis[1], Nikolaos Papailiou[1],
Victor Giannakouris[1], Dimitrios Tsoumakos[2], and Nectarios Koziris[1]

[1] Computing Systems Laboratory, National Technical University of Athens,
Athens, Greece
{katerina,gmytil,npapa,vgian,nkoziris}@cslab.ntua.gr
[2] Department of Informatics, Ionian University, Corfu, Greece
dtsouma@ionio.gr

Abstract. We present *IReS*, the *Intelligent Resource Scheduler* that is able to abstractly describe, optimize and execute any batch analytics workflow with respect to a multi-objective policy. Relying on cost and performance models of the required tasks over the available platforms, IReS allocates distinct workflow parts to the most advantageous execution and/or storage engine among the available ones and decides on the exact amount of resources provisioned. Moreover, IReS efficiently adapts to the current cluster/engine conditions and recovers from failures by effectively monitoring the workflow execution in real-time. Our current prototype has been tested in a plethora of business driven and synthetic workflows, proving its potential of yielding significant gains in cost and performance compared to statically scheduled, single-engine executions. IReS incurs only marginal overhead to the workflow execution performance, managing to discover an approximate pareto-optimal set of execution plans within a few seconds.

1 Introduction

Over the last two decades, a plethora of diverse execution engines and datastores, both centralized and distributed, have emerged to cope with the challenges posed by the volume, velocity and variety of Big Data and the analysis thereof (e.g., [1–3,8], etc.). In the course of time, Big Data analytics platforms become faster, more efficient and sophisticated, but also more specialized, excelling at certain types of data and processing tasks. Moreover, although many approaches in the relevant literature manage to optimize the performance of single engines by automatically tuning a number of configuration parameters (e.g., [26,31]), they bind their efficacy to specific data formats and workloads.

However, there is no one platform to rule them all: No single execution model is suitable for all types of tasks and no single data model is suitable for all types of data. Thus, the task of architecting an analytics environment that best suits specific scientific or business needs can be frustrating to prospective users. Especially when having to orchestrate long and complex processing pipelines that contain diverse operators and crunch multiple data formats from various sources,

M. Castellanos et al. (Eds.): BIRTE 2015/2016/2017, LNBIP 337, pp. 133–154, 2019.
https://doi.org/10.1007/978-3-030-24124-7_9

analysts can easily go down the wrong technology path. Modern business logic and scientific simulations are encoded into workflows that include a multitude of diverse tasks. Such tasks range from simple Select-Project-Join (SPJ) and data movement to complex NLP-, graph- or custom business-related tasks over a variety of data formats and origins, such as relational data from a legacy DBMS, key-value pairs from a NoSQL cluster, graph data, etc. To add insult to injury, such workflow execution may involve multiple and often conflicting constraints, including time, cost, resource utilization and other execution aspects.

To help address such challenges, many organizations are deploying multiple platforms to handle different parts of their data and workflows (e.g., Facebook [12], Twitter [11], Uber [27], etc.). Even cloud vendors currently offer software solutions that incorporate a multitude of processing frameworks, data stores and libraries to alleviate the burden of managing multiple installations and configurations (e.g., [5,6,10]). The new paradigm of *multi-engine analytics* [36] has recently been proposed as a promising solution that can abstract away the specifics of the underlying platforms and hide the details of how and where each task is executed. This approach aims to unify runtimes and storage backends and promote a declarative way of specifying and executing processing tasks on arbitrary datasets. One of the most compelling, yet daunting challenges in a multi-engine environment is the design and creation of a *meta-scheduler* that automatically allocates workflow subtasks to the right engine(s) according to multiple criteria, deploys and runs them without manual intervention.

Related work mostly revolves around storage engines. Traditional data federation approaches (e.g., [32,35]) solely focus on SQL analytics, while modern ones [28] consider data lake scenarios where historical data stored in HDFS are combined with operational data residing in OLTP systems or NoSQL stores. Polystores, on the other hand, migrate data across various data stores, creating additional load (e.g., [16,21,38]). Very few recent approaches exist for both data and execution engines, which are either proprietary tools with limited applicability and extension possibilities for the community (e.g., [34]) or focus more on the translation of scripts from one engine to another, being thus tied to specific programming languages and engines (e.g., [13,23]). Contrarily, we would ideally opt for a solution that (i) adopts a declarative approach for expressing workflows, (ii) is able to accommodate new platforms, implementation languages and tools as they emerge or as business needs change, (iii) supports multiple optimization goals, (iv) executes workflows in a fail-safe manner and (v) is open-source.

To this end, we design and implement *IReS* [19,20], the open-source *Intelligent Multi-Engine Resource Scheduler*[1] that acts as an "umbrella" for multiple execution engines and datastores, allowing for their seamless integration in the context of a single analytics workflow. IReS handles the whole life cycle of a workflow, from its declarative description to its optimization, planning, execution and monitoring in a transparent to the user way, masking the specifics of the underlying platforms.

---

[1] https://github.com/project-asap/IReS-Platform.

Given a high-level description of the analytics tasks and data at hand using an extensible meta-data framework, IReS is able to optimize, schedule, execute and monitor any workflow that contains them. First, IReS models the cost and performance characteristics of the required tasks over the available platforms in an offline manner. Based on the produced, incrementally updatable models, the planner of IReS is able to map distinct parts of a workflow to the most advantageous store and execution engine and decide on the exact amount of resources provisioned in order to optimize any multi-objective, user-defined policy. The resulting optimization is orthogonal to (and in fact enhanced by) any optimization effort within an engine. Finally, IReS executes the optimized workflow, efficiently adapting to the current cluster and engine conditions and recover from failures by effectively monitoring the workflow execution in real-time.

In this paper we thoroughly present IReS and its internals, delving into the design and implementation details of its modules. Our key contributions are:

- A multi-engine planner that selects the most prominent workflow execution plan among existing runtimes, datastores and operators and elastically provisions the correct amount of resources, based on cost and performance estimations of the various operators over the available platforms.
- A modelling methodology that provides performance and cost estimations of the available analytics operators for different engine configurations. The resulting models are utilized by the planner for multi-engine workflow optimization.
- An execution layer that enforces and monitors the selected multi-engine execution plan, allowing for fine grained resource control and fault tolerance.
- An extensible meta-data description framework for operators and data, which allows for declarative workflow description and automatic discovery of all alternative execution paths.
- An extensive evaluation of our open-source prototype operating over both real-life and synthetic workflows. The results prove that IReS is able to (i) efficiently decide on the best execution plan based on the optimization policy and the available engines within a few seconds, even for large-scale workflow graphs and multiple optimization objectives, (ii) tolerate engine and hardware failures and, most importantly, (i) speed-up the fastest single-engine workflow executions by up to 30% by exploiting multiple engines.

2 IReS Architecture

IReS follows a modular architecture, as depicted in Fig. 1. IReS comprises three layers, the *Interface*, which serves as the point of interaction with the outside world, the *Optimizer*, which constructs the execution plan that best serves the current business objectives and the *Executor*, which enforces it. In the following, we describe in more detail the role, functionality and internals of these layers, delving into the specifics of the most important modules of the platform.

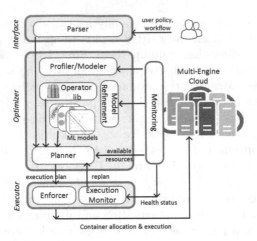

Fig. 1. Architecture of the IReS platform.

2.1 Interface Layer

The Interface layer is responsible for handling the interaction between IReS and its users. It allows users to declaratively describe execution artefacts such as operators, data and workflows, along with their inter-dependencies, properties and restrictions using a unified description framework. It thus enables the user to focus on *what* she wants to achieve rather than *how* to achieve it, abstracting away the details and specifics of underlying platforms. The user-provided workflow is parsed as a dependency graph by the *Parser* and is handed over to the IReS Optimizer along with the user-defined optimization policy.

The IReS description framework sets the guidelines for recording all the information necessary to define and plan a workflow. The two core entities of the framework are *data* and *operators*, which are connected in directed graphs to form workflows. Both data and operators need to be accompanied by a set of metadata, i.e., properties that describe them. Data and operators can be either *abstract* or *materialized*. Abstract operators and datasets are defined and used when composing a workflow, whereas materialized ones refer to specific implementations and existing datasets and are usually provided by the operator developer or the dataset owner respectively. For instance, an abstract operator could simply signify that tf-if is applied on one input dataset and provides one output dataset, while a materialized operator is tied to a specific implementation of tf-idf in Spark/MLlib. Materialized operators, along with their descriptions, are stored in the *Operator library* (Fig. 1). The role of IReS is to eventually map the abstract operators and datasets to materialized ones based on the compliance of their metadata, in order to provide a tangible execution plan.

The metadata that describe operators, such as input types, execution parameters, etc., and data, such as schemata, location of objects, etc., are organized in a generic tree format. To allow for flexibility, only the first levels of the metadata tree are pre-defined. Users can add their ad-hoc subtrees to define custom data

(a)

```
#Reviews
Constraints.Engine.FS=HDFS
Constraints.type=text
Execution.path=hdfs:///user/ires/data
Optimization.documents=2000
```

(b)

```
#tf-idf
Constraints.Input.number=1
Constraints.Output.number=1
Constraints.OpSpecification.Algo=tf-idf
```

Fig. 2. Metadata description of (a) the dataset and (b) an abstract tf-idf operator.

or operator properties. Some fields, mostly the ones related to operator and data requirements, such as the number of inputs/outputs of an operator or the format of a dataset, are *compulsory*, since the workflow planning and execution is impossible without them. The rest, e.g., cost models, statistics, etc. are *optional*: They either serve as extra matching fields for more fine-grained execution planning or they provide additional hints to facilitate the adherence to the workflow optimization policy. Most metadata fields of abstract data and operators are optional, to allow for any desired level of abstraction. Moreover, they support regular expressions. In general, we pre-define the following metadata fields:

Constraints, which contain the information required to discover all possible execution plans that correspond to the abstractly defined workflow. This discovery entails the matching of (a) abstract operators to materialized ones and (b) data to operators in the corresponding metadata fields. Mandatory fields include specifications of operator inputs/outputs, algorithms implemented and underlying engines.

Execution, which provides (a) the execution parameters of a materialized operator, such as the path of its executable or the required execution arguments, and (b) access info of a materialized dataset, such as its path.

Optimization, which is optional and holds additional information that assists in the optimization of the workflow. This information may include a performance/cost function provided by the developer of a materialized operator or dataset statistics (e.g., number of documents in a dataset) provided by its owner. In case a performance/cost function is not a priori known, optimization metadata fields provide IReS with instructions on how to create one by profiling over specific metrics, such as execution time, required RAM, etc. More details on the profiling process can be found in Sect. 2.2.

As a motivating example, imagine an e-commerce website that decides to summarize reviews for a specific product, i.e., perform tf-idf over the corpus of the product reviews, followed by a k-means clustering. First, the input dataset, Reviews, needs to be described as depicted in Fig. 2(a): It is a text file stored in HDFS, as recorded in the Constraints.type and Constraints.Engine.FS fields respectively, following the path specified by the Execution.path field. The information under Optimization tracks down the number of documents contained in the dataset. This information will be used during the planning phase (see Sect. 2.2) to help obtain more accurate performance and cost estimations for the operators using Reviews as input. Then, we need to specify the

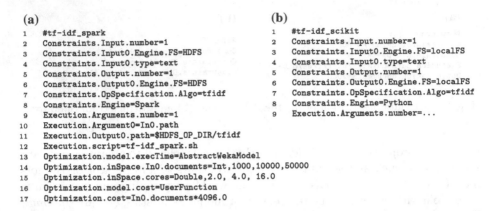

(a)
```
1   #tf-idf_spark
2   Constraints.Input.number=1
3   Constraints.Input0.Engine.FS=HDFS
4   Constraints.Input0.type=text
5   Constraints.Output.number=1
6   Constraints.Output0.Engine.FS=HDFS
7   Constraints.OpSpecification.Algo=tfidf
8   Constraints.Engine=Spark
9   Execution.Arguments.number=1
10  Execution.Argument0=In0.path
11  Execution.Output0.path=$HDFS_OP_DIR/tfidf
12  Execution.script=tf-idf_spark.sh
13  Optimization.model.execTime=AbstractWekaModel
14  Optimization.inSpace.In0.documents=Int,1000,10000,50000
15  Optimization.inSpace.cores=Double,2.0, 4.0, 16.0
16  Optimization.model.cost=UserFunction
17  Optimization.cost=In0.documents*4096.0
```

(b)
```
1   #tf-idf_scikit
2   Constraints.Input.number=1
3   Constraints.Input0.Engine.FS=localFS
4   Constraints.Input0.type=text
5   Constraints.Output.number=1
6   Constraints.Output0.Engine.FS=localFS
7   Constraints.OpSpecification.Algo=tfidf
8   Constraints.Engine=Python
9   Execution.Arguments.number=...
```

Fig. 3. Metadata description of tf-idf operator in (a) Spark/MLlib and (b) python.

operations to be performed. In its most abstract form, the `tf-idf` operator (see Fig. 2(b)) just needs to define the number of input/output parameters as well as the implemented algorithm (under `OpSpecification.Algo`). The same holds for the `k-means` operator.

We assume that the IReS operator library already contains two materialized tf-idf operators, one in Python/scikit and one in Spark/MLlib, provided by the company developers. The metadata of the materialized operators include all information required in order to execute the operations on an engine. For instance, the description of the `tf-idf_spark` materialized operator in Fig. 3(a) states that this is a Spark implementation (l. 8) of the tf-idf algorithm (l. 7) that reads its input from HDFS (l. 3) in the form of a text file (l. 4) and outputs its results in HDFS (l. 6). The operator is executed via a shell script (l. 12), having the path of the input file as an execution argument (l. 10). The `Optimization` metadata designate time and cost as possible optimization objectives of the specific operator (l. 13, l. 16). Execution time estimations are provided by a model (l. 13), which is constructed by the IReS profiler/modeler as instructed in l. 14–15, through a process which will be described subsequently, while cost estimations are given by a developer-provided function (l. 16–17). The `tf-idf_scikit` materialized operator is described similarly (see Fig. 3), indicating Python as the implementation engine (l. 8) and the local filesystem as the input source (l. 3).

To discover the actual tf-idf implementations that match the abstract `tf-idf` operator and comply with the `Reviews` dataset, we employ a tree matching algorithm to ensure that all compulsory fields match. This is performed during planning and optimization, described subsequently. In our example, both `tf-idf_scikit` and `tf-idf_spark` match `tf-idf` in the fields designated in blue. Moreover, the `Reviews` dataset can be directly used as input to `tf-idf_spark`, as the matched metadata fields in red suggest. Thus, `tf-idf_spark` is considered when constructing the optimized execution plan. `tf-idf_scikit` cannot operate on `Reviews` as is, since the fields in red do not match: `tf-idf_scikit` reads from the local filesystem while `Reviews` is stored in HDFS. However, we will see in the next Section how we can circumvent this incompatibility.

2.2 Optimizer Layer

The *Optimizer layer* is responsible for optimizing the execution of an analytics workflow with respect to the policy provided by the user. The core component of this layer is the *Planner*, which determines the execution plan that best satisfies the - possibly multiple - user objectives in real-time. This entails deciding on where each subtask is to be run, under what amount of resources provisioned and whether data need to be moved to/from their current locations and between runtimes (if more than one is chosen).

Such a decision must rely on the characteristics of the analytics tasks that reside within the IReS *Operator library*. To that end, each operator is modeled and the corresponding models are stored in the IReS *ML models library*. The initial model of an operator results from the offline profiling of it using the *Profiler/Modeler* module, which directly interacts with the pool of physical resources and the monitoring layer in-between. Moreover, while the workflow is being executed, the initial models are refined in an online manner by the *Model Refinement* module, using monitoring information of the actual run. This mechanism allows for dynamic adjustments of the models and enables the Planner to base its decisions on the most up-to-date knowledge.

▶**Profiler/Modeler.** While accurate models do exist for relational operators over RDBMSs, which usually include their own cost-based optimizer, this is not the case for other analytics operators (e.g., natural language processing, machine learning, graph processing, etc.) and modern runtimes (be they distributed or centralized): Only a very limited number of operators and engines has been studied, while most of the proposed models entail knowledge of the code to be executed (e.g., [33,39]). Moreover, there is no trivial way to compare or correlate cost estimations derived from different engines at a meta-level.

To that end, we adopt an engine-agnostic approach that treats materialized operators as "black boxes" and models them using profiling and machine learning. The profiling mechanism adopted builds on prior work [22]. Its input parameters fall into three categories: (a) *data specific*, which describe the data to be used for the operator profiling (e.g., type and size, dimensionality, distribution, etc.), (b) *operator specific*, which relate to the algorithm of the operator (e.g., number of output clusters in k-means, number of iterations in pagerank, etc.), and (c) *resource specific*, which define the resources to be tweaked during profiling (e.g., cluster size, main memory, etc.). The sampling of the configuration space follows an adaptive approach, picking the most representative instances of the deployment space to achieve high accuracy given a certain budget of runs.

The output is the profiled operator's performance and cost (e.g., completion time, average memory, CPU consumption, etc.) under each combination of the input parameter values. Both the input parameters as well as the output metrics are specified by the user/developer in the materialized operator's metadata (Fig. 3, l. 14–15). The collected metrics are then used to create estimation models, making use of neural networks, SVM, interpolation and curve fitting techniques for each operator running on a specific engine. The cross validation technique [29] is used to maintain the model that best fits the available data.

▶**Model Refinement.** The offline produced models assure the system a warm start, as they can provide accurate cost and performance estimations from the very first workflow planning. However, as the system is put to use, online measurements of executing tasks can contribute to the increase of the models' prediction accuracy and to the better adjustment to the current conditions. Upon execution of a workflow, the currently monitored execution metrics provide feedback to the existing models in order to refine them and capture possible changes in the underlying infrastructure (e.g., hardware upgrades) or temporal degradations (e.g., due to unbalanced use of engines, collocation of competing tasks, surges in load etc.). This mechanism contributes to the adaptability of IReS, ameliorating the accuracy of the models while the platform is in operation.

▶**Planner.** This module, in analogy to traditional query planners, intelligently explores all the available execution plans to discover the (near-)optimal one with respect to the user-defined, possibly multiple optimization objectives.

The Planner's input is the abstract workflow graph, expressed as a DAG of operator and data nodes. As a first step, for each abstract operator of the input workflow the Planner needs to explore the IReS Operator library to discover all matching materialized operators, i.e., operators that share the same metadata. To speedup this procedure, we use string labelled and lexicographically ordered metadata trees, which allow for efficient, one pass tree matching. The matching is performed by simultaneously iterating over both trees using a recursive merge procedure to match children nodes. The complexity of matching two metadata trees with up to t nodes is $O(t)$. We further improve the matching procedure by indexing the IReS library operators using a set of highly selective metadata attributes (e.g., algorithm name). Only operators that contain the correct attributes are considered as candidate matches and are further examined.

The discovery of the best materialized operator combinations out of all feasible ones that simultaneously optimize more than one execution criterion, e.g., both execution time and memory utilization, translates to a multi-objective optimization problem that, in the case of conflicting objectives, has a possibly large number of pareto-optimal solutions.

A simplistic algorithm would exhaustively try all possible combinations and check their validity by consulting the input/output specifications of the materialized operators and datasets. In case an input dataset can not be used as is by a materialized operator, or if subsequent operators are incompatible in their input/output formats, the Planner searches the IReS library for *auxiliary operators*, which can be interposed to "glue" different engines. Such auxiliary operators include move and transformation operations (e.g., the copyToLocal and copyFromLocal mechanisms of HDFS, which move datasets from HDFS to the local filesystem and vice versa), are provided by the developers and treated as common materialized operators. Thus, invalid combinations are those that contain incompatible elements for which no auxiliary operator exists that can render them compatible.

After the elimination of invalid combinations, the objective functions for each valid one should be evaluated based on the prediction models of the involved operators, including the auxiliary ones. Finally, the algorithm should return the combinations that provide the pareto-optimal solutions that minimize or maximize the objective functions.

While such a naive algorithm would provide optimal solutions, it would only be practical for small workflow instances. Assuming a workflow graph of n abstract nodes and m materialized matches for each of them, the complexity of the algorithm is $\mathcal{O}(m^n)$, meaning that the size of combinations to be checked grows exponentially with the number or workflow nodes. Thus, to be able to accommodate large and complex workflow instances within a reasonable time-frame, we opt for a heuristic planning algorithm, *H-Planner*, which relies on genetic algorithms to find near-optimal solutions.

More specifically, H-Planner uses NSGA-II [18], the most prevalent evolutionary algorithm that has become the standard approach to generating pareto-optimal solutions to a multi-objective optimization problem. All candidate materialized operators of each abstract one are provided as input to the algorithm. NSGA-II initially creates random permutations of the input, i.e., different combinations of materialized operators, validates them, adding - if necessary - auxiliary operators, and evaluates for each of them a set of scores. This set contains the aggregate of the estimations of all involved operators for each objective function (consulting the models). Combinations that best fit the optimization criteria are selected and their crossover, along with some mutations (i.e., small changes at random), are provided as input to the next iteration of NSGA-II. After a fixed number of iterations or if no significant progress is achieved, the process results in a set of approximate pareto-optimal execution plans.

In the special case of (1) a single optimization objective and (2.a) workflows that exhibit compatibility of input/output operator specification or (2.b) a linear structure, we can employ a more accurate and efficient algorithm, the *DP-Planner*, which relies on dynamic programming (DP) to select the truly optimal execution plan. The aforementioned conditions are deemed necessary to guarantee the principle of optimality: When all workflow operators are compatible, i.e., use the same input/output format and engine, or when the workflow does not contain operators that branch and merge again at any point, we can ensure that optimizing each step of the workflow will result in the optimization of the entire workflow. As Big Data workflows commonly use HDFS as their common data substrate and often follow simple linear structures, we believe that this algorithm can find application in many practical cases.

The abstract workflow of our motivating example performs tf-idf feature-extraction over Reviews and clusters the output using k-means. Assuming each operator has two implementations, using either Spark/MLlib or Python/scikit, we have the possible alternative execution plans of Fig. 4. Note that the Planner

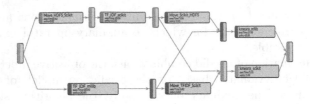

Fig. 4. Materialized workflow and optimal plan.

automatically adds the necessary `move` operators in order to match `Reviews`, which resides in HDFS, with `tf-idf_scikit`, which reads from the local filesystem, and transfer intermediate results between the two engines (i.e., match the output of an operator to the input of the subsequent one).

Let us assume an optimization policy that targets execution time minimization. Intuitively, small datasets run faster in a centralized manner while distributed implementations prevail for bigger datasets. Indeed, the Python implementation is estimated to be the fastest for both steps, even with the additional cost of transferring data from HDFS to the local filesystem, due to the small input size and is thus included in the selected execution path, marked in green.

▶**Resource Provisioning.** Apart from deciding on the specific implementation/engine of each workflow operator, the Planner of IReS aims to provision the correct amount of resources so that the workflow execution conforms as much as possible to the user-defined optimization policy. The possible resource-related parameters that need to be defined include, for instance, the number of cores or the amount of memory which will be allocated to the execution of a materialized operator. The resource provisioning process builds again on the NSGA-II genetic algorithm: The range of possible values for each resource-related parameter is provided as input to the genetic algorithm and various combinations of them are iteratively tested to discover the one that achieves local optima of the trained models. The estimated parameter values are passed as arguments to the workflow execution during run-time.

2.3   Executor Layer

The *Executor layer* is the layer that enforces the optimal plan over the physical infrastructure. Its main responsibilities include the execution of the ensuing plan, a task undertaken by the *Enforcer*, and the assurance of the platform's fault tolerance, carried out by the *Execution Monitor*.

▶**Enforcer.** The Enforcer orchestrates the execution of the materialized operators, over the appropriate platforms and resources, as chosen by the Planner. The enforcer adopts methods and tools that translate high level "start runtime under x amount of resources", "move data from site Y to Z" type of commands to a series of primitives as understood by the specific runtimes and storage engines. Such actions might entail code and/or data shipment, if necessary.

Our working prototype relies on YARN [37], a cluster management tool that enables fine-grained, container-level resource allocation and scheduling over various processing frameworks. Apart from requesting from YARN the necessary container resources for each workflow operator, the enforcer needs to pay special attention to the workflow execution orchestration. To that end, IReS extends Cloudera Kitten [7], a set of tools for configuring and launching YARN containers as well as running applications inside them, in order to add support for the execution of a DAG of operators instead of just one. Concisely, each workflow is deployed over the physical resources as a YARN application: An application master container is launched to coordinate all containers required to execute each workflow operator. The number and size of those containers are designated by the Planner's resource provisioning mechanism.

▶**Execution Monitor.** This module captures failures that might occur, both at node and engine levels, on-the-fly through real-time monitoring. Thus, it ensures the availability and fault tolerance of the system by employing two mechanisms:

- A *node health check mechanism* provided by YARN, which monitors the health status of the underlying infrastructure by periodically executing customizable and parametrized scripts in all cluster nodes. The health check script may include rules for the per node usage of memory, CPU, network, etc. Any node failing to adhere to the script rules is characterized as unhealthy. For instance, a health script may check a node's current memory usage and report the node as unhealthy if it exceeds 95%. The health status (HEALTHY/UNHEALTHY state per cluster node) is reported back to the IReS server. No execution will be scheduled to unhealthy cluster nodes.
- A *service availability check mechanism* that examines the availability of all engines needed for the enforcement of an execution plan. Essentially, a daemon running on the YARN application master container periodically pings the available services and stores their status (ON/OFF) in memory. This information is served, whenever needed, to the IReS Planner. The period of the availability check is customizable, currently set to 5 s.

This information is used during the phases of both planning and execution of a workflow: **During workflow planning**, unavailable engines are excluded when constructing the optimal execution plan and resources are provisioned exclusively taking into account the currently healthy ones. **During workflow execution**, engine failures are detected in real-time. When failures affect an operator's execution, the workflow enters a REPLANNING state, which triggers the following steps: (a) The operator currently running is stopped and all subsequent operators pending for execution are cancelled; (b) The YARN application master checks for the existence of any intermediate materialized datasets and determines which part of the workflow needs to be re-scheduled for execution; (c) The Planner is invoked to select the new execution plan of the remaining workflow; (d) The new plan is enforced.

As a checkpointing mechanism, IReS persists in HDFS the output of successfully executed operators. Taking advantage of any intermediate materialized data, it effectively reduces the workflow part that needs to be re-scheduled.

Table 1. Operators with their associated engines

Operator	Compute Engine (version)/Data Engine
PageRank	Spark(2.1.1)/HDFS, Hama(0.7.1)/HDFS, Java(1.8)/localFS
k-means	Spark(2.1.1)/HDFS, Python scikit-learn(1.19.0)/localFS
tf-idf	Spark(2.1.1)/HDFS, Python scikit-learn(1.19.0)/localFS
UserProfiling	Spark(2.1.1)/HDFS
Classifier	Spark(2.1.1)/HDFS
tokenization	Spark(2.1.1)/HDFS, Java Stanford CoreNLP(3.9.0)/localFS
stop-word removal	Spark(2.1.1)/HDFS, Java Stanford CoreNLP(3.9.0)/localFS
sentence detection	Spark(2.1.1)/HDFS, Java Stanford CoreNLP(3.9.0)/localFS

3   Experimental Evaluation

Our prototype is implemented in Java 1.8 and uses the YARN scheduler and
the Cloudera Kitten 0.2.0 project for the management of the deployed compute
and data engines. IReS is open-source and available on GitHub. In the following
experiments, IReS orchestrates a number of runtimes and data stores presented
in Table 1. For all engines, we maintain the default configuration. Both our multi-
engine framework and the available engines are deployed over a 8-node cluster,
where each node features eight Intel(R) Xeon(R) CPU E5405 @ 2.00 GHz cores
and 8 GB of main memory. In our experiments, we make the assumption that
there is only one workflow executing at any given time. The scheduling of multiple concurrent workflows is a subject of future work.

▶**Workflows and Data.** For our experiments we use both real and synthetic
workflows. Real workflows are driven by actual business needs and have been
specified in the context of the EU-funded ASAP project[2]. They cover complex
data manipulations in the areas of *telecommunication analytics* and *web data
analytics*, provided by a large telecommunications company and a well-known
web archiving organization respectively. The tasks involved include *machine
learning (ML)*, *graph processing* and *natural language processing (NLP)* operators (see Table 1) over datasets that consist of anonymized telecommunication
traces and web content data. By selecting workflows that cover different and
representative areas (ML, graph, text) of Big Data applications, we showcase
the general applicability of our framework.

Synthetic workflows are used for stressing our system in terms of workflow
size and complexity and evaluating various aspects of it in a controlled manner.
They include workflows produced by the Pegasus workflow generator [15], as
well as sequential workflow topologies. The Pegasus-generated workflow graphs
fall into four scientific workflow categories (Montage, CyberShake, Epigenomics
and Inspiral) and contain patterns derived from different scientific application

---

[2] ASAP (Adaptive Scalable Analytics Platform) envisions a unified execution framework for scalable data analytics. www.asap-fp7.eu/.

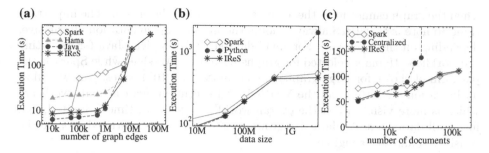

Fig. 5. Execution times for the (a) Influencer Detection, (b) Tourism Observation and (c) Document similarity workflows vs. various input sizes.

domains, such as astronomy, biology, gravitational physics and earthquake science. All these graphs present complex topologies, where nodes have high in- and out-degrees. Montage is the most complex workflow to process, as it is the most interconnected one, while Epigenomics and Inspiral contain more sequential patterns that render processing easier.

3.1 Execution of Real-Life Workflows

In this set of experiments, we use IReS to optimize the execution of real-life applications in a multi-engine environment. We assume a single optimization objective, minimizing execution time. The execution time of the plan produced by IReS is compared against that of the whole workflow exclusively running on a single engine. The goal for IReS is to discover execution plans at least as efficient as the fastest single-engine choice (plus a small overhead). As the combination of different engines within the same plan reveals chances for further optimization, there exist cases where IReS outperforms the fastest single engine alternative.

▶**Influencer Detection.** The first application, derived from the telecommunication analytics domain, calculates the influence score of a subscriber on a telecommunications network (to be used in a recommendation system). Data input is in the form of csv call detail records (CDR). For solving the problem, we first model the CDR data as a graph: Each customer (i.e., phone number) represents a vertex and each call corresponds to an edge. This way, we can directly apply the Pagerank algorithm. The available execution engines are: (i) Spark, (ii) Hama and (iii) a centralized Java implementation.

Figure 5a depicts the execution time of the workflow for various graph sizes when executed over the available engines and when IReS is used. As expected, the centralized (Java) implementation outperforms the others for small-scale graphs. However, as input size grows and exceeds the memory limits of a single node, this approach fails. Distributed platforms expose a different behavior. They incur overheads for small graphs but scale well for larger datasizes. The Hama-based implementation achieves good performance for medium-sized graphs, but as it relies on a distributed main-memory execution model, it also seizes to scale when the graph cannot fit in the aggregate memory of the cluster. The important thing to note is that IReS always adopts the fastest implementation alternative, depending on the input size: For small data sizes, IReS picks Java for executing the workflow; Hama is selected for graphs with over 1M edges while Spark is the platform of choice for large graphs having more than 10M edges. The workflow optimization algorithm and the YARN-based execution incur a small overhead, which is more visible when the overall workflow execution time is limited, i.e., for small data sizes. As data size grows, this overhead is amortized and can be considered almost negligible.

▶**Tourism Observation.** This application builds a tourism observation service based on CDR data. The workflow consumes two datasets: (i) the CDRs and (ii) a dataset that maps the GSM cells of the mobile network to geographical regions. Both datasets reside in HDFS. The first operator, called *user_profiling*, joins the two datasets and outputs records that encode the temporal behaviour of users. These vectors are subsequently clustered by a k-means algorithm to discover typical calling behaviours. Both the user profiles and the clusters are finally handed over to a proprietary classification algorithm that labels the calling behaviours and returns the percentage of each label in each spatial region. For example, we can deduce that in New York, 75% of the callers are residents and 25% commuters. For all the operators, IReS chooses between two alternative implementations: (i) a centralized Python code based on the scikit-learn library (ii) a Spark job based on the MLlib library.

Figure 5b plots the workflow execution time as the size of the CDR dataset increases. The centralized implementation performs better than Spark for CDR datasets smaller than 1GB while Spark scales better as size grows. IReS always adapts to the fastest engine. When the join selectivity of the *user_profiling* operator is high, leading to small join results, IReS opts for a hybrid execution plan, selecting the Spark implementation for the first operator and the centralized Python implementations for the remaining two. This way, for large datasets, IReS manages to outperform even the best single-engine execution.

▶**Document Similarity.** This application, which falls into the web data analytics category, aims to cluster similar documents together. The input dataset, provided by a large, European web archiving organization, comprises text files of 40 KB each. As a first step, documents go through an NLP pipeline consisting of sentence detection, tokenization and stop-words removal. Documents are vectorized according to a vocabulary and the tf-idf metric is computed for each of them. Finally, k-means clustering is used to group similar document-vectors. For each operator, two implementations are available: (i) a distributed, Spark-based implementation, and (ii) a centralized implementation (a Java-based implementation using the Stanford CoreNLP library for the NLP operator and a Python-based implementation using scikit-learn for the tf-idf and k-means operators).

Figure 5c presents the performance results of the Document Similarity workflow when varying the number of input documents. We observe that the centralized implementation outperforms Spark only for small datasets (less than 10 K documents in our case). Using our trained cost estimators, IReS selects the

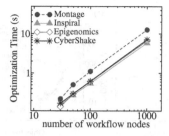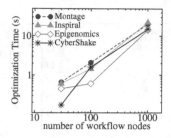

Fig. 6. Optimization time vs. workflow size, 4 engines/operator: (a) Single-objective optimization with DP-Planner (b) 2-objective optimization with H-Planner.

proper engines and always performs as good as the fastest engine does. What is more, for a range of input sizes, IReS picks hybrid plans that combine different execution engines. Indeed, from 10 K to 40K number of input documents IReS maps the tf-idf operator to Python and the *k-means* operator to Spark. This way, it outperforms even the fastest single-engine execution by up to 30%.

3.2 Workflow Planner

In this section we experimentally evaluate the performance of the IReS multi-engine workflow planner when performing single- or multi-objective optimization with respect to: (i) the optimality of yielded plans, (ii) the number of available alternative implementations of each operator and (iii) the workflow complexity. For these experiments, we use the synthetic, Pegasus-generated workflows. This gives us the flexibility to create arbitrarily large workflow graphs and test complex topologies that are more difficult to obtain in practice. To perform optimization, IReS requires performance profiles for every operator available in the IReS library. As these operators are part of a synthetic workflow, models have to be simulated. To every targeted optimization objective M_i (e.g., execution time, cost, memory utilization, etc.), we randomly assign a domain of the form $R_i = (0, N_i]$, i.e., a range where M_i can obtain a value from. The M_i value of each materialized operator is selected uniformly at random in R_i. To further stress the Planner in terms of the number of possible execution plans that need to be processed, we make the assumption that all operators are compatible in their inputs/outputs. As a side effect, no auxiliary operators are required.

In Fig. 6a we assess the performance of the DP-Planner algorithm for the single-objective optimization problem, while Fig. 6b presents the performance of the H-Planner algorithm for the 2-objective optimization problem, when ranging the number of workflow nodes from 30 to 1000, considering 4 alternative execution engines per operator. Here we should note that DP-Planner discovers the exact optimal plans, while H-Planner trades optimality for speed, returning approximate, near-optimal solutions.

Both planning algorithms exhibit similar behaviour, scaling linearly with the graph size. The CyberShake, Epigenomics and Inspiral workflows of the

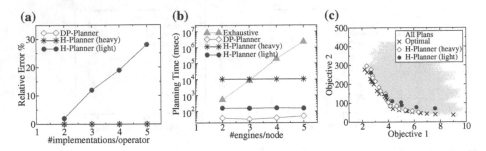

Fig. 7. (a) Relative error and (b) planning time of various algorithms for a synthetic 10-node workflow (single-objective). (c) Pareto frontiers (multi-objective).

same size require comparable times to be processed by each of the algorithms. Only Montage deviates in the single-objective case, exhibiting slightly increased planning times due to its dense structure: The Montage graph is more connected, having multiple nodes with high in- and out-degrees. Since the complexity of DP-Planner is $\mathcal{O}(op \cdot m^2 \cdot k)$, k being the number of inputs of each operator, the high in-degrees of Montage have a linear impact on optimization time.

For both the single- and multi-objective optimization cases, even under the extreme scenario of 1000-node workflows, the overhead of IReS is less than 12 s in all runs. An average 30-node workflow, can be optimized and scheduled for execution with IReS in the sub-second time-scale. This also holds for all of the real-life workflows utilized throughout this section, which require planning times in the order of milliseconds. This allows us to expect that the IReS Planner can handle the most complex multi-engine workflow scenarios under any single- or multi-objective optimization policy with negligible overhead compared to the total execution time of the analytics workflow itself.

In the next experiment, we investigate the quality of the execution plans that IReS selects in both the single- and multi-objective policy scenarios, as well as the cost for discovering them for all planning algorithms employed. As a baseline, we implement an exhaustive algorithm that enumerates all possible execution plans of a workflow and selects the optimal one(s). The complexity of it is exponential to the number of workflow nodes and highly affected by the number of available engines for each operator. As the cost of constructing the optimal solution for the Pegasus graphs is prohibitive, for this experiment we use a smaller synthetic graph of 10 nodes. This is the largest graph size on which the exhaustive algorithm successfully runs in our machine. The synthetic graph has been created by removing nodes from the smallest available Montage graph until we end up with 10 nodes. We assume that all operators have the same number of alternative implementations, which ranges from 2 to 5.

Figure 7a plots the relative error between the cost of the selected and the cost of the optimal plan as the number of operator alternatives increases, when using three algorithms: DP-Planner and two variations of H-Planner, the *light* one that runs for 100 generations and the *heavy* one that runs for 1000 generations.

The more the generations, the longer it takes for the algorithm to execute but the closer the results are to the optimum. As expected, DP-Planner always achieves optimal results. Zero relative error is also observed for the heavy version of H-Planner, since it performs a more extensive search to discover the optimal plan. The light version of H-Planner, configured to run for an order of magnitude less generations, deviates from the optimum, but still less than 30%. Moreover, in that case, the number of alternative implementations has a monotonically increasing effect on the relative error.

Figure 7b presents the corresponding planning times. We see that the exhaustive algorithm, denoted as *Exhaustive*, very soon becomes unaffordable even for small graphs: For 5 implementations per operator, the algorithm needs almost an hour to investigate all possible plans. The fastest planning algorithm is DP-Planner, requiring at most 35msec for discovering the optimal plan (in the case of 5 alternatives/engine). The light version of H-Planner follows, with a constant planning time of around 110ms, regardless of the number of alternatives per engine. The heavy version of H-Planner is 2 orders of magnitude slower than the light one. Even so, it requires less than 10 s to provide results, time certainly affordable especially when the quality of results is the desideratum.

Next, we consider two optimization objectives, *Objective 1* and *Objective 2*, under the same experiment configuration. In this case the Planner returns a set of approximate pareto-optimal execution plans. DP-Planner is unable to handle multi-objective planning, thus only the two variations of H-Planner are evaluated. Figure 7c plots all possible execution plans in terms of their Objective 1 and Objective 2 values in grey, considering 4 alternatives/operator. The black marks depict the pareto optimal frontier [18], as designated by the exhaustive algorithm. The heavy version of H-Planner produces the plans in red while the light version the plans in blue. Both H-Planner variations result in plan sets that lie close to the pareto optimal ones and cover their entire frontier, with H-Planner heavy producing results closer to optimal. To quantify the quality of the two H-Planner versions, we calculate the *Hausdorff distance* [25] between resulting plan sets and the pareto optimal one (as calculated by the exhaustive algorithm). The Hausdorff distance is a metric that measures how far two subsets of a metric space are from each other and is defined as the greatest of all distances from a point in one set to the closest point in the other set. More formally, assuming A is the approximate plan set and P the pareto optimal one, the Hausdorff distance between the two sets is $d_H(A, P) = \max_{\forall a \in A}\{\min_{\forall p \in P}\{d(a, p)\}\}$, where $d(a, p)$ is the Euclidean distance between points a and p. For the experiment of Fig. 7c, it holds that $d_H(A, P) = 15.6$ for H-Planner heavy and $d_H(A, P) = 60.7$ for the H-Planner light. The plan set produced by the heavy version of the H-planner is 4× closer to the pareto-optimal than the one produced by the light version. Experiments with ranging the number of alternative implementations per operator show no qualitative difference.

(a)   **(b)**

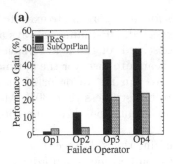 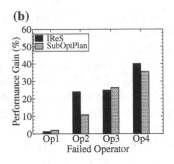

Fig. 8. Total execution time in the presence of failures. (a) *Eng1* is the fastest for all operators. (b) The fastest engine alternates between *Eng1* and *Eng2*

3.3 Fault-Tolerance Mechanism

In this section, we test IReS under the presence of failures and evaluate its resilience. To have a better control over the experiment, we assume a synthetic, sequential workflow of four operators, Op1 to Op4, each having two implementations (*Eng1, Eng2*). Each operator/engine combination has a performance model drawn from a uniform distribution.

We conduct four experiments, simulating the failure of Op1 to Op4 respectively, by disabling the engine selected by IReS during operator execution. As explained in Sect. 2.3, IReS will cancel the execution of the failed operator and all subsequent ones, it will determine the subgraph of the initial workflow that needs to be re-planned and will issue a request to the Planner for a new plan. The IReS fault-tolerance mechanism is compared to two alternative strategies: (a) *TrivialReplan*, which does not materialize intermediate datasets and thus requires re-scheduling of the whole workflow and (b) *SubOptPlan*, which represents the hypothetical case where the initial execution plan had been selected excluding the failed engine, i.e., the workflow execution is ab initio suboptimal, but not affected by the engine failure.

Figure 8 plots the gain in workflow execution time achieved by the IReS and SubOptPlan strategies compared to TrivialReplan when each of the Op1 to Op4 fails. In Fig. 8a, *Eng1* is the fastest alternative for all operators. Since IReS does not need to re-execute the successfully completed operators, the workflow performance ameliorates as failures occur later in the execution path. Contrarily, the performance of workflows executed with TrivialReplan naturally degrades as the position of the failed operators moves towards the end of the workflow, since larger parts of the workflow need to be re-executed. Thus, IReS exhibits increasing performance gains that reach 50%. The performance gain of SubOpt-Plan, which always runs the whole workflow in *Eng2*, is always worse than that of IReS, with the exception of Op1 failure: When Op1 fails, IReS can not take advantage of any intermediate result and has to re-schedule the whole workflow from scratch. The new plan coincides with the SubOptPlan plus the replanning overhead. When failures occur at later stages, IReS exploits the performance gains of the operators successfully executed on *Eng1*, thus the performance gain compared to SubOptPlan increases.

In the setup of Fig. 8b, we randomly pick which of *Eng1* or *Eng2* is the best alternative for each operator. Once again, IReS plans always outperform the TrivialReplan ones, with an increasing performance gain as failures occur later in the execution. Compared to SubOptPlan, we see that there are still cases where IReS performs better (failure of Op2 and Op4). When the selected engine of Op1 or Op3 fails, SubOptPlan slightly outperforms IReS due to the extra cost that the replanning and launching of new containers incurs.

4   Related Work

Data federation approaches have a long tradition, having extensively studied query execution across multiple data sources for decades [17,32,35]. However, these approaches focus solely on SQL analytics and fail to optimize query execution over datasets split between multiple sources. On the contrary, recent attempts in the field of data management aim to provide a unified query language or API over various datastores. SparkSQL [14], part of the Apache Spark project [3], and PrestoDB [9], powered by Facebook, are two production systems that provide a query execution engine with connectors to various external systems such as PostgreSQL, MemSQL, Hive, etc. However, to perform any operation on external data they both need to fetch and distribute them internally, missing out on many engine-specific optimizations.

Polystores have recently been proposed as a means to combine data from heterogeneous sources [21,38]. They consist of a multitude of data stores, each accommodating different query types. In a polystore environment, data migration among stores is frequent and cumbersome, requiring pairwise, bi-directional connections between the available data stores and creating additional load. Data move can be facilitated by special communication frameworks like PipeGen [24], which use binary buffers to transfer data. Such frameworks can complement IReS, providing efficient move operators whenever data transfer is required.

Recent research works like the Cascading Lingual project [4] and CloudMdsQL [30] try to optimize query resolution over heterogeneous environments by pushing query processing to the datastores that manage the data as much as possible. They mostly provide rule-based optimizations while considerable effort is devoted to the translation between the involved storage engines' native query languages. All of the above approaches, unlike IReS, focus solely on storing and querying Big Data, rather than performing any complex analytics workflow.

In the field of workflow management, HFMS [34] aims to create a planner for multi-engine workflows, but focuses more on lower-level database operators, emphasizing on their automatic translation from/to specific engines via an XML-based language. Yet, this is a proprietary tool with limited applicability and extension possibilities for the community. Contrarily, IReS is a fully open-source platform that targets both low and high level operators.

Musketeer [23] and Rheem [13] also address multi-engine workflow execution, acting as mediators between an engine's front- and back-end. They first map a user's workflow to an internal representation and then apply a set of rule-based optimizations before sending it for execution. They focus more on the translation of scripts from one engine to another, being thus tied to specific programming languages and engines. Contrarily, IReS is engine agnostic, treating operators as black boxes. This allows for extensibility to new engines and easy addition of new operators regardless of their implementation language.

5   Conclusions

Deciding on the exact platforms, configurations and resources to execute long and complex Big Data workflows on, especially when multiple execution criteria are involved, is a daunting task, even for the most knowledgeable and experienced system architect. IReS alleviates this burden, by automatically planning the execution of workflow parts over different platforms, abstracting away their specifics. Based on cost and performance estimations, IReS is able to make the most out of each available platform, matching tasks to the most beneficial runtimes and data to the most suitable stores. IReS proves extremely useful in the case of large workflows with complex structure or of tasks with unknown and hard-to-predict behaviour. Moreover, depending on the workflow and the operators involved, IReS has the potential of yielding significant gains in cost and performance compared to statically scheduled, single-engine executions. The IReS prototype already supports a number of compute and data engines and has been extensively evaluated in optimizing and scheduling a variety of diverse, business-driven as well as synthetic workflows. The experiments showcase (a) a speedup of up to 30% in the execution of the tested workflows, (b) the efficiency of the multi-objective optimizer, which discovers the close-to-optimal pareto plans within a few seconds and (c) the reliability of the system, which manages to recover from failures with minimum impact on the workflow execution time.

References

1. Apache Flink. https://flink.apache.org/
2. Apache Hadoop. http://hadoop.apache.org/
3. Apache Spark. https://spark.apache.org/
4. Cascading Lingual. www.cascading.org/projects/lingual/
5. Cloudera Distribution CDH 5.2.0. http://www.cloudera.com/content/cloudera/en/downloads/cdh/cdh-5-2-0.html
6. Hortonworks Sandbox. http://hortonworks.com/products/hortonworks-sandbox/
7. Kitten. https://github.com/cloudera/kitten
8. monetdb. https://www.monetdb.org/
9. Presto. http://www.teradata.com/Presto
10. Running Databases on AWS. http://aws.amazon.com/running_databases/
11. The Infrastructure Behind Twitter: Scale. https://blog.twitter.com/engineering/en_us/topics/infrastructure/2017/the-infrastructure-behind-twitter-scale.html
12. What is Facebook's architecture? https://www.quora.com/What-is-Facebooks-architecture-6

13. Agrawal, D., et al.: Rheem: enabling multi-platform task execution. In: SIGMOD (2016)
14. Armbrust, M., et al.: SparkSQL: relational data processing in spark. In: SIGMOD, pp. 1383–1394. ACM (2015)
15. Bharathi, S., et al.: Characterization of scientific workflows. In: Workshop on Workflows in Support of Large-Scale Science (2008)
16. Bugiotti, F., et al.: Invisible glue: scalable self-tuning multi-stores. In: CIDR (2015)
17. Chawathe, S., et al.: The TSIMMIS project: integration of heterogenous information sources. In: IPSJ, pp. 7–18 (1994)
18. Deb, K., et al.: A fast and elitist multiobjective genetic algorithm: NSGA-ii. IEEE Trans. Evol. Comput. **6**(2), 182–197 (2002)
19. Doka, K., Papailiou, N., Tsoumakos, D., Mantas, C., Koziris, N.: IReS: intelligent, multi-engine resource scheduler for big data analytics workflows. In: Proceedings of the 2015 ACM SIGMOD, pp. 1451–1456. ACM (2015)
20. Doka, K., et al.: Mix "n" match multi-engine analytics. In: Big data, pp. 194–203. IEEE (2016)
21. Duggan, J., et al.: The bigDAWG polystore system. ACM Sigmod Rec. **44**(2), 11–16 (2015)
22. Giannakopoulos, I., Tsoumakos, D., Koziris, N.: A decision tree based approach towards adaptive profiling of cloud applications. In: IEEE Big Data (2017)
23. Gog, I., et al.: Musketeer: all for one, one for all in data processing systems. In: Eurosys, p. 2. ACM (2015)
24. Haynes, B., Cheung, A., Balazinska, M.: Pipegen: data pipe generator for hybrid analytics. arXiv:1605.01664 (2016)
25. Henrikson, J.: Completeness and total boundedness of the hausdorff metric. MIT Undergrad. J. Math. **1**, 69–80 (1999)
26. Herodotou, H., et al.: Starfish: a self-tuning system for big data analytics. In: CIDR (2011)
27. Johnson, N., Near, J.P., Song, D.: Towards practical differential privacy for SQL queries. Vertica 1, 1000
28. Karpathiotakis, et al.: No data left behind: real-time insights from a complex data ecosystem. In: SoCC, pp. 108–120. ACM (2017)
29. Kohavi, R., et al.: A study of cross-validation and bootstrap for accuracy estimation and model selection. In: IJCAI (1995)
30. Kolev, B., et al.: CloudMdsQL: querying heterogeneous cloud data stores with a common language. Distrib. Parallel Databases **34**, 1–41 (2015)
31. Lim, H., Herodotou, H., Babu, S.: Stubby: a transformation-based optimizer for mapreduce workflows. In: VLDB (2012)
32. Roth, M.T., Schwarz, P.M.: Don't scrap it, wrap it! a wrapper architecture for legacy data sources. In: VLDB, vol. 97 (1997)
33. Sharma, B., Wood, T., Das, C.R.: HybridMR: A Hierarchical MapReduce Scheduler for Hybrid Data Centers. In: ICDCS (2013)
34. Simitsis, A., et al.: HFMS: managing the lifecycle and complexity of hybrid analytic data flows. In: ICDE. IEEE (2013)
35. Tomasic, A., Raschid, L., Valduriez, P.: Scaling access to heterogeneous data sources with DISCO. IEEE TKDE **10**(5), 808–823 (1998)
36. Tsoumakos, D., Mantas, C.: The case for multi-engine data analytics. In: an Mey, D., et al. (eds.) Euro-Par 2013. LNCS, vol. 8374, pp. 406–415. Springer, Heidelberg (2014). https://doi.org/10.1007/978-3-642-54420-0_40
37. Vavilapalli, V.K., et al.: Apache hadoop yarn: yet another resource negotiator. In: SoCC, p. 5. ACM (2013)

38. Wang, J., et al.: The myria big data management and analytics system and cloud services. In: CIDR (2017)
39. Zhang, Z., et al.: Automated profiling and resource management of pig programs for meeting service level objectives. In: ICAC, pp. 53–62. ACM (2012)

Ubiq: A Scalable and Fault-Tolerant Log Processing Infrastructure

Venkatesh Basker, Manish Bhatia, Vinny Ganeshan, Ashish Gupta,
Shan He, Scott Holzer, Haifeng Jiang, Monica Chawathe Lenart,
Navin Melville, Tianhao Qiu, Namit Sikka, Manpreet Singh[✉],
Alexander Smolyanov, Yuri Vasilevski, Shivakumar Venkataraman,
and Divyakant Agrawal

Google Inc., Mountain View, USA
manpreet@google.com

Abstract. Most of today's Internet applications generate vast amounts
of data (typically, in the form of event logs) that needs to be processed and analyzed for detailed reporting, enhancing user experience
and increasing monetization. In this paper, we describe the architecture
of Ubiq, a geographically distributed framework for processing continuously growing log files in real time with high scalability, high availability
and low latency. The Ubiq framework fully tolerates infrastructure degradation and data center-level outages without any manual intervention. It
also guarantees exactly-once semantics for application pipelines to process logs as a collection of multiple events. Ubiq has been in production
for Google's advertising system for many years and has served as a critical log processing framework for several dozen pipelines. Our production deployment demonstrates linear scalability with machine resources,
extremely high availability even with underlying infrastructure failures,
and an end-to-end latency of under a minute.

Keywords: Stream processing · Continuous streams · Log
processing · Distributed systems · Multi-homing · Fault tolerance ·
Distributed consensus protocol · Geo-replication

1 Introduction

Most of today's Internet applications are data-centric: they are driven by back-
end database infrastructure to deliver the product to their users. At the same
time, users interacting with these applications generate vast amounts of data
that need to be processed and analyzed for detailed reporting, enhancing the
user experience and increasing monetization. In addition, most of these applications are network-enabled, accessed by users anywhere in the world at any time.
The consequence of this ubiquity of access is that user-generated data flows continuously, referred to as a *data stream*. In the context of an application, the data
stream is a sequence of events that effectively represents the history of users'

© Springer Nature Switzerland AG 2019
M. Castellanos et al. (Eds.): BIRTE 2015/2016/2017, LNBIP 337, pp. 155–174, 2019.
https://doi.org/10.1007/978-3-030-24124-7_10

interactions with the application. The data is stored as a large number of files, collectively referred to as an input log (or multiple input logs if the application demands it, e.g., separate query and click logs for a search application). The log captures a wealth of information that can be subsequently analyzed for obtaining higher-level metrics as well as deep insights into the operational characteristics of the application. In general, this analysis typically relies on complex application logic that necessitates joining [3], aggregation and summarization of fine-grained information. Most contemporary Internet-based applications must have backend infrastructure to deal with a constant ingestion of new data that is added to the input logs. Furthermore, this processing should be scalable, resilient to failures, and should provide well-defined consistency semantics.

The goal of Ubiq is to provide application developers a log processing framework that can be easily integrated in the context of their application without worrying about infrastructure issues related to scalability, fault tolerance, latency and consistency guarantees. Ubiq expects that the input log is made available redundantly at multiple data centers distributed globally across multiple regions. The availability of identical and immutable input logs enables the system to withstand complete data center outages, planned or unplanned. Ubiq processes the input log at multiple data centers, and is thus *multi-homed* [13]: processing pipelines are run in multiple data centers in parallel, to produce a globally synchronous output stream with multiple replicas.

Although it is often argued that data center failures are rare and dealing with them at the architectural level is overkill, at the scale at which Google operates such failures do occur. We experience data center disruptions for two reasons: (i) partial or full outages due to external factors such as power failures and fiber cuts; and (ii) shutdowns for planned maintenance. It can be argued that planned outages can be managed by migrating operational systems from one data center to another on the fly. In practice, however, we have found that such a migration is extremely difficult, primarily due to the large footprint of such operational systems; precisely checkpointing the state of such systems and restoring it without user downtime is a significant undertaking. During the past decade, we have explored numerous approaches to the operational challenge of recovering or migrating processing pipelines from an unhealthy data center to another data center. Our current conclusion is that the best recourse is to ensure that such systems are multi-homed [13].

Over the last decade, many stream processing systems have been built [1, 4,6,9,10,14,17]. We are unaware of any published system other than Google's Photon [3] that uses geo-replication and multi-homing to provide high availability and full consistency even in the presence of data center failures. Photon is designed for applications that need state to be tracked at the *event* level, such as joining different log sources. However, this is a very resource-intensive solution for other data transformation applications such as aggregation and format conversion, where it is sufficient to track state at the granularity of *event bundles*, that is, multiple events as a single work unit. Event bundling demands far fewer machine resources, and entails different design/performance considerations and failure semantics from those of Photon. Ubiq uses different mechanisms for backup workers, work allocation, and has different latency and resource utilization characteristics. See Sect. 7 for a detailed comparison of the differences between Photon and Ubiq.

1.1 System Challenges

We next describe the challenges that must be overcome to make the Ubiq architecture generic enough to be deployed in a variety of application contexts.

- **Consistency semantics:** Log processing systems consume a continuous stream of data events from an input log and produce output results, in an incremental fashion. A critical design challenge is to specify and implement the consistency semantics of incremental processing of input events. Given the mission-critical nature of the applications that Ubiq supports, such as billing, it needs to be able to assure exactly-once semantics.
- **Scalability:** The next challenge is scalability. Ubiq needs to support applications with varying amounts of traffic on its input log. Furthermore, Ubiq needs to be dynamically scalable to deal with varying traffic conditions for a single application. Finally, Ubiq must be able to handle ever-increasing amounts of traffic. Currently, it processes millions of events per second; this is bound to increase in the future.
- **Reliability:** As mentioned earlier, Ubiq needs to automatically handle not only component failures within a data center but also planned and unplanned outages of an entire data center.
- **Latency:** The output of Ubiq is used for several business-critical applications such as analyzing advertising performance and increasing monetization. Keeping the infrastructure latency overhead to under a minute assures the effectiveness of these business processes.
- **Extensibility:** To support multiple use cases and deployments, Ubiq needs to be generic enough to be used by different applications, and to be easily integrated in a variety of application contexts.

1.2 Key Technical Insights

Here are some of the main design ideas that help Ubiq address the system challenges mentioned above:

- All framework components are stateless, except for a *small amount of globally replicated state*, which is implemented using Paxos [15]. In order to amortize the synchronization overhead of updating the global state, Ubiq batches multiple updates as a single transaction. For scalability, the global state is partitioned across different machines.
- From an application developer's perspective, Ubiq simplifies the problem of continuous distributed data processing by transforming it into processing *discrete* chunks of log records *locally*.

– Ubiq detects data center failures by introducing the notion of *ETAs*, which capture the expected response time of work units, so appropriate avoidance measures can be taken in the presence of failures.

The paper is organized as follows. In Sect. 2, we start by presenting the overall architecture of Ubiq followed by some of the implementation details of its key components. In Sect. 3, we describe the key features of Ubiq's design that deliver exactly-once processing, fault tolerance and scalability, in both single and multiple data centers. In Sect. 4, we demonstrate how Ubiq can be deployed in the context of a data transformation and aggregation application. Section 5 summarizes the production metrics and performance data for a log processing pipeline based on Ubiq. In Sect. 6, we report our experiences and lessons learned in using Ubiq for several dozens of production deployments. Section 7 presents related work and Sect. 8 concludes the paper.

2   The Ubiq Architecture

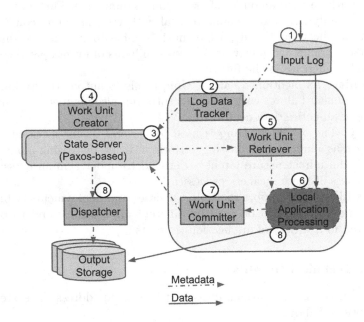

Fig. 1. Ubiq architecture in a single data center

2.1   Overview

Figure 1 illustrates the overall architecture of Ubiq in a single data center. The numbers in the figure capture the workflow in the Ubiq system, which is as follows:

1. *Input log creation:* New log events are written to the input log, which is physically manifested as a collection of files. This step is outside the scope of Ubiq, though we enumerate it here to show the end-to-end workflow.
2. *Tailing of input logs:* The first responsibility of Ubiq is to continuously monitor the files and directories associated with the input log. This functionality is performed by the *Log Data Tracker* component.
3. *Storage of metadata:* Once newly arrived data is discovered, its metadata (that is, file name and current offset) is delivered to a metadata repository, which stores the state about what has been processed and what has not (to ensure exactly-once semantics). This metadata is stored inside the *State Server*, which replicates it globally.
4. *Work unit creation:* The continuously growing log is converted into *discrete work units*, or *event bundles*, by the *Work Unit Creator*.
5. *Work unit distribution:* After the work units are created, they need to be delivered to the application for executing application logic. The *Local Application Processing* component *pulls* work units from the State Server via the *Work Unit Retriever* component.
6. *Application processing:* The *Local Application Processing* component locally applies application-specific logic such as data transformation and other business logic. See Sect. 4 for a sample application.
7. *Work unit commitment:* Once the Local Application Processing component completes processing the work unit, it invokes the *Work Unit Committer*, which coordinates the commit of the work unit by updating the metadata at the State Server. The Work Unit Retriever and Work Unit Committer together decouple the local application processing completely from the rest of the Ubiq framework.
8. *Dispatch of results:* If the results of the local application processing are fully deterministic and the output storage system expects at-least-once semantics, the Local Application Processing component may dispatch the results to output storage directly. Otherwise, the results need to be delivered to output storage after they are committed to the State Server. This is accomplished by the *Dispatcher* component, using a two-phase commit with the output storage.

As described above, the Ubiq framework is relatively simple and straightforward. The challenge, as described in Sect. 1.1, is to make this system strongly consistent, scalable, reliable and efficient.

2.2 Ubiq Architecture in a Single Data Center

Expectations for Input Log Data: Ubiq expects input files in multiple data centers to reach eventual consistency byte by byte. For example, new files may get added or existing files may keep growing. When created redundantly, the corresponding files in different regions may have different sizes at any time, but should become identical at some point in the future. If a file has size S_1 in one data center and size S_2 in another and $S_1 < S_2$, the first S_1 bytes in the two files must be identical.

State Server: The State Server is the globally replicated source of truth about log processing status, and the center of communication among all other Ubiq components. It is implemented using a synchronous database service called PaxosDB [8] that performs consistent replication of data in multiple data centers using Paxos [15], a distributed consensus protocol. It stores the metadata about what has been processed and what has not. For each input log file and offset, it maintains three possible states:

- Not yet part of a work unit
- Already part of a work unit in progress
- Committed to output storage

It maintains this information efficiently by merging contiguous byte offsets in the same state; that is, maintaining state at the granularity of <filename, begin_offset, end_offset>.

All other framework components interact with the State Server. The State Server receives information about newly arrived data from the Log Data Tracker, uses this meta-information to create work units that will be delivered via the Work Unit Retriever to the Local Application Processing component, and commits the work units that have been completed. The metadata information stored at the State Server is critical to ensure the exactly-once semantics of Ubiq. The State Server suppresses any duplicate information received from the Log Data Tracker. All metadata operations, such as work unit creation, work retrieval by the Work Unit Retrievers, and work commitment by the Work Unit Committers, are executed as distributed transactions using atomic read-modify-write on the underlying storage at the State Server.

Log Data Tracker: The primary task of the Log Data Tracker is to discover growth of data in the input logs, which occurs in two ways: new input log files, and increases in the size of existing files. The Log Data Tracker continuously scans input directories and registers new log filenames in the State Server with their current sizes. It also monitors the sizes of existing files and informs the State Server when new bytes are discovered.

The Tracker runs independently in or near each input logs data center and only notifies the State Server of updates in its local logs data center. Since the State Server de-duplicates the information received from the Tracker, the design for the Tracker is simplified, to provide at-least-once semantics. Every file is tracked by at least one Tracker worker. Every update is retried until successfully acknowledged by the State Server.

Work Unit Creator: The Work Unit Creator runs as a background thread inside the State Server. Its goal is to convert the continuously growing log files into *discrete work units*, or *event bundles*. The Work Unit Creator maintains the maximum offset up to which the file has grown at each of the input logs data centers. It also stores the offset up to which work units have been created in the past for this file. As it creates new work units, it atomically updates the offset to ensure that each input byte is part of exactly one work unit. In order to prevent starvation, the Work Unit Creator prioritizes bytes from the oldest file while creating work units. The Work Unit Creator also tries to ensure that a work unit has chunks from several different files, as these could be read in parallel by the application.

Work Unit Retriever and Work Unit Committer: The goal of these two framework components together is to decouple the local application processing completely from the rest of the Ubiq framework. The Work Unit Retriever is responsible for finding uncommitted work units in the State Server. It delivers these work units to the Local Application Processing component (whenever the latter *pulls* new work units) and tracks this delivery through the global system state. Once the Local Application Processing component completes processing a work unit, it requests a commit by invoking the Work Unit Committer. This initiates an atomic commit, and if successful, the global system state is updated to ensure that the data events in the completed work unit will not be processed again. On the other hand, if the commit fails, the work unit will be retried again to ensure exactly-once semantics.

Dispatcher: If the results of an application are deterministic and the output storage system expects at-least-once delivery, the Local Application Processing component can directly deliver the results to output storage system. Otherwise, a dedicated framework component, the Dispatcher, delivers the results of the Local Application Processing to output storage. The Dispatcher needs to perform a two-phase commit between the State Server and the output storage system to ensure exactly-once semantics. Ubiq currently supports dispatching to Mesa [12] and Colossus (Google's distributed file system). Ubiq has a generic API that can be extended to support more output storage systems in future.

Garbage Collector: Once a work unit is dispatched to the output storage, a background thread in the State Server is responsible for garbage-collecting the work unit and all the metadata associated with it. This thread also garbage-collects input filenames once these get older than a certain number of days (e.g., d days) and they are fully processed. The State Server guarantees that if it receives an input filename (from the Log Data Tracker) with a timestamp older than d, it will drop the filename. The Log Data Tracker only tracks files at most d days old.

2.3   Ubiq Architecture in Multiple Data Centers

So far we have focused on the Ubiq design in the context of a single data center. Figure 2 shows the detailed architecture of the Ubiq system deployed over two data centers.

Replication of Critical State: In Ubiq, the critical component that must remain consistent across data centers is the *global system state maintained at the State Server*. In particular, the global state information must be synchronously maintained with strong consistency across multiple data centers to ensure that we do not violate the exactly-once property of the log processing framework. This is accomplished by using PaxosDB, as described in the previous section on the

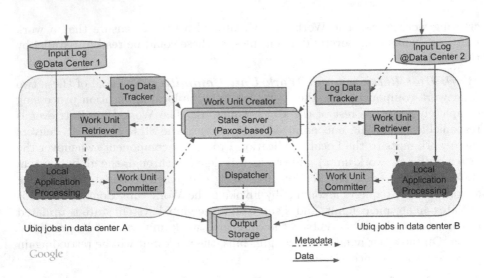

Fig. 2. Ubiq architecture in two data centers

State Server. All metadata operations, such as work creation, work retrieval by the Work Unit Retrievers, and work commitment by the Work Unit Committers, are executed inside State Server as distributed transactions across multiple data centers globally. In order to amortize the overhead of individual transactions, we use several system-level optimizations such as batching multiple transactions.

De-duplication of Input from Multiple Logs Data Centers: As mentioned earlier, Ubiq expects input bytes in multiple data centers to reach eventual consistency byte by byte. The Log Data Tracker in each data center independently tracks growth of data in the corresponding input log data center. The Work Unit Creator unifies data from multiple input log data centers to create *global* work units. It does this by maintaining a key-value data structure inside the State Server. The *key* is the basename of a file (i.e., name of the file without the path). Inside the *value*, it stores metadata about the file in all input logs data centers. If the input bytes are available in only one input data center, it will mark this in the work unit so that the work unit is preferably processed only in a nearby data center. The State Server assigns work units uniformly amongst all healthy data centers, or proportionally to the fraction of resources provisioned by the user for local application processing in each data center.

Replication of Output Data: It is possible that the data center containing the output of the Local Application Processing component may go down before the results are consumed by output storage. In order to handle this, Ubiq must be able to either roll back a committed work unit to regenerate the output or replicate the output of the Local Application Processing component into another data center, before committing the work unit into the State Server. If the application's business logic is non-deterministic and output storage has partially consumed the output, rollback is not an option. In order to address this,

Ubiq provides a *Replicator* component as a first-class citizen. The Replicator copies a file from the local filesystem to one or more remote filesystems in other data centers.

Preventing Starvation: Even though Ubiq does not provide any hard ordering guarantees, it ensures that there is no starvation. Each framework component prioritizes the oldest work unit. For example, the Work Unit Creator adds the oldest bytes when creating work units; the Work Unit Retriever retrieves the oldest work unit, and so on.

3   Ubiq System Properties

3.1   Consistency Semantics

Depending upon the nature of the underlying applications, processing of input data events can be based on (i) at-most-once semantics; (ii) at-least-once semantics; (iii) exactly-once semantics; or (iv) in the extreme case, no consistency guarantees. Given that Ubiq has to be generic to be used in multiple application contexts, it provides *exactly-once semantics*. Supporting this consistency guarantee introduces significant synchronization overhead; however, our experience is that a large class of applications, especially those with financial implications (e.g., billing advertisers, publisher payments, etc.), warrant exactly-once processing of data events in the input log. As mentioned in Sect. 2.3, Ubiq achieves exactly-once semantics by de-duplicating input from multiple logs data centers, executing all metadata operations on input byte offsets as distributed Paxos transactions inside the State Server, and ensuring that there is no starvation.

Note that for applications to leverage the exactly-once guarantees of Ubiq, they must write code that does not have side effects outside the Ubiq framework (e.g., updating a global counter in an external storage system). The Ubiq design does not provide any ordering guarantees; it restricts the processing logic of input events to be independent of each other. However, Ubiq ensures that input events are not starved.

3.2   Fault Tolerance in a Single Data Center

Here is how Ubiq handles machine failures in a single data center:

- *All components in Ubiq are stateless*, except the State Server, for which the state is stored persistently. Within a single data center, every Ubiq component can be executed on multiple machines without jeopardizing the correctness of the system. Hence, each component is relatively immune to machine failures within a data center.
- The State Server leverages PaxosDB [8] for fault tolerance. If an application is running entirely in a single data center, Ubiq enables running multiple PaxosDB group members as replicas in the same data center to handle machine failures.

– To handle *local application processing failures*, we use a notion called *Estimated Time of Arrival*, or *ETA*, to capture the expected amount of time processing a work unit should take. Violations of ETAs are clues that something might be wrong in the system. To handle local application processing failures within a single data center, we define a *local ETA* with each work unit. When a Work Unit Retriever obtains a work unit W from the State Server, the State Server marks it with an ETA of t time units. When a mirrored Work Unit Retriever approaches the State Server within t time units, W is blocked from distribution. On the other hand, if the Retriever requests work after t time units have elapsed, then W becomes available for distribution. This allows backup workers in the same data center to start processing the work unit if the original worker is unable to process before the local ETA expires. Duplicate requests to commit a work unit (either because two workers were redundantly assigned the work unit or the request to commit got duplicated at the communication level due to timeout) are suppressed at the State Server since only one of them will be accepted for commit and the others will be aborted.

3.3   Fault Tolerance in Multiple Data Centers

As mentioned in [13], a data center is in *full outage* mode if it is completely unresponsive. A data center in *partial outage* mode is responsive but its performance/availability may be significantly degraded. Although both partial and full outages are handled by migrating workloads from a malfunctioning data center to a healthy one, there are some major differences in how such workload migration takes effect.

Impact of Full Data Center Outage: Google has dedicated services that continuously monitor full data center outages and notify interested systems; Ubiq learns about full data center outages proactively using these external signals. In the normal case, Ubiq assigns new work units uniformly amongst all the active data centers. During a full data center outage, Ubiq stops assigning any work unit to the unhealthy data center. Existing work units assigned to the unhealthy data center are immediately re-assigned to one of the healthy data centers. The entire workload is handled by the remaining healthy data centers as soon as the full outage occurs. Assuming that the healthy data centers are provisioned to handle the entire load, there is no impact on end-to-end latency.

Impact of Partial Data Center Outage: Unlike full data center outages, there are no direct signals or monitors to detect partial data center outages. Hence, we need to build mechanisms inside Ubiq to deal with partial outages. As mentioned in Sect. 3.2, the notion of local ETA allows us to have backup workers in the same data center. However, in the case of a partial data center outage, backup workers in the unhealthy data center may continue to process the same work unit, leading to starvation of work units. In order to prevent this from happening, we have another ETA inside the State Server, known as the *data center ETA*. We give a work unit to one data center by default and set the data center ETA to T minutes. If the work unit is not committed within T minutes, it is made available to another data center. This ensures that if one processing data center goes down or is unable to complete the work within the specified SLA, backup workers in the other processing data center will automatically take over the pending workload. Therefore, when a partial data center outage occurs, the workload migration does not take effect immediately, but needs to wait for the timeout of the data center ETA. The healthy data center picks up the timed-out work units from the slow data center only after the data center ETA expires. In practice, the data center ETA is set to be an order of magnitude larger than the local ETA. This ETA timeout contributes to increased latency. If an application does not want to see these latency spikes, it can set a lower value for the data center ETA at the expense of higher resource cost.

Note that the existence of the data center ETA does not remove the need to have a local ETA. Local application processing often performs intermediate local checkpoints of partial data processing. Having a local ETA allows a backup worker in the same data center to resume processing from these checkpoints.

The consequence of this design is that the overall Ubiq architecture is resilient to both partial and full data center outages; furthermore, it can be dynamically reconfigured from N data centers to N' data centers, which makes our operational task of running log processing pipelines in a continuous manner 24×7 significantly more manageable.

3.4   Scalability

As mentioned above, all components in Ubiq, with the exception of the State Server, are stateless. This means that they can be scaled to run on multiple machines without compromising on consistency.

To ensure that the *State Server* does not suffer from scalability bottlenecks, the configuration information uses a key concept to partition the work among multiple machines: input filenames are hashed to an integer domain, which is configured in terms of a certain number of partitions; i.e., $\langle integer \rangle$ MOD $\langle number\_of\_partitions \rangle$. Each machine is responsible for a single partition.

To make the State Server design extensible, we need to allow the partitioning information to be dynamically re-configured without bringing the system down. We do this by maintaining configuration information for different time ranges. Each input filename encodes an immutable timestamp based on a global time server utility (TrueTime [11]) to ensure that the timing information is consistent across all filenames and across all regions. The configuration of the State Server has a time range associated with it. That is, it may be that from $\langle 5{:}00\,\text{AM}\,Today \rangle$ to $\langle 5{:}00\,\text{PM}\,Today \rangle$ the State Server has 10 partitions whereas from $\langle 5{:}01\,\text{PM}\,Today \rangle$ onward it has 20 partitions. During the transition, the State Server decides which partition mechanism to use based on the encoded timestamp, until it is safe to transition to a new configuration.

3.5   Extensibility

Finally, Ubiq's design is extensible. From an application developer's perspective, Ubiq simplifies the problem of continuous distributed data processing by transforming it into processing discrete chunks of log records locally. Ubiq's API can be used by any application-specific code, and hence can be easily integrated in a variety of application contexts. The application developer only needs to provide the log processing code and some configuration information such as the input log source filename(s), the number of workload partitions, and number of data centers.

4   Data Transformation and Aggregation: An Application Using Ubiq

We now describe how the Ubiq framework is used to deploy a critical application at Google. The goal of this application is to continuously transform and aggregate log events into higher-level measures and dimensions, and to materialize the results into downstream storage systems such as Mesa [12], an analytical data warehousing system that stores critical measurement data. As mentioned in Sect. 2, Ubiq separates the processing responsibilities into (i) a common framework that focuses on incremental work management, metadata management, and work unit creation; (ii) specialized *local application processing*, which focuses on the application logic required to process a new set of input events. This application logic has the following responsibilities:

- Transforming input events: The local application processing transforms the input events based on application needs. Such transformation may involve data cleaning and standardization, splitting a single event into multiple rows destined to multiple tables in the underlying database, annotating each input event with information from databases, applying user-defined functions, executing complex business logic, etc.
- Partially aggregating input events: Although downstream systems can perform aggregation internally, given the massive size of input, it is much more resource-efficient if the input is partially aggregated. The local application processing performs a partial GROUP BY operation on each bundle of input events.
- Converting data into requisite storage format: Input data is stored in a row-oriented format that needs to be transformed into a columnar data layout.

Note that this application could be built using the Photon [3] architecture as well. However, it would be very resource-intensive to store state at the event level.

Figure 3 illustrates the above application using the Ubiq framework. The application developer is responsible only for the development of the subcomponent that encodes the application logic, the Data Transformer & Aggregator. This subcomponent relies on a well-defined API that is provided to the application developer for interfacing with the Ubiq components. This deployment uses the *Replicator* component of Ubiq since the underlying business logic is non-deterministic.

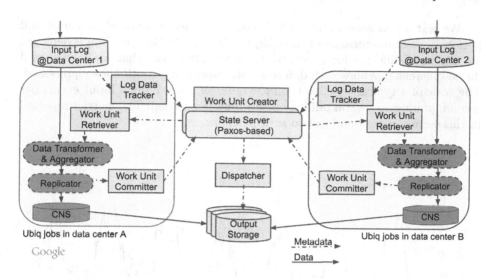

Fig. 3. Data transformation and aggregation: an application using Ubiq

5   Production Metrics

Deployment Setup: Ubiq in production is deployed in a highly decentralized manner (see Fig. 4). As shown in the figure, the input logs are made available redundantly in at least two regional data centers, e.g., data centers 1 and 2. The Ubiq pipelines are active in at least three data centers, e.g., A, B, and C. To preserve data locality, data centers A and C are close to 1 while data center B is close to 2. The global system state, although shown as a centralized component, is in general actively maintained in a synchronous manner in at least 5 different data centers. If data center B, for example, experiences either a partial or complete outage, then data centers A and C will start sharing the workload without any manual intervention and without any breach of SLA. This assumes that there are enough resources available at data centers A and C for scaling Ubiq components for additional workloads.

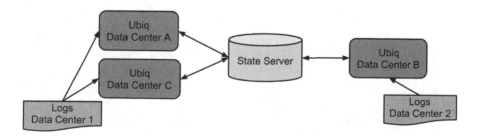

Fig. 4. A distributed deployment of Ubiq over multiple data centers

We next report some of the critical production metrics to highlight the overall performance characteristics of the Ubiq framework. At Google, Ubiq is deployed for dozens of different log types, which effectively means that we have several dozen different pipelines with different data rates being continuously processed. The scale of a typical pipeline is on the order of a few million input events per second, producing several million output rows per second. The metrics reported in this section correspond to two such pipelines.

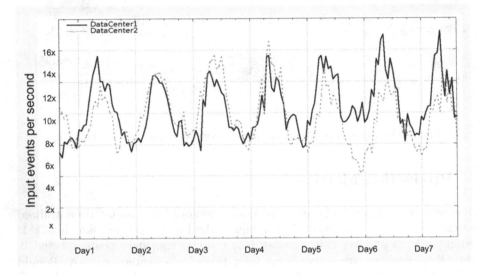

Fig. 5. Throughput during normal period

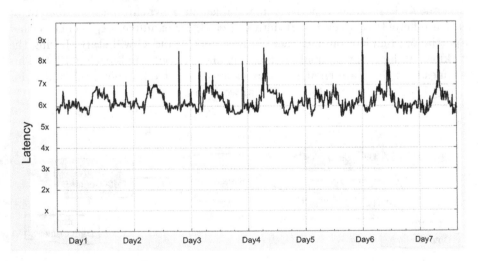

Fig. 6. Latency during normal period

Throughput and Latency During Normal Periods: Figure 5 illustrates the throughput that is processed by Ubiq at each data center. One observation we make is that the load is evenly distributed across both data centers. Figure 6 illustrates the 90th percentile latency associated with processing the input events for the same log type during the same period as Fig. 5. These latency numbers correspond to the difference between the time when the bytes are first tracked by Ubiq and the time when the bytes are dispatched to output storage. Note that the latency corresponds to global results produced at both data centers. Based on our internal instrumentation, when there is no application processing in the pipeline, latency is approximately under a minute for the 90th percentile. All the additional latency therefore comes from the application processing of this particular log type.

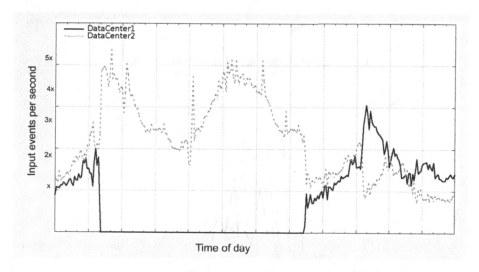

Fig. 7. Throughput during full data center outage

Impact of Full Data Center Outage: Figures 7 and 8 analyze the system behavior in the presence of a full data center outage. In Fig. 7, we observe that one of the data centers experiences a full outage, resulting in the increased workload at the other data center. However, the 90th percentile latency metrics in Fig. 8 demonstrate that latency is not adversely impacted during workload migration. As explained in Sect. 3.3, Ubiq gets an external signal for a full data center outage, and immediately shifts the entire workload to the healthy data centers. Each data center is provisioned to handle the complete load. Note that there is a huge spike in latency for a very brief period during the full data center outage. This is because of a big increase in the number of input events (due to minor upstream disruptions).

Impact of Partial Data Center Outage: Figures 9 and 10 depict the behavior of the system in the presence of a partial data center outage. In Fig. 9, around

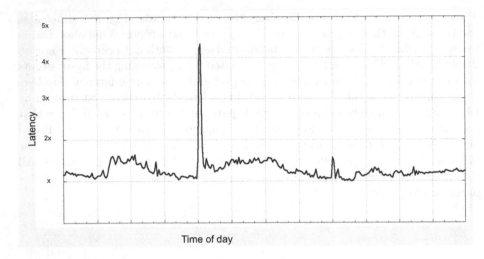

Fig. 8. Latency during full data center outage

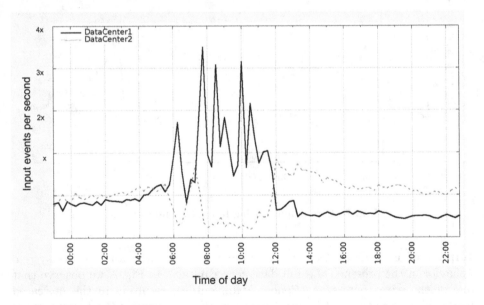

Fig. 9. Throughput during partial data center outage

5:30 am, one of the data centers experiences a partial outage and as a result, its throughput declines sharply, while the other data center picks up the additional load. Figure 10 reports the latency for the 90th percentile: indeed, during the partial outage, the latency in processing input log events increases considerably. As explained in Sect. 3.3, this is because the shift of the workload to the healthy data center happens after the data center ETA expires.

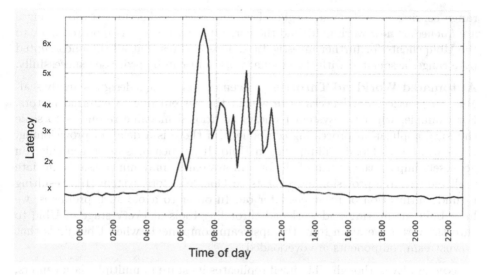

Fig. 10. Latency during partial data center outage

In summary, we note that both partial and full data center outage are handled transparently by the Ubiq framework and no manual intervention is required.

6 Experiences and Lessons Learned

In this section, we briefly highlight the main lessons we have learned from build-ing a large-scale framework for continuous processing of data streams in a pro-duction environment. One key lesson is to prepare for the unexpected when engi-neering large-scale infrastructure systems since at our scale many low-probability events do occur and can lead to major disruptions.

Data Corruption: As an infrastructure team, we account for software and hardware failures of individual components in the overall system design. How-ever, a major challenge arises in accounting for data corruption that occurs because of software and hardware failures much lower in the stack. The scale at which Ubiq runs increases the chance of seeing these bugs in production. Also, there may be bugs in the business logic inside the Local Application Processing component or in an upstream system. This may cause the Local Application Processing component embedded in Ubiq to fail an entire work unit due to a handful of bad events.

We have built several solutions to address the issue of data corruption. The first approach is to provide a detailed reporting tool that allows the application developer to identify the exact byte range of the input work unit where the problem occurs. In addition, we have gone one step further, where a failed work unit with diagnostics about corrupted byte range is automatically split into multiple parts: the corrupted byte range and the uncorrupted byte ranges. A byte range consists of <filename, begin_offset, end_offset>. The uncorrupted ranges are queued as new work units and the corrupted byte range is reported back to the Ubiq clients for further investigation. This ensures that all the uncorrupted byte ranges associated with the original work unit can be processed successfully.

Automated Workload Throttling: Even though Ubiq's design is highly scalable, in practice, bottlenecks arise within the system due to external factors. For example, when the system requests additional machine resources to scale the local application processing component, if there is a delay in provisioning, there will be workload buildup within Ubiq. If no measures are taken this can adversely impact the health of the overall system or may unnecessarily initiate multiple resource provisioning requests to Google's Borg system [16], resulting in under-utilization of resources later on. In order to avoid such problems, we have built monitoring and workload throttling tools at every stage of Ubiq to throttle work generation from the upstream components when Ubiq finds that downstream components are overloaded.

Recovery: Even though Ubiq itself replicates its state in multiple data centers, for critical business applications we guard against the failure of the entire Ubiq pipeline by keeping additional metadata inside the output storage system for each work unit. This metadata tracks the list of input filenames/offsets used to generate the output. In the case of Ubiq failure, we can read this metadata from both the output storage system and the input logs to bootstrap the state of Ubiq in the State Server. In theory, if the majority of the machines on which a Paxos partition is running go unhealthy, this can lead to corrupted state at the State Server. In practice, a more likely cause of Ubiq failure is an accidental bug in the code that leads to inconsistent state in the State Server.

7   Related Work

During the past decade, a vast body of research has emerged on continuous processing of data streams [1,2,7,9,10]. Most of these systems are research prototypes and the focus has been to develop declarative semantics for processing continuous queries over data streams. Over the past few years, the need for managing continuous data has become especially relevant in the context of Internet-based applications and services. Systems such as Storm [6], Samza [5], Spark Streaming [17], Apache Flink [4] and Heron [14] are available in the open-source domain for continuously transforming granular information before it is stored. However, none of these systems are *multi-homed*; they operate in a single data center and hence are vulnerable to data center outages.

The only published system that is geo-replicated and provides both multi-homing and strong consistency guarantees even in the presence of data center failures is Google's Photon [3]. The main distinction between Ubiq and Photon is that Photon is targeted for *event-level* processing whereas Ubiq supports processing *multiple events as a single work unit* (i.e., event bundles). The difference in processing granularity between Photon and Ubiq leads to the following differences in design and performance tradeoffs:

- *Principal use cases:* One canonical application for Photon is *log joining*, where each log event is joined independently with other log sources and output as a new augmented event. In contrast, Ubiq works best for applications like *partial aggregation* and *data format conversion* where multiple events are processed together to generate new output, which can then be efficiently consumed by downstream applications.
- *Resource efficiency:* In contrast with Photon, Ubiq does not need to maintain global state at the event level, and hence requires significantly fewer machine and network resources to run. Although it is feasible to trivially perform every data transformation, event by event, using Photon, it would be wasteful in machine resources for those data transformations where event-level state information is not necessary.
- *Backup workers:* The bundle processing in Ubiq allows for global, ETA-based work unit distribution (to all processing sites), which results in near-zero duplicate work. In contrast, all processing sites in a Photon system need to read all events and the de-duplication takes place later.
- *Failure semantics:* For applications where the processing of each event may fail and needs to be retried (e.g., transient lookup failures to an external backend), Ubiq would have to fail the entire work unit if the number of failed events is beyond a threshold, which renders the idea of work-unit splitting prohibitively expensive. By contrast, even in the worst-case scenario, if every alternate event fails processing and needs to be retried, Photon would process the successful events and commit them to the output since it maintains event-level state.
- *Work allocation:* As Ubiq is based on bundle-level granularity, it is much easier to allocate work to local application processing using a *pull-based* mechanism. Photon, on the other hand, leverages *push-based* work allocation.
- *Latency:* Ubiq incurs noticeably higher latency (on the order of tens of seconds) compared to Photon (on the order of seconds). Ubiq needs to wait to create event bundles while Photon does not need to incur this cost. Pull-based work allocation also contributes to higher latency in Ubiq. As a result of the different strategy for backup workers, partial data center outages impact overall latency in Ubiq while Photon handles partial data center outages seamlessly without any latency impact.

8   Concluding Remarks

In this paper, we have presented the design and implementation details of an extensible framework for continuously processing data streams in the form of event bundles. We illustrated how the Ubiq framework is used in real production applications in Google. One of the key aspects of Ubiq's design is to clearly separate the system-level components of the framework from the application processing. This extensibility allows a myriad of applications to leverage the processing framework without duplication of effort. Ubiq's extensibility has proven to be a powerful paradigm used by dozens of applications, even though it was originally envisioned to simplify the operational issues for a handful of very large customers. Another key feature of Ubiq is that it provides exactly-once semantics. Although there are no ordering guarantees, exactly-once semantics make application logic considerably simpler: application developers do not have to complicate processing logic to handle missing or duplicate data. To deal with the high variability of input data rates, Ubiq's design is highly scalable and elastic: additional resources can be provisioned or removed dynamically without impacting the operational system. Component failures at the data center level are handled by redundantly processing the work units in a staggered manner. Finally, the multi-homed design of Ubiq makes it effective in dealing with full and partial data center outages transparently, without any manual intervention. In the future, we plan to develop a service-oriented architecture for Ubiq for more effective accounting, access control, isolation, and resource management. We are also exploring the use of machine learning models for fine-level resource management and predictive control.

References

1. Abadi, D.J., et al.: Aurora: a new model and architecture for data stream management. VLDB J. **12**(2), 120–139 (2003)
2. Abadi, D.J., et al.: The design of the borealis stream processing engine. In: CIDR, pp. 277–289 (2005)
3. Ananthanarayanan, R., et al.: Photon: fault-tolerant and scalable joining of continuous data streams. In: SIGMOD, pp. 577–588 (2013)
4. Apache Flink (2014). http://flink.apache.org
5. Apache Samza (2014). http://samza.apache.org
6. Apache Storm (2013). http://storm.apache.org
7. Arasu, A., et al.: STREAM: the Stanford stream data manager. In: SIGMOD, p. 665 (2003)
8. Chandra, T.D., et al.: Paxos made live - an engineering perspective. In: PODC, pp. 398–407 (2007)
9. Chandrasekaran, S., et al.: TelegraphCQ: continuous dataflow processing. In: SIGMOD, p. 668 (2003)
10. Chen, J., et al.: NiagaraCQ: a scalable continuous query system for internet databases. In: SIGMOD, pp. 379–390 (2000)
11. Corbett, J.C., et al.: Spanner: Google's globally distributed database. ACM Trans. Comput. Syst. **31**(3), 8 (2013)
12. Gupta, A., et al.: Mesa: geo-replicated, near real-time, scalable data warehousing. PVLDB **7**(12), 1259–1270 (2014)
13. Gupta, A., Shute, J.: High-availability at massive scale: building Google's data infrastructure for ads. In: BIRTE (2015)
14. Kulkarni, S., et al.: Twitter Heron: stream processing at scale. In: SIGMOD, SIGMOD 2015, pp. 239–250 (2015)
15. Lamport, L.: The part-time parliament. ACM Trans. Comput. Syst. **16**(2), 133–169 (1998)
16. Verma, A., et al.: Large-scale cluster management at Google with Borg. In: EuroSys, pp. 18:1–18:17 (2015)
17. Zaharia, M., et al.: Discretized streams: fault-tolerant streaming computation at scale. In: SOSP, pp. 423–438 (2013)

BIRTE 2017

Towards Interactive Data Exploration

Carsten Binnig[1,2(✉)], Fuat Basık[4], Benedetto Buratti[1], Ugur Cetintemel[2],
Yeounoh Chung[2], Andrew Crotty[2], Cyrus Cousins[2], Dylan Ebert[2],
Philipp Eichmann[2], Alex Galakatos[2], Benjamin Hättasch[1], Amir Ilkhechi[2],
Tim Kraska[2,3], Zeyuan Shang[2], Isabella Tromba[3], Arif Usta[4],
Prasetya Utama[2], Eli Upfal[2], Linnan Wang[2], Nathaniel Weir[2],
Robert Zeleznik[2], and Emanuel Zgraggen[2]

[1] TU Darmstadt, Darmstadt, Germany
carsten.binnig@cs.tu-darmstadt.de
[2] Brown University, Providence, USA
[3] Massachusetts Institute of Technology, Cambridge, USA
[4] Bilkent University, Ankara, Turkey

Abstract. Enabling interactive visualization over new datasets at
"human speed" is key to democratizing data science and maximizing
human productivity. In this work, we first argue why existing analytics infrastructures do not support interactive data exploration and outline the challenges and opportunities of building a system specifically
designed for interactive data exploration. Furthermore, we present the
results of building IDEA, a new type of system for interactive data exploration that is specifically designed to integrate seamlessly with existing data management landscapes and allow users to explore their data
instantly without expensive data preparation costs. Finally, we discuss
other important considerations for interactive data exploration systems
including benchmarking, natural language interfaces, as well as interactive machine learning.

1 Introduction

Truly interactive visualization applications allow users to make data-driven decisions at "human speed," but traditional analytical DBMSs for OLAP workloads
are ill-suited to serve this class of applications. Historically, DBMSs for OLAP
workloads are optimized for data warehousing scenarios that can afford long data
loading times (e.g., for index construction), and only have to support a fixed number of pre-defined reports. Moreover, traditional analytical DBMS implement an
execution paradigm that run OLAP queries until completion before returning
an exact result to the user which can take seconds or minutes on large data sets.
All these reasons make traditional analytical DBMS solutions an exceptionally
bad fit for interactive data exploration (IDE). At the same time, the expectation
that a new system supporting interactive data exploration will replace existing
data management stacks for analytics is, simply, unrealistic. Instead, a system
designed specifically for interactive data exploration must integrate and work
seamlessly with existing data infrastructures (e.g., data warehouses, distributed
file systems, analytics platforms).

M. Castellanos et al. (Eds.): BIRTE 2015/2016/2017, LNBIP 337, pp. 177–190, 2019.
https://doi.org/10.1007/978-3-030-24124-7_11

We thus argue that we need to rethink the design of the data management stack to better support interactive data exploration scenarios. To illustrate the needs for a new backend, we illustrate an example workflow as shown in Fig. 1. In this example, a user wants to determine which features (shown as boxes on the left) in the US census dataset [19] affect whether an individual earns a salary of more than $50k annually. To answer this question, the user first drags out the sex attribute to the canvas (Step A) to view the distribution of males and females. The user then drags out the salary attribute, links these two visualizations, and selects the female bar to view the filtered salary distribution for females only (Step B). A duplicate of the salary visualization connected with a negated link (dotted line) allows a comparison of the relative salaries of males and females (Step C). After some analysis, the user decides to check whether an individual's education level coupled with sex has an impact on salary. Finally, linking education to each of the salary visualizations and selecting only individuals with a PhD (a rare subpopulation) creates a complex workflow comparing the respective salaries of highly educated males and females (Step D). From this analysis, the data seem to suggest that highly educated females earn less money annually than their male counterparts. To further explore this finding, the user might continue the analysis by testing the impact of additional attributes, applying statistical techniques (e.g., a t-test) to validate the finding, or performing various ML tasks (e.g., classification, clustering) to test other hypotheses. A more complete demonstration of this scenario in Vizdom is available at https://vimeo.com/139165014.

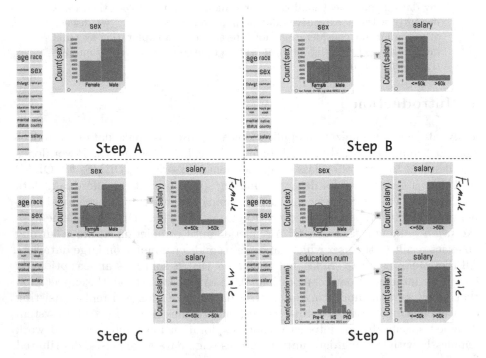

Fig. 1. Example workflow to analyze salary distributions

We therefore suggest dropping the assumptions of traditional DBMSs for OLAP workloads and propose a new breed of systems that supports (1) immediate exploration of new datasets without the need for expensive data preparation, (2) a progressive query execution model that supports interactive query response times and refines results over time, and (3) more "conversational" query interfaces that allow domain experts to incrementally explore all facets of a new data set in order to better support query processing for visual data exploration tools such as Vizdom [8].

One of the most important aspects is that throughout the data exploration process, the database backend system must be able to consistently provide response times low enough to guarantee fluid user interactions in the frontend to all queries. In fact, a recent study [20] shows that even small delays (more than 500ms) significantly decrease a user's activity level, dataset coverage, and insight discovery rate. No existing techniques, though, can guarantee interactive latencies while also addressing all of our previously stated goals. For example, existing data warehouses require a full copy of the data and suffer from long loading times, which contradicts our goal of being able to start exploring a new dataset immediately without expensive data preparation (e.g., indexing, compression). Furthermore, many existing data warehouse indexing techniques suffer from the "curse of dimensionality" and do not scale well beyond a handful of attributes [5]. Restricting the number of attribute combinations is also not an option, since the core idea of data exploration is to look for new, unexplored relationships in the data. Finally, dynamic data reorganization techniques (e.g., cracking [17]) do not solve the high-dimensionality problem and require sorting the data based on user access patterns, thereby violating the key randomness assumption of many online algorithms.

In order to return early results for long-running queries over large datasets and refine results progressively, online aggregation techniques [16,23] provide approximate answers with an estimated error, and several newer analytics frameworks (e.g., Spark [29], Flink [2]) now support online aggregation using a streaming execution model. We therefore believe that online aggregation is a good starting point since these techniques will allow the system to quickly provide initial results that are refined over time as more data is scanned. However, while online aggregation techniques work well for approximating results to queries on common subpopulations in the data, they start to break down when applied to increasingly rare subpopulations (e.g., when the user in the example selected individuals with a PhD), since scanning the base data in a random order might not provide enough of these instances to provide an accurate estimate. This problem is quite common in many interactive data exploration use cases, where rare events often contain the most interesting insights (e.g., the habits of the few highly valued customers). Although disproportionate stratified sampling can help in these cases by overrepresenting rare data items, these samples typically need to be fully constructed before data exploration even begins [1,6], contradicting our goal of enabling immediate exploration of new datasets. More importantly, though, most of these systems make the strong assumption that the entire workload is known a priori in order to create appropriate samples, whereas our goal is to allow users to explore data in new and potentially unanticipated directions.

This paper gives an overview of our keynote given at BIRTE 2017[1] and assembles results from different previously published papers [3,4,9,10,12,13,15, 32]. In summary, in this paper we make the case for a new bread of systems for interactive data exploration and present the results of our own implementation called IDEA (Interactive Data Exploration Accelerator), which allows users to connect to existing data sources and immediately begin the process of interactive data exploration. The outline of the paper is organized as follows:

- We first outline the overall challenges and opportunities associated when building a new system for interactive data exploration (Sect. 2).
- We then describe the design and unique contributions of our system called IDEA (Sect. 3).
- We discuss other important considerations for interactive data exploration including benchmarking, natural language interfaces, as well as interactive machine learning and outline our contributions in those directions as well (Sect. 4).
- We finally conclude in Sect. 5.

2   Challenges and Opportunities

Designing a system for interactive data exploration with a human-in-the-loop frontend requires solving a set of very unique research challenges while also opening the door to several interesting opportunities. In this section, we first outline some of the requirements and challenges, followed by an overview of some of the unique opportunities to address them.

2.1   Challenges

Interactive data exploration has a very unique set of requirements (e.g., response time guarantees), many of which are pushing the boundaries of what is feasible today.

Interactive Latencies: By far, the most important challenge in supporting interactive data exploration is to display a result within the latency requirement. As [20] showed, even small delays of more than 500 ms can significantly impact the data exploration process and the number of insights a user makes. Therefore, a new system for IDE need to maintain certain response time guarantees in order to provide a fluid user experience. Moreover, we believe that a system should be able to refine the query answer progressively. This allows users to get a more accurate answer while visually inspecting the query results.

---

[1] http://db.cs.pitt.edu/birte2017/keynote.html.

Conversational Queries: Different from classical OLAP workloads, users want to explore all different factets of a data set instead of browsing a fixed set of reports. This is very different from whart existing analytical databases assume since they expect that the workload is known a priori to create the "right" indexes/samples, whereas the goal of data exploration is to explore and visualize the data in new ways. Moreover, indexes and data cubes suffer from the curse of dimensionality, since memory required is exponential with the number of attributes, making it almost impossible to build an index over all attributes or without knowing the data exploration path ahead of time.

Rare Data Items: Data exploration often involves examining the tails of a distribution to view the relatively rare data items. For example, real world datasets are rarely perfectly clean and often contain errors (which are typically rare) that can still have a profound effect on the overall results. Similarly, valid outliers and the tails of the distribution are often of particular interest to users when exploring data (e.g., the few billionaires in a dataset, the super users, the top-k customers, the day with the highest traffic). Unfortunately, for rare events and the tail of the distribution, sampling techniques do not work well since they often miss rare items or require a priori knowledge of the workload, a challenge when designing an system for IDE.

Connect and Explore: Ideally, the user should be able to connect to a dataset and immediately start exploring it. However, this requirement implies that there is no time for data preparation and the system has to build all internal storage structures such as indexes on the fly. Another implication of the *connect and explore* paradigm is that the system has to stream over larger datasets (from the sources) and may not be able to hold the entire dataset in memory (or even on disk). As outlined in the introduction, online aggregation methods are a good fit to overcome this challenge, since they provide an immediate estimate (with error bars) over the incoming stream. However, online aggregation techniques assume that the data is random, which might be false since some data sources (e.g., data warehouses) often sort the data on some attribute. This can result in a biased estimate of the result and invalid error bars. Similarly, no good estimates are possible if the source returns the data in some chronological order and if there is some (unknown) correlation between time and the value of interest (e.g., the sales are increasing over time).

Quantifying Risk: An interactive data exploration system with a visual interface allows users to explore hundreds of hypotheses in a very short amount of time. Yet, with every hypothesis test (either in the form of an explicit statistical test or through a more informal visualization), the chance of finding something by chance increases. Additionally, the visual interface can make it easier to overlook other challenges, (e.g., "imbalance of labels" for a classifier) which can lead to incorrect conclusions. Therefore, quantifying the risk is extremely important for an interactive data exploration system.

2.2 Opportunities

Although there are several challenges to address, there are many unique opportunities, since data exploration involves close interactions between analysts and the system. Many of these challenges have not yet been explored within the data management community.

Think Time: Although the user expects subsecond response times from the system, the system's expectation from the user is different; there might be several seconds (or sometimes even minutes) between user interactions. During this time, the system not only has the chance to improve the current answers on the screen, but also prepare for any future operations. For instance, in our running example, the user might have already dragged out the sex and salary attribute, but not yet linked them together. Given that both attributes are on the screen, the system might begin creating an index for both attributes. Should the user decide to link the two visualizations and use one as a filter, the index is already created to support this operation.

Interaction Times: Similar to think time, the system can also leverage the user interaction time to provide faster and more accurate answers. For example, it takes several hundred valuable milliseconds to drag an attribute on the interactive whiteboard or to link two visualizations together. In contrast to the previous think time, user interactions are much shorter but usually provide more information to the system about the intent of the user.

Incremental Query Building: In contrast to one-shot DBMS queries, data exploration is an iterative, session-driven process where a user repeatedly modifies a workflow after examining the results until finally arriving at some desired insight. For example, think of the session shown in Fig. 1 where the user first filteredn salary by gender and then added a filter on education. This session-driven discovery paradigm provides a lot of potential to reuse results between each interaction and modification.

Data Source Capabilities: Traditional analytics systems like Spark and streaming systems like Streambase assume that they connect to a "dumb" data source. However, many data sources are far from "dumb". For instance, commonly the data source is a data warehouse with existing indexes, materialized views, and many other advanced capabilities. While these capabilities do not directly fulfill the needs for interactive data exploration, they can still be used to reducing load and network traffic between the data warehouse and the accelerator. Furthermore, there has been work on leveraging indexes [22] to retrieve random samples from a DBMS. These techniques, together with the possibility to push down user-defined functions (UDFs) to randomize data, provide a feasible solution to the previously mentioned bias problem.

Human Perception: One of the most interesting opportunities stems from the fact that all results are visualized. Therefore, often precise answers are not needed and approximations suffice. Furthermore, the human eye has limitations and humans are particularly bad at understanding the impact of error bars [11]. The system can exploit both of these properties to provide faster response times (i.e., only compute what is perceived by the user).

Modern Hardware: Finally, there are several modern hardware trends that can significantly improve the amount of work that can be done in less than 500 ms. While there has been already a lot of work in leveraging GPUs for data exploration [21], most of the existing solutions focus on single machine setups and ignore the potential of small high-performance clusters. Small high performance clusters can help to significantly increase the amount of available main memory (1–2 TB of main memory is not uncommon with 8 machine cluster), which is crucial for interactive speeds, while avoiding the problems of fault-tolerance and stragglers that come with large cloud deployments. At the same time, fast network interconnects with RDMA capabilities are not only more affordable for smaller clusters, but also offer unique opportunities to decrease latencies. However, taking full advantage of the network requires carefully redesigning the storage layer of the system in order to enable remote direct memory access [4].

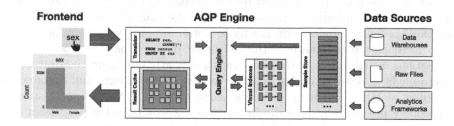

Fig. 2. The IDEA system architecture overview

3   The IDEA System

The IDEA system is the first system built specifically to enable users to visually explore large datasets through "conversational" interactions. Our prototype addresses many of the previously mentioned challenges (Sect. 2), applying novel progressive sampling, indexing, and query optimization techniques in order to provide interactive response times. In this section, we first provide an overview of our proposed architecture, followed by highlights of research insights and contributions.

3.1   Architecture

The architecture of IDEA is shown in Fig. 2. The Vizdom frontend provides a visual data exploration environment specifically designed for pen and touch interfaces, such as the recently announced Microsoft Surface Hub. A demo video of Vizdom can be found here [7]. Currently, Vizdom connects to IDEA using a standard REST interface, which in turn connects to the data sources using the appropriate protocols (e.g., ODBC). These data sources can include anything from legacy data warehouses to raw files to advanced analytics platforms (e.g., Spark [30], Hadoop [26]). As shown in Fig. 2, Vizdom connects to IDEA, which acts as an intelligent cache for those data sources and executes user queries interactively using a novel AQP engine.

IDEA's AQP engine is the core of IDEA and divides the memory into three parts: the *Result Cache*, the *Sample Store*, and space for *Indexes*. When triggered by an initial user interaction, IDEA translates it into a query and begins ingesting required data from the various data sources, speculatively performing operations and caching the results in the *Result Cache* to support possible future interactions. At the same time, IDEA also caches all incoming data in the *Sample Store* using a compressed row format. When the available memory for the *Sample Store* is depleted, IDEA starts to update the cache using a reservoir sampling strategy to eventually create a representative sample over the whole dataset. Furthermore, IDEA might decide to split up the reservoir sample into several stratified subsamples to overrepresent the tails of the distribution, or to create specialized *Indexes* on the fly to better support visual workloads. All these decisions are constantly optimized based on both past and current user interactions. For example, if the user drags a new attribute onto the canvas, the system might allocate more resources to the dragged attribute and preparation for potential follow-up queries. At the same time, IDEA constantly streams increasingly precise results to the frontend as the computation progresses over the data, along with indications about both the completeness and current error estimates.

3.2   Research Findings and Contributions

In this section, we highlight a few selected research findings and contributions of IDEA.

Progressive AQP Engine: IDEA's engine is neither a classical DBMS execution engine nor a streaming engine, instead has an entirely unique semantics. Unlike DBMSs, queries are not one-shot operations that return exact results; rather, data exploration workflows are constructed incrementally, requiring fast response times and progressive results that refine over time. At the same time, streaming engines traditionally deploy predefined queries over infinite data streams, whereas IDEA is meant to enable free-form exploration of data sampled from a deterministic system (e.g., a finite data source).

Fundamentally, IDEA acts as an intelligent, in-memory caching layer that sits in front of the much slower data sources, managing both progressive results and the samples used to compute them. Oftentimes, IDEA has the opportunity to offload pre-filtering and pre-aggregation operations to an underlying data source (e.g., perform a predicate pushdown to a DBMS), or even transform the base data by executing a custom UDF in an analytics framework. Finally, in contrast to traditional DBMSs and streaming engines, users compose queries incrementally, therefore resulting in simultaneous visualizations of many component results with varying degrees of error. Maintaining different partial results rather than a single, exact answer imposes a completely new set of challenges for both expressing and optimizing these types of queries. Currently, our IDEA prototype uses a preliminary interaction algebra to define a user's visual queries [10].

Probabilistic Query Formulation: While developing the AQP enfine of IDEA, we observed that many visualizations rely on the observed frequencies in the underlying data, or estimates of the probability of observing certain data items. For example, a bar chart over a nominal attribute is simply a visualization of the relative frequencies of the possible attribute values (i.e., a probability mass function), and a histogram of a continuous attribute visually approximates the attribute's distribution (i.e., a probability density function). Although seemingly trivial, this observation prompted us to reconsider online aggregation as a series of probability expressions.

This novel probability formulation actually permits a wide range of interesting optimizations including taking advantage of the Bayes' theorem to maximize the reuse of results. Our current implementation of IDEA therefore manages a cache of results that stores previously computed frequencies and error estimates for reuse in future queries [15].

Visual Indexes: Similar to the algebra and optimizer, we also found that traditional indexes are not optimal for interactive data exploration tasks. Most importantly, existing techniques either sort the data (e.g., database cracking) or do not naturally support summary visualizations. As previously mentioned, sorting can destroy data randomness and, consequently, the ability to provide good estimates. Similarly, indexes generally index every tuple without considering any properties of the frontend (e.g., human perception limitations, visualization characteristics). This approach often results in very large indexes, especially with increasingly large samples or highly dimensional data.

For example, some visualizations (e.g., histograms) require the system to scan all leaf pages in a traditional B-tree, since this index is designed for single range requests rather than providing visual data summaries. We therefore developed VisTrees [13], a new dynamic index structure that can efficiently provide approximate results specifically to answer visualization requests. The core idea is that the nodes within the index are "visually-balanced" to better serve visual user interactions and then compressed based on perception limitations. Furthermore, these indexes are built on the fly during the think-time of users to avoid heavy upfront cost which would violate out connect-and-explore paradigm.

Sample Store: As previously mentioned, IDEA caches as much data as possible from the underlying data sources in order to provide faster approximate results, since most data sources are significantly slower. For example, the memory bandwidth of modern hardware ranges from 40–50 GB/s per socket [4], whereas we recently measured that PostgreSQL and a commercial DBMS can only export 40–120 MB/s, even with a warm cache holding all data in memory. Although DBMS export rates may improve in the future, IDEA's cache will still remain crucial for providing approximate answers to visual queries and supporting more complex analytics tasks (e.g., ML algorithms).

If the cached data exceeds the available memory, IDEA needs to carefully evict stored tuples while retaining the most important data items in memory. For example, caching strategies like LRU do not necessarily maintain a representative sample. Therefore, IDEA uses reservoir sampling instead to evict tuples while preserving randomness. Furthermore, IDEA also needs to maintain a set of disproportionate stratified samples that overrepresent uncommon data items in order to support operations over rare subpopulations. The necessity to maintain different types of potentially overlapping samples poses many interesting research challenges. For example, deciding when and what to overrepresent is a very interesting problem, and IDEA uses a cost model to make this decision as described in [15].

Inconsistencies: Interactive response times often require computing approximate answers in parallel, which can lead to inconsistencies in concurrent views (e.g., the combined `salary` bars shown in Fig. 1(B) may not sum to the total number of females). Similarly, an outlier that appears in one result visualization may not yet be reflected in another, causing the user to draw a potentially incorrect conclusion.

Although initially assuming that inconsistencies would pose an important challenge for IDEA, we found that this problem only arises in a few corner cases, and we did not observe any consistency issues during various user studies [10,15,31]. In particular, IDEA's result reuse and sampling techniques work together to mitigate many potential consistency problems, and any noticeable differences tend to disappear before the user can even recognize them.

4   Other Considerations

In addition to the core challenges that we address in IDEA to support a backend, there are many other considerations when building a novel data management system for interactive data exploration.

4.1   Benchmarking IDE Systems

Existing benchmarks for analytical database systems such as TPC-H [28] and TPC-DS [27] are designed for static reporting scenarios. However, those benchmarks are not suitable for evaluating new backends for interactive data exploration because of different reasons. For instance, the main metric of these benchmarks is the performance of running individual SQL queries to the end, thereby not supporting more recent systems which return approximate results such as IDEA [10], approXimateDB/XDB [18], or SnappyData [24]. More importantly, workloads of traditional analytical benchmarks do not meet the complexity of actual data exploration workflows where queries are built and refined incrementally.

We have therefore started to work a novel benchmark called *IDEBench* [12] that can be used to evaluate the performance of IDE systems under realistic conditions in a standardized, automated, and re-producible way. An initial version of the benchmark and results of running the benchmark on several data analytics backends for interactive data exploration is available[2].

4.2   Natural Language Interfaces

While visual exploration tools have recently gained significant attention, Natural Language Interfaces to Databases (NLIDB) appeared as a high-promise alternative as it enables users to pose complex ad-hoc questions in a concise and convenient manner. For example, imagine that a medical doctor starts her new job at a hospital and wants to find out about the age distribution of patients with the longest stays in the hospital. This question typically requires the doctor—when using a standard database interface directly—to write a complex nested SQL query. Even with a visual exploration tool such as Tableau [25] or Vizdom [8], a query like this is far from being trivial since it requires the user to execute multiple query steps and interactions. Alternatively, with an exploration tool that provides a natural language interface, the query would be as simple as stating "What is the age distribution of patients with the longest stays in the hospital?". However, understanding natural language questions and translating them accurately to SQL is a complicated task, and thus NLIDBs have not yet made their way into commercial products.

We therefore developed *DBPal*, a relational database exploration tool that provides an easy-to-use natural language (NL) interface aimed at improving the transparency of the underlying database schema and enhancing the expressiveness and flexibility of human-data interaction through natural language. Different from existing approaches, our system leverages deep models to provide a more robust query translation. Our notion of model robustness is defined as the effectiveness of the translation model to map linguistically varying utterances to finite pre-defined relational database operations. Take, for example, a SQL expression *SELECT * FROM patients WHERE diagnosis='flu'*. There are numerous corresponding natural language utterances for this query, such as *"show all patients*

---

[2] https://idebench.github.io/.

with diagnosis of flu" or simply *"get flu patients"*. We aim to build a translating system that is invariant towards these linguistic alterations, no matter how complex or convoluted. The video at https://vimeo.com/user78987383/dbpal shows a recording of a representative user session in our system.

4.3   Interactive Model Curation

Extracting actionable insights from data has been left to highly trained individuals who have a background in machine learning. For example, it is common practice for corporations to employ teams of data scientists that assist stakeholders in building models to find qualitative, data-driven insights to inform possible business decisions. Having such a high-entry bar to data analysis however presents several challenges. For one, it presents a bottleneck. While research is trying to understand and promote visualization and data literacy and educational institutions are ramping up their data science curricula there is still a shortage of skilled data scientists. And second, and more importantly, restricting data analysis to those with a computational and machine learning background creates an inequality. Small business owners without those skills or research domains where computational background might not be as prevalent are at a disadvantage as they can not capitalize on the power of data.

We believe that there is an opportunity for tool builders to create systems for people who are domain experts but neither ML experts. We are therefore working on a new system for Quality-aware Interactive Curation of Models, called *QuIC-M* [3]. Through *QuIC-M* domain experts can build these pipelines automatically from high level tasks specification and at a fast pace without the need to involve a data scientist and without sacrificing quality. Making sense of data is exploratory by nature, and demands rapid iterations and all but the simplest analysis tasks, require humans-in-the-loop to effectively steer the process. *QuIC-M* exposes a simple model building interface allowing domain experts to seamlessly interleave data exploration with curation of machine learning pipelines. However, empowering novice users to directly analyze data also comes with drawbacks. It exposes them to "the pitfalls that scientists are trained to avoid" [14]. We discussed and described such "risk" factors and QuIC-M's user interface in related works [9,32].

5   Conclusion

In this paper, we presented the case for a new bread of data management systems which seek to maximize human productivity by allowing users to rapidly gain insights from new large datasets. We outlined the research challenges and opportunities when building such a new system and discussed the insights we gained from building our system called IDEA. Finally, we discussed other important considerations in the context of building interactive data exploration systems including benchmarking, natural language interfaces, as well as interactive machine learning.

References

1. Agarwal, S., et al.: BlinkDB: queries with bounded errors and bounded response times on very large data. In: EuroSys, pp. 29–42 (2013)
2. Apache Flink. http://flink.apache.org/
3. Binnig, C., et al.: Towards interactive curation & automatic tuning of ML pipelines. In: 1st Inaugural Conference on Systems ML (SysML) (2018)
4. Binnig, C., et al.: The end of slow networks: it's time for a redesign. In: VLDB, pp. 528–539 (2016)
5. Böhm, C., Berchtold, S., Kriegel, H., Michel, U.: Multidimensional index structures in relational databases. J. Intell. Inf. Syst. **15**, 51–70 (2000)
6. Chaudhuri, S., Das, G., Narasayya, V.R.: Optimized stratified sampling for approximate query processing. TODS **32**, 9 (2007)
7. Crotty, A., et al.: Vizdom Demo Video. https://vimeo.com/139165014
8. Crotty, A., et al.: Vizdom: interactive analytics through pen and touch. In: VLDB, pp. 2024–2035 (2015)
9. Crotty, A., Galakatos, A., Zgraggen, E., Binnig, C., Kraska, T.: Vizdom: interactive analytics through pen and touch. Proc. VLDB Endow. **8**(12), 2024–2027 (2015)
10. Crotty, A., Galakatos, A., Zgraggen, E., Binnig, C., Kraska, T.: The case for interactive data exploration accelerators (IDEAs). In: HILDA@SIGMOD, p. 11. ACM (2016)
11. Cumming, G., Finch, S.: Inference by eye: confidence intervals and how to read pictures of data. Am. Psychol. **60**, 170–180 (2005)
12. Eichmann, P., Zgraggen, E., Zhao, Z., Binnig, C., Kraska, T.: Towards a benchmark for interactive data exploration. IEEE Data Eng. Bull. **39**(4), 50–61 (2016)
13. El-Hindi, M., Zhao, Z., Binnig, C., Kraska, T.: VisTrees: fast indexes for interactive data exploration. In: HILDA (2016)
14. Fisher, D., DeLine, R., Czerwinski, M., Drucker, S.: Interactions with big data analytics. Interactions **19**(3), 50–59 (2012)
15. Galakatos, A., Crotty, A., Zgraggen, E., Binnig, C., Kraska, T.: Revisiting reuse for approximate query processing. PVLDB **10**(10), 1142–1153 (2017)
16. Hellerstein, J.M., Haas, P.J., Wang, H.J.: Online aggregation. In: SIGMOD, pp. 171–182 (1997)
17. Idreos, S., Kersten, M.L., Manegold, S.: Database cracking. In: CIDR, pp. 68–78 (2007)
18. Li, F., Wu, B., Yi, K., Zhao, Z.: Wander join: online aggregation via random walks. In: ACM SIGMOD, pp. 615–629. ACM (2016)
19. Lichman, M.: UCI Machine Learning Repository (2013)
20. Liu, Z., Heer, J.: The effects of interactive latency on exploratory visual analysis. TVCG **20**, 2122–2131 (2014)
21. Liu, Z., Jiang, B., Heer, J.: imMens: real-time visual querying of big data. In: EuroVis, pp. 421–430 (2013)
22. Olken, F., Rotem, D.: Random sampling from relational databases. In: VLDB, pp. 160–169 (1986)
23. Pansare, N., Borkar, V.R., Jermaine, C., Condie, T.: Online aggregation for large MapReduce jobs. In: VLDB, pp. 1135–1145 (2011)
24. Snappy data. https://www.snappydata.io/. Accessed 02 Nov 2017
25. Tableau. http://www.tableau.com. Accessed 02 Nov 2017
26. The Apache Software Foundation. Hadoop. http://hadoop.apache.org
27. TPC-DS (2016). http://www.tpc.org/tpcds/. Accessed 02 Nov 2017

28. TPC-H (2016). http://www.tpc.org/tpch/. Accessed 02 Nov 2017
29. Zaharia, M., Das, T., Li, H., Hunter, T., Shenker, S., Stoica, I.: Discretized streams: fault-tolerant streaming computation at scale. In: SOSP, pp. 423–438 (2013)
30. Zaharia, M., et al.: Resilient distributed datasets: a fault-tolerant abstraction for in-memory cluster computing. In: NSDI, pp. 15–28 (2012)
31. Zgraggen, E., Galakatos, A., Crotty, A., Fekete, J., Kraska, T.: How progressive visualizations affect exploratory analysis. IEEE Trans. Vis. Comput. Graph. **23**(8), 1977–1987 (2017)
32. Zhao, Z., De Stefani, L., Zgraggen, E., Binnig, C., Upfal, E., Kraska, T.: Controlling false discoveries during interactive data exploration. In: Proceedings of the 2017 ACM International Conference on Management of Data, pp. 527–540. ACM (2017)

DCS: A Policy Framework
for the D̲etection of C̲orrelated
Data S̲treams

Rakan Alseghayer[1](✉), Daniel Petrov[1], Panos K. Chrysanthis[1](✉),
Mohamed Sharaf[2], and Alexandros Labrinidis[1]

[1] University of Pittsburgh, Pittsburgh, PA, USA
{ralseghayer,dpetrov,panos,labrinid}@cs.pitt.edu
[2] Department of Computer Science and Software Engineering,
College of Information Technology, United Arab Emirates University, Al Ain, UAE
msharaf@uaeu.ac.ae

Abstract. There is an increasing demand for real-time analysis of large
volumes of data streams that are produced at high velocity. The most
recent data needs to be processed within a specified delay target in order
for the analysis to lead to actionable result. To this end, in this paper,
we present an effective solution for detecting the correlation of such data
streams within a micro-batch of a fixed time interval. Our solution,
coined DCS, for D̲etection of C̲orrelated Data S̲treams, combines (1)
incremental sliding-window computation of aggregates, to avoid unnecessary re-computations, (2) intelligent scheduling of computation steps
and operations, driven by a utility function within a micro-batch, and
(3) an exploration policy that tunes the utility function. Specifically, we
propose nine policies that explore correlated pairs of live data streams
across consecutive micro-batches. Our experimental evaluation on a real
world dataset shows that some policies are more suitable to identifying
high numbers of correlated pairs of live data streams, already known
from previous micro-batches, while others are more suitable to identifying previously unseen pairs of live data streams across consecutive
micro-batches.

1 Introduction

Motivation. More and more organizations (commercial, health, government,
and security) currently base their decisions on real-time analysis of business and
operational data in order to stay competitive. Towards this, they deploy a variety
of monitoring applications to analyze large volumes of live data streams, that
are produced at high velocity. Data analysts explore such large volumes of data
streams, typically representing time series of raw measures, looking for valuable
insights and interesting events.

A common method for getting a better understanding of the observed behavior conveyed in a set of data streams is to find correlations in the data streams

© Springer Nature Switzerland AG 2019
M. Castellanos et al. (Eds.): BIRTE 2015/2016/2017, LNBIP 337, pp. 191–210, 2019.
https://doi.org/10.1007/978-3-030-24124-7_12

[1]. The correlation can be also used as a source for finding similarity measures faster [2], running threshold queries [3], or reducing the size of the data, but preserving some of its characteristics [4].

Challenges. Finding correlations in data streams is a challenging task. Current methodologies approach this challenge by employing some prediction techniques [5], Discrete Fourier Transform approximations [6,7], or using clustering and Markov chain modeling [8]. All those approaches have their limitations, whether due to lack of absolute precision as a result of using approximations or predictions, or due to the usage of computationally expensive operations. Other approaches address this challenge by indexing the data series [9–11]. Predominantly the users are looking for pairs of (positively or negatively) correlated data streams over a short period of time. The high number of data streams implies an even bigger number of pairs—precisely $\frac{n*(n-1)}{2}$ pairs for n data streams. The time to explore completely all pairs on one computer may be prohibitively long. The challenge is exacerbated when the demand is for answers in *real-time* and for a large set of *live* data streams.

Problem Statement. Clearly there is a need for algorithms that quickly identify windows of correlated data streams. In our prior work [12,13], we proposed such algorithms, called *iBRAID-DCS* and *PriCe-DCS*, which detect pairs of correlated data streams within micro-batches of data streams with specific intervals. They both uses the Pearson Correlation Coefficient to correlate two windows of pairs of data streams.

As long as the detection of correlated pairs is considered independent across micro-batches, *PriCe-DCS* executes in the same fashion within each micro-batch, identifying the highest possible number of correlated pairs. However, there are exploration tasks that *do* consider the detection of correlated pairs across micro-batches. For example, in some tasks, the goal is to detect as many *unique* pairs of correlated data streams as possible across two consecutive micro-batches, while in others, the goal is to *assure* the perpetual correlation between them.

To that end, in this paper, we study nine policies to address the different requirements of exploration tasks. These policies may leverage prior knowledge (i.e., exploit already detected correlated data streams in preceding micro-batches) to steer the detection of correlated pairs in the current micro-batch.

Contributions. In summary, in this paper:

- We present our *DCS* (*Detection of Correlated Data Streams*) framework that employs the two base algorithms *iBRAID* and *PriCe* and is driven by a utility function [12,13], (Sect. 2).
- We propose nine different policies that our novel *PriCe-DCS* algorithm can employ when analyzing consecutive micro-batches. These policies can increase the efficiency when detecting correlated live data streams and/or address different exploration requirements. By appropriately tuning the parameters of the utility function, the different policies exhibit different *detection-recall, overlapping-recall,* and *diversity* results (Sect. 3).

- We experimentally evaluate and compare our algorithms, along with the behavior of the nine detection policies. Our results using a real world dataset show that our *PriCe-DCS* outperformed all the other algorithms. Furthermore, with the policies *Blind* and *X% Probing* (i.e., 1% Probing and 5% Probing), *PriCe-DCS* was able to identify more diverse correlated data streams across micro-batches than the *Informed* policy. On the other hand, *P-Alternating* and *Informed* policies were able to assure the existence of correlation in already identified correlated data streams (i.e., high *overlapping-recall*). The other policies exhibited mixed behavior (Sect. 4).

We discuss related work in Sect. 5 and conclude in Sect. 6.

2   DCS Framework

In this section, we review our *DCS* mode of operation, introduced in [13], its optimization objective, and our novel algorithm *PriCe-DCS* that implements its objective.

2.1   System Model

Without loss of generality, we consider a (monitoring) system that receives data from n data streams. Each data point in a data stream is a tuple t consisting of a timestamp ts and a numeric value val ($t = (ts, val)$). The timestamp captures the moment in time when the tuple was produced.

The data is produced at high velocity. The different streams produce the consecutive tuples at the same rate, and they are all synchronized. However, there are techniques to determine missing values, and to synchronize data which arrives at different rates, but they are beyond the scope of this paper.

The real-time analytical processing is performed in *micro-batches*.

Definition 1. *A micro-batch is a group of synchronized tuple subsequences over a set of data streams defined by a timestamp interval I.*

Each micro-batch, whether of the same or different data streams, is of the same size, i.e., contains the same number of tuples with consecutive timestamps within the interval. The inter-arrival time of two consecutive micro-batches specifies the maximum computational time for processing a micro-batch.

Definition 2. *The inter-arrival time is the delay target or deadline d by which the last result can be produced while analyzing a micro-batch.*

In real-time processing, ideally, the deadline d equals to the interval ($d = I$) so that there is no delay gap in processing between two consecutive micro-batches. However, it is expected to be a bit longer due to various overheads in the system, including any pre-processing of micro-batches.

2.2   Optimization Objective

Our *DCS* framework focus on analytical processing that finds correlated data streams in real-time, using the Pearson Correlation Coefficient (PCC) as a correlation metric for pairs of sliding windows of data streams.

Definition 3. *Given two numeric data streams x and y of equal length m, the PCC is calculated with the following formula:*

$$corr(x, y) = \sum_{i=1}^{m} \frac{(x_i - \mu_x)(y_i - \mu_y)}{\sigma_x \sigma_y} \tag{1}$$

where μ_x is the average (or mean) of the values of x, μ_y is the mean of the values of y, σ_x and σ_y are the standard deviations of the values of x and y, respectively.

Definition 4. *Two sliding windows of the same range w with a slide of 1 are correlated when the PCC is more than a given threshold τ (PCC $\geq \tau$).*

Definition 5. *A pair of data streams in a micro-batch is correlated when it contains at least A correlated sliding windows with threshold τ.*

The windows, which meet the criterion, may be consecutive or stratified over the interval defining a micro-batch.

The formalization of the algorithmic problem is as follows:

Problem: *Given a micro-batch B of a set of data streams DS with an arrival interval I, perfectly synchronized and with no missing tuples, and a deadline d, detect the number of correlated pairs of data streams, each of which has A correlated sliding windows, not necessary consecutive, with a PCC threshold of τ, by the deadline d.*

The optimum solution will be when the number of identified correlated pairs in a micro-batch are equal to the actual total number of correlated pairs. Hence, the optimization goal in DCS is to maximize the number of identified pairs by a deadline. Formally, the ratio of number of detected correlated pairs to the total number of correlated pairs is close to 1 and the metric is defined as:

$$Detection\text{-}Recall = \frac{\#\ identified\ correlated\ pairs}{Actual\ \#\ correlated\ pairs} \tag{2}$$

2.3   Base Algorithms

IBRAID-DCS is an enhancement over the work BRAID [14], where the *PCC* can be calculated by computing five sufficient statistics—sum of the tuples in each window, the sum of the squares of the tuples of each window, and the inner cross-product of the tuples of the two windows, for which the correlation is calculated. The sum ($sumx$) and the sum of the square of the tuples ($sumxx$)

of a window of length m of a data stream x, and corresponding inner product ($sumprodxy$) are denoted as

$$sumx = \sum_{i=1}^{m} x_i \qquad sumxx = \sum_{i=1}^{m} x_i^2 \qquad sumprodxy = \sum_{i=1}^{m} x_i y_i$$

The covariance of the two data streams x and y is

$$cov = sumprodxy - \frac{sumx \times sumy}{m}$$

and the variance of the window can be calculated as according to the following formula

$$varx = sumxx - \frac{(sumx)^2}{m}$$

Similarly, the variance for data stream y will be denoted $vary$. Then PCC can be calculated, applying the following formula

$$corr(x, y) = \frac{cov}{\sqrt{varx \times vary}}$$

The sufficient statistics can be computed either from scratch or incrementally each time a pair of data streams is explored by a new tuple. In the case of incremental calculation, the sums stored in memory are incremented by the new values and decremented by the values that are not part of the windows anymore. The same operations are performed for the sums of the squares and the inner cross products, using the respective tuples.

With that in mind, $iBRAID\text{-}DCS$ is a round-robin scanning algorithm that uses the incremental computation of PCC. It analyzes the pairs of data streams in a micro-batch sequentially, starting from the first tuple for all data streams. It calculates the sufficient statistics that are needed to calculate the PCC efficiently (i.e., single pass over tuples). Next, it calculates the PCC for the first tuple for all pairs of windows. Once this is done, the windows are slid further by one tuple, the sufficient statistics are updated incrementally—the first tuple is expired/subtracted from them, and the new tuple is added. The PCC is calculated again for all pairs. Then, it keeps analyzing all data streams by a single tuple, augmenting the sufficient statistics incrementally, and recalculating the PCC. This is done until the whole micro-batch is analyzed.

$iBRAID\text{-}DCS$ has four key advantages: (1) it is accurate, (2) easy to implement, (3) does not cause "starvation" among the pairs, and (4) it reduces the computations by half due to the usage of the sufficient statistics. $iBRAID\text{-}DCS$ is experimentally shown to perform well for data streams whose data is uniformly distributed and for low correlation thresholds ($\tau < 0.5$).

PriCe-DCS is a scanning algorithm that uses a utility function to analyze the pairs of windows while reusing partial PCC computations. It analyzes the most promising pair first, which is the one with the highest utility function value:

$$Pr = PCC * (M/totalExp)/C \tag{3}$$

where PCC is the most recently calculated Pearson Correlation Coefficient for a pair of sliding windows that belong to the same pair of data streams, M is the number of correlated sliding windows found in the corresponding pair of data streams so far, $totalExp$ is the total number of analyzed pairs of sliding windows, and C is the cost of analyzing a pair of sliding windows in terms of number of computations (i.e., the number of operations needed to calculate the sufficient statistics for a pair of sliding windows). The default values are $PCC = 1$, $M = 0$, $totalExp = 1$, and $C = 1$.

Early termination happens when the A criterion of the number of correlated windows is reached for a pair, and pruning happens according to the following condition:

$$(A - correlatedWindows) > (I - slidingWindowPosition)$$

where $correlatedWindows$ are the total number of windows that are correlated in a pair of streams according to PCC τ, and $slidingWindowPosition$ is the pair's analysis location in the interval. Recall, I is the interval of the data streams.

3   Detection Policies

When the very first micro-batch arrives at the system, the system has no prior knowledge about any correlated pairs of streams. However, this is not the case after the analysis of any micro-batch that produces a set of correlated pairs of data streams. This raises the question of how to exploit the results of past micro-batch analyses, such as, picking the first pair in a new micro-batch to analyze. This question has a major impact on $PriCe\text{-}DCS$'s behavior in supporting *exploration, exploitation* or *fairness*, and its answer determines the initialization of the parameters of $PriCe\text{-}DCS$'s utility function.

In fact, we propose nine policies, which differ in the way each initializes the utility function of $PriCe\text{-}DCS$.

Blind. When the analysis of a micro-batch starts with no prior knowledge of correlated pairs of streams, *Blind* policy initializes $PriCe\text{-}DCS$'s utility function to its default values (as discussed in Sect. 2.3). It is to be noted, however, that the very first micro-batch analysis in all approaches follows the *Blind* approach[1].

Informed. The utility function is initialized based on the results of the latest micro-batch analysis. In *Informed* starting phase, $PriCe\text{-}DCS$'s utility function is initialized to the same parameter values of the correlated pairs used by the immediately previous micro-batch. The rationale behind this policy is to keep analyzing closely those pairs that already exhibited high correlation in the previous micro-batch, potentially indicating an insight of interest.

---

[1] In DCS [12,13], Blind was referred to as Cold Start whereas the other proposed policies here are instances of Warm Start.

Untouched. The focus is on the pairs that were not processed at all in the previous micro-batch due to the lack of any correlated windows (i.e., not chosen for analysis due to their low values of Pearson Correlation Coefficient) at the beginning of *PriCe-DCS*'s execution. Specifically, such pairs are jumpstarted by altering their previous number of correlated windows (i.e., the parameter that reflects this information) to have the value A. This increases their priority, preventing their starvation and giving them another chance to be analyzed in the new micro-batch. The rationale behind this policy is to allow such pairs another chance, potentially identifying different behavior, which remained undetected in the previous micro-batch.

Alternating. This policy gives the pairs that were not correlated in the previous micro-batch a chance to be explored through a hybrid round-robin fashion. In *Alternating* starting phase, alternately, a pair from those that are not correlated in the previous micro-batch, is picked and explored using *PriCe-DCS* followed by a pair from those which were correlated. When the starting phase concludes (i.e., touched all the pairs at least once), the pairs are processed with *PriCe-DCS* according to the utility function. By doing this, we hope to reduce the effect of starvation for those that were not correlated in the previous micro-batch.

X% Non-correlated. This policy tries to achieve fairness of exploration through jumpstarting the lowest X% pairs in priority. The pair with the highest priority among those lowest X% is picked and explored. This continues until all those X% pairs are jumpstarted. Subsequently, *PriCe-DCS* carries out the exploration process as it usually does.

Decaying History. This policy regards the significance of the whole historical correlation information of a pair differently from recent micro-batches information. In the utility function, it alters the parameter M, which reflects the number of correlated sliding windows found for a corresponding pair, such that it becomes weighted. It gives the historical correlation information (i.e., data from micro-batches earlier than the most recent one) a weight, and then gives a higher weight to the most recent correlation information. Then, the total of both becomes the new parameter M. The goal behind this policy is to consider higher the most recent information along the exploration process as opposed to older ones.

Shared Stream. Its focus is on the group of pairs, that were not correlated in the previous micro-batch but share a data stream that was part of a correlated one in the preceding micro-batch. The idea in this policy is that a data stream that is correlated with another one, might be correlated with a third different stream as well. Thus, this policy picks a pair from this group of non-correlated pairs according to *PriCe-DCS* and explores it. Shared Streams starts all those pairs, and then, carries on using *PriCe-DCS*.

X% Probing. This policy explores the first few windows for all the pairs in a round-robin fashion. This is done to set the utility function with actual current values instead of artificial hand-crafted ones. After those few windows, *PriCe-DCS* kicks in and continues the exploration process using the utility function that had its parameters filled with actual data through the probing process.

The rational behind this policy is to take advantage the good properties of *iBRAID-DCS* during the starting phase. In some respect, this policy is a hybrid of *iBRAID-DCS* and *PriCe-DCS*.

P-Alternating. This policy mimics the multilevel queue scheduling, whereby the pairs are explored in a round-robin fashion between two groups. Those are the previously correlated pairs and the non-correlated ones. This is to give the pairs that were not correlated in the previous micro-batch a chance to be persistently processed. It picks a pair from the non-correlated ones and processes it using *PriCe-DCS*, then, it picks a pair from those that were correlated. It does that until the end of the micro batch (i.e., not only the starting phase), and carries on in this fashion by picking the pair from each group of pairs according to the utility function. By doing this, the hope is to alleviate the effect of starvation for those pairs, that were not correlated in the previous micro-batch in a persistent way, for they might exhibit some correlation beyond the starting phase.

4   Experiments and Analysis

In this section we present the evaluation of the *DCS* framework and its algorithms. Furthermore, we evaluate the nine different policies with *PriCe-DCS*, and how each policy addresses different exploration requirements. For consistency, we used the same dataset and settings as in [13].

4.1   Experimental Framework

Algorithms. We compared a baseline algorithm *Random* against our two algorithms *iBRAID* and *PriCe*, along with their *DCS* variants *Random-DCS*, *iBRAID-DCS*, and *PriCe-DCS*. Also, we studied the nine different policies that modify *PriCe-DCS* default behavior.

Testbed. We implemented all the discussed algorithms and policies in C++ 11. We ran the experiments on a computer with 2 Intel CPUs, running at 2.66 GHz, and 96 GB of RAM memory. The operating system used was CentOS 6.5 and the compiler was GCC version 4.8.2.

Metrics. We evaluated the performance of the policies in terms of *detection-recall*, *overlapping-recall*, and *diversity*. We also measure the *cost*, which is used to determine the deadlines in our experiments. Those metrics are discussed next.

Cost: This is our efficiency metric. We measured the deadline latency as the number of operations performed to detect correlated pairs of data streams. We used the number of operations as it provides the asymptotic efficiency of the policies compared to one another. This does not depend on factors such as the hardware characteristics and the operating system of the computer, on which the experiments are run, nor the efficiency of the compiler. We examined how the policies meet deadlines and how many correlated pairs they could detect under such a requirement.

Table 1. Experimental parameters

Parameter	Value(s)	Parameter	Value(s)
PCC τ	[0.75, 0.90]	w	8
A	[112, 225, 450]	# data streams	72
I	900 (180 s)	# *micro-batches*	4

Detection-Recall: This is our detection optimization criterion (Eq. 2). It reflects how capable the policy is in detecting correlated pairs out of the total actual correlated pairs. Thus, it is a ratio of the number of detected correlated pairs to the total number of correlated pairs.

Overlapping-Recall: An overlapping pair is a detected correlated pair in a given micro-batch, which was also detected as correlated in the immediately preceding micro-batch. In this metric, we find the ratio of the detected overlapping pairs to the total number of overlapping pairs in a micro-batch. Note that this metric does not apply to the very first micro-batch.

Diversity: We measure how many new pairs (i.e., not seen as a result in the most recent micro-batch) are detected in each micro-batch. This is our exploration *vs* exploitation criterion.

Dataset. *Yahoo Finance Historical Data* [15]*:* The dataset we have used in our experiments consists of 318 data streams. Those reflect the trading of 53 companies on the NYSE for the last 28 years. This gives us a total of 50,403 different pairs to analyze. The data granularity is a day, which includes the price of the stock of the company at opening, the price at the end of the day (closing), the highest price for the day, the lowest price for the day, the amount of shares traded that day, and the adjusted close (calculated according to the standards of the CRSP, Center for Research in Security Prices). The length of each data stream is about 7,100 tuples. Those tuples are divided into micro-batches.

Experiments. We ran four experiments in total. The first two evaluate our base algorithms, and the latter two assess the ability of our proposed policies to detect and diversify the correlated pairs of data streams using *PriCe-DCS*. We conducted the experiments for two PCC threshold τ's, 75% and 90%, and for three different values of A, 112, 225 and 450. The values of A correspond to the 1/8, 1/4 and 1/2 of the micro-batch interval. The micro-batch interval is set to 900 tuples to simulate an inter-arrival time of 180 seconds, where each tuple is produced each 200 ms. Finally, we experimented with three deadlines corresponding to 25%, 50%, and 75% of the total operations needed to determined all the correlated pairs in a micro-batch, i.e., achieve total *detection-recall.* The experimental parameters are summarized in Table 1. In all experiments, we have divided the dataset into four mutually exclusive groups, and we ran our experiments on all of them, we found that the results are similar. Thus, we reported the results of one of those groups. Moreover, we did pick 10% for the *X% Non-Correlated* as a middle point between the policies *Untouched* and *Alternating.*

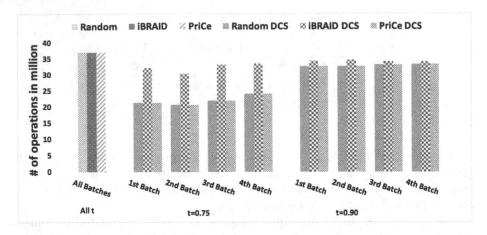

Fig. 1. The cost in number of operations for 4 consecutive micro-batches ($A = 112$).

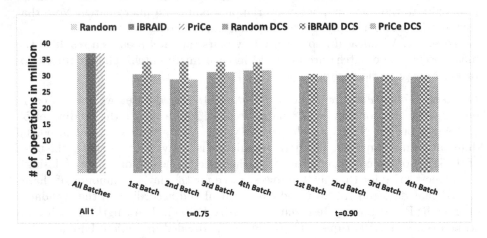

Fig. 2. The cost in number of operations for 4 consecutive micro-batches ($A = 225$).

4.2   Experimental Results

In this section, we present the results of four experiments that we conducted to evaluate the ability of the policies to detect and diversify in real-time the correlated pairs in data streams.

Experiment 1 (Figs. 1, 2 and 3). In our first experiment, we measured the execution *cost* or latency in *number of operations* of each algorithm to detect the specified number A of correlated pairs of sliding windows in four consecutive micro-batches.

As expected, *Random*, *iBRAID*, and *PriCe* have the same number of operations due to exhaustive processing of the pairs. These do not use A for either early termination nor pruning. Thus, with fixed number of data streams, intervals,

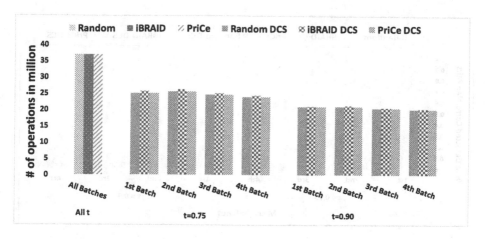

Fig. 3. The cost in number of operations for 4 consecutive micro-batches ($A = 450$).

and window range, the number of operations induced by the three algorithms is identical. They always consume the same amount of operations regardless of the other parameters (i.e., PCC τ and A). The impact of DCS mode on all three algorithms is clearly visible in all figures.

In Fig. 1, we notice that the higher the PCC τ, the more operations are executed by the algorithms. This is due to the fewer number of windows that are highly correlated according to the PCC τ. This results in higher latency in detecting them by the algorithms. On the other hand, in case of low PCC τ, we see that DCS terminates the analysis process early, as soon as it reaches the A criterion of number of correlated sliding windows. We also observe that $iBRAID$-DCS consistently underperforms the other DCS algorithms in latency. This is a consequence of the $iBRAID$ scheduling scheme, where it processes all the pairs in a round-robin fashion to avoid starvation. This leads to having a pair pruned at a late stage of the analysis.

In Fig. 2, we notice that $iBRAID$-DCS exhibited higher latency in the cases where PCC $\tau = 0.75$. This is counter intuitive. To clearly state the reason, we observe that the lower the A criterion, the later the pruning will occur in case of no high correlated windows were processed. With that in mind, we say that the pairs of data streams in Fig. 2 in the case of PCC $\tau = 0.75$ has produced high amount of correlated windows, enough to delay the pruning towards the end, but not enough to terminate the analysis early. Therefore, the performance of $iBRAID$-DCS was lower with low PCC τ.

Our last explanation is also supported by our experimental results in Fig. 3, which show clearly that with high A, the DCS mode is able to reach a better performance than low A. The reason is that with $A = 450$, if a pair encounters no correlated windows yet, it can be pruned by midway of the analysis process.

Finally, DCS mode of operation was able to enhance the performance of the algorithms up to 1.8 times (Fig. 3).

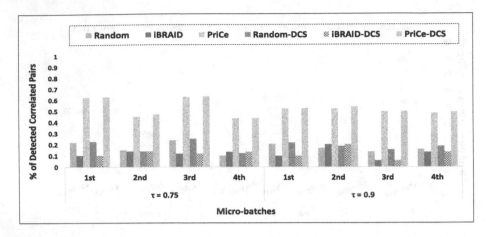

Fig. 4. The % of correlated pairs of streams detected by all algorithms at 25% of the interval I ($A = 112$).

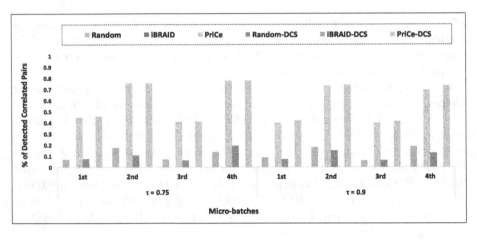

Fig. 5. The % of correlated pairs of streams detected by all algorithms at 25% of the interval I ($A = 225$).

Experiment 2 (Figs. 4, 5, 6, 7 and 8). In this experiment, we studied the *Detection-Recall* of each algorithm with respect to a given deadline. We set the deadline to be 25%, 50%, and 75% of the processing duration of each interval and measured the percentage of the number of correlated pairs each algorithm was able to detect. The results are shown in Figs. 4, 5 and 6 for the deadline 25%, in Fig. 7 for the deadline 50%, and in Fig. 8 for the deadline 75%.

In general, we notice that *DCS* mode of operation in all cases for all algorithms outperforms the original algorithms. This is attributed to the pruning and early termination features of *DCS*, which allow the algorithms to analyze other pairs and detect more correlated data streams.

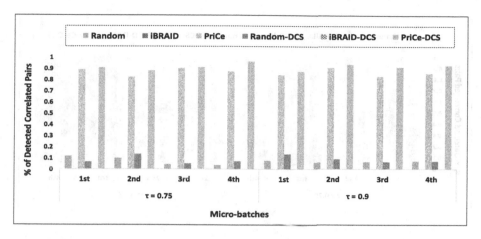

Fig. 6. The % of correlated pairs of streams detected by all algorithms at 25% of the interval I ($A = 450$).

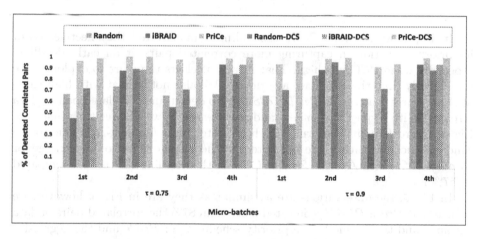

Fig. 7. The % of correlated pairs of streams detected by all algorithms at 50% of the interval I ($A = 225$).

In Fig. 4, we notice that *iBRAID* and *iBRAID-DCS* detected lower percentage of correlated pairs of data streams than *PriCe* and *PriCe-DCS*, while *PriCe* and *PriCe-DCS* have comparable performance. We attribute this to the fact that with a low value of A, we are expecting the required A number of correlated pairs to be detected quickly by *PriCe* and *PriCe-DCS*, while the round-robin scheduling of *iBRAID* and *iBRAID-DCS*, which process all the pairs one pair at a time, is not affected by the value of A. We also notice that *Random* performed slightly better than *Random-DCS* in the 2nd micro-batch, and this is due to the random scheduler nature that picks a pair in a random fashion. In addition, we observe that the average detection percentages for *Random* with $A = 112$ for all PCC τ at the deadline 25% is 18% comparing to 52% for *PriCe*.

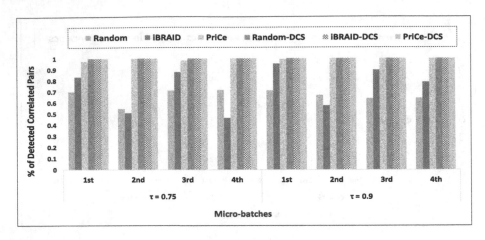

Fig. 8. The % of correlated pairs of streams detected by all algorithms at 75% of the interval I ($A = 450$).

In Fig. 5, we see that *PriCe* scheduling demonstrated the effectiveness of its priority function in capturing more correlated pairs at an early deadline, especially when PCC τ is high. That means, it elects the pairs to explore more intelligently than the other two algorithms. We also notice that with high value of A and early deadline, *iBRAID-DCS* fails to detect any correlated pair of data streams. With respect to *Random* and *Random-DCS*, we observe the same as in Fig. 4, where *Random* performed slightly better than *Random-DCS* due to the random scheduler nature. We also note that the average detection percentage for *Random-DCS* with $A = 225$ for all PCC τ at the deadline 25% is 12% compared to 57% for *PriCe*.

In Fig. 6, the observations are as similar as they are in Fig. 5, however, we realize that *PriCe-DCS* has detected more than 87% the correlated pairs of data streams, and this is due to the priority scheduling of *PriCe* and the aggressive pruning at high A. The *Random-DCS* fails to meet that, since it picks pairs in an unpredictable way, and this delays the analysis duration for each pair, hence, delaying its pruning.

In Fig. 7, we note that *PriCe-DCS* outperforms all the other algorithms. This is for the obvious reason of having more processing time to advance the sliding windows and capture more correlated windows between a pair of data streams. As a result, it reaches the criterion A (=225) of declaring the pair as a correlated one quickly. For $A = 112$ and $A = 450$, our observations are similar as in Fig. 7.

Finally, towards the end of the micro-batch analysis process, we see clearly in Fig. 8 that all the algorithms are detecting pairs with an overall relatively higher percentage than the earlier deadlines, and this is expected with more time to analyze the pairs of data streams. We also observe the effect of pruning clearly on all algorithms under *DCS* mode. This is a result of the A criterion being very high, which leads to early pruning for non promising pairs of data streams.

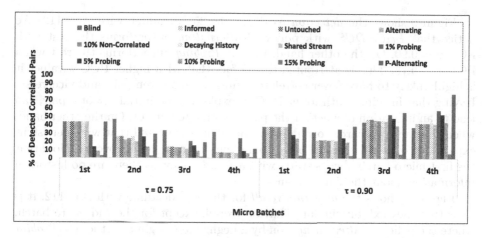

Fig. 9. The % of correlated pairs of streams detected by all policies at 25% of the interval I ($A = 112$).

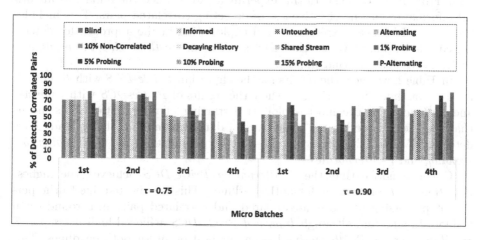

Fig. 10. The % of correlated pairs of streams detected by all policies at 50% of the interval I ($A = 112$).

Thus, all the correlated pairs of data streams were detected earlier than the 75% deadline. The same holds for $A = 112$ and $A = 225$.

Experiment 3 (Figs. 9 and 10). Our previous two experiments show that *PriCe-DCS* exhibits the best performance overall. In our third experiment, we studied the *detection-recall* of each policy with respect to a given deadline. We set the deadline to be 25%, 50%, and 75% of the processing duration of each interval and measured the percentage of the number of correlated pairs each policy was able to detect. We experimented with the values of PCC τ and A, shown in Table 1. All experiments produced similar results; thus, we report the results for the deadline 25% and 50% only.

Figure 9 shows the *detection-recall* for the 25% deadline with $A = 112$. We notice that *PriCe-DCS* with policy *P-Alternating* outperforms the rest with PCC $\tau = 0.90$. On the other hand, the *1% Probing* outperforms the rest when PCC $\tau = 0.75$. This is attributed to the fact that with higher PCC τ values it is highly likely to have fewer correlated windows in a given pair, and vice versa. Having that in mind, with lower PCC τ, exploring the initial 1% of a pair, can lead to an indication of whether the pair is correlated or not. On the other hand, when the pair has scarce correlated windows, it is expected that with persistent exploration of non-correlated pairs, to find new correlation discoveries. Note that the first micro-batch always starts with a *Blind* policy, as there are no historical information about the data streams.

Figure 10 shows the *detection-recall* for the 50% deadline with $A = 112$. It is clear that they exhibit similar behavior overall, except for the 2nd micro-batch, where the policy *P-Alternating* won by a negligible margin over the *X% Probing* policies.

Experiment 4 (Table 2). In this experiment, we studied the impact of historical information on the effectiveness of detecting correlated pairs. This includes the trade-off between exploration and exploitation in the approach for detecting correlated pairs. We use the metrics *detection-recall*, *overlapping-recall*, and *diversity* to illustrate that impact.

In Table 2, we show the results for the algorithm *PriCe-DCS* with *Blind* policy as a baseline. In addition, we show the results of *PriCe-DCS* with *Informed* and *Untouched* as the most exploitative starting phase varieties. This means that they keep detecting the same pairs of data streams that they already have detected. We also show the winners from Experiment 3 (i.e., *1% Probing*, *5% Probing*, and *P-Alternating*).

One can notice that the *P-Alternating PriCe-DCS* achieved the highest *detection-recall* on average for both deadlines. This is expected due to the persistent processing of the non-correlated and correlated pairs in a round-robin fashion. In addition, although *Informed PriCe-DCS* achieved high *overlapping-recall* on average, *P-Alternating* has the highest of all for both deadlines. This is to be expected because *Informed PriCe-DCS* does not alter the parameters of the utility function, instead, it carries all the information of pairs from previous micro-batches as they are, and in the case of *P-Alternating*, the persistent processing of the already correlated pairs manifests itself in the highest *overlapping-recall*.

Finally, the explorative policies (i.e., *Blind*) achieved the highest *diversity* in detecting correlated pairs than the exploitative ones (i.e., *Informed*, *Untouched*, and *P-Alternating*), in fact, they have achieved the lowest *diversity* on average. This can be explained because the exploitative policies have some kind of informative approach on how to analyze the data streams, whether this is from previous micro-batches or some other source. Thus, they will keep exploring the pairs that were already correlated in previous micro-batches.

Take Away: In our first two experiments, we found that *PriCe-DCS* outperformed all other algorithms. In the third, we found that *PriCe-DCS* with *X%*

Table 2. Results of Experiment 4

	Batches	25% Deadline					50% Deadline				
		1st	2nd	3rd	4th	Avg.	1st	2nd	3rd	4th	Avg.
	Full Correlated	429	580	236	234	–	429	580	236	234	–
	Full Overlapped	–	364	215	181	–	–	364	215	181	–
PriCe Blind	Correlated	163	184	103	88	–	231	298	135	130	–
	Overlapped	–	70	67	54	–	–	140	98	84	–
	Unseen Before	163	114	36	34	–	231	158	37	46	–
	Detection-Recall	0.380	0.317	0.436	0.376	0.377	0.538	0.514	0.572	0.556	0.545
	Overlap-Recall	–	0.192	0.312	0.298	**0.267**	–	0.385	0.456	0.464	**0.435**
	Diversity	1	0.620	0.350	0.386	**0.589**	1	0.530	0.274	0.354	**0.540**
PriCe Informed	Correlated	163	126	111	99	–	231	232	144	141	–
	Overlapped	–	81	99	87	–	–	144	136	118	–
	Unseen Before	163	45	12	12	–	231	88	8	23	–
	Detection-Recall	0.380	0.217	0.470	0.423	0.373	0.538	0.400	0.610	0.603	0.538
	Overlap-Recall	–	0.223	0.460	0.481	0.388	–	0.396	0.633	0.652	0.560
	Diversity	1	0.357	0.108	0.121	**0.397**	1	0.379	0.056	0.163	**0.399**
PriCe Untouched	Correlated	163	126	111	99	–	231	232	144	141	–
	Overlapped	–	81	99	87	–	–	144	136	118	–
	Unseen Before	163	45	12	12	–	231	88	8	23	–
	Detection-Recall	0.380	0.217	0.470	0.423	0.373	0.538	0.400	0.610	0.603	0.538
	Overlap-Recall		0.223	0.460	0.481	0.388	–	0.396	0.633	0.652	0.560
	Diversity	1	0.357	0.108	0.121	**0.397**	1	0.379	0.056	0.163	**0.399**
PriCe 1% Probing	Correlated	179	203	124	135	–	295	323	178	156	–
	Overlapped	–	123	101	90	–	–	178	129	111	–
	Unseen Before	179	80	23	45	–	295	145	49	45	–
	Detection-Recall	0.417	0.350	0.525	0.577	0.467	0.688	0.557	0.754	0.667	0.666
	Overlap-Recall	–	0.338	0.470	0.497	0.435	–	0.489	0.600	0.613	0.567
	Diversity	1	0.394	0.185	0.333	0.478	1	0.449	0.275	0.288	0.503
PriCe 5% Probing	Correlated	121	143	114	124	–	281	278	173	182	–
	Overlapped	–	110	100	96	–	–	184	145	134	–
	Unseen Before	121	33	14	28	–	281	94	28	48	–
	Detection-Recall	0.282	0.247	0.483	0.530	0.385	0.655	0.479	0.733	0.778	0.661
	Overlap-Recall	–	0.302	0.465	0.530	0.433	–	0.505	0.674	0.740	0.640
	Diversity	1	0.231	0.123	0.226	0.395	1	0.338	0.162	0.264	0.441
PriCe P-Alternating	Correlated	163	224	131	182	–	231	375	202	191	–
	Overlapped	–	108	124	130	–	–	209	187	173	
	Unseen Before	163	116	7	52	–	231	166	15	18	–
	Detection-Recall	0.380	0.386	0.555	0.778	**0.525**	0.538	0.647	0.856	0.816	**0.714**
	Overlap-Recall	–	0.297	0.577	0.718	**0.531**	–	0.574	0.870	0.956	**0.800**
	Diversity	1	0.518	0.053	0.286	0.464	1	0.443	0.074	0.094	0.403

Probing is the best policy for detecting correlated live data streams for low values of PCC τ. On the contrary, *PriCe-DCS* with *P-Alternating* is the best policy for detecting correlated live data streams for high values of PCC τ. In the last experiment, we found that *P-Alternating, Informed* and *Untouched* policies are more suitable for exploiting the space of exploration, and for finding correlated pairs regardless of *diversity*. However, *Blind* policy does detect more diverse pairs across micro-batches along the exploration process.

5   Related Work

The processing of data and fast discovery of correlated subsequences of time series is tackled in two scenarios with respect to the production of data: (1) static, when the data is collected upfront and it forms the search space for finding the correlated subsequences [14,16,17], and (2) dynamic, when the data is processed as it is produced [5–8,18]. The former is beyond the scope of our work. In this section, we focus on the latter, and in particular the state-of-the-art of computationally cheap identification of correlated data streams.

RainMon [5] proposes a 3-stage technique to mine bursty data streams. The received signals are first decomposed, in order to obtain a smoothed representation of the data. In the next stage, called summarization, the received data goes through incremental principal component analysis in an effort to outline the long-term trends in the streams and to identify anomalies, if there are any. In the last stage, named Prediction, the system forecasts trends, relying on the output from the summarization stage. In our work, we do not make predictions and use the data as it is delivered to identify correlated data streams.

A framework for identification of highly correlated pairs of data streams is also presented in StatStream [6]. One of the assumptions of the work is that only an approximation of the PCC is sufficient to identify the pairs of highly correlated data streams. Based on this assumptions, the authors proposed a twofold approach to efficiently identify the pairs of interest. They employ a computationally cheap Discrete Fourier Transformation (DFT) technique to calculate an approximation of the PCC. Furthermore, they proposed an n-dimensional grid structure, which stores the DFT statistics and PCC approximations of each stream, whereby neighboring cells reflect highly correlated streams. This is the springboard for identification of the highly correlated pairs of data streams. However, DFT is known for its poor performance on data streams, which mimic white noise, thereby the required number of DFT coefficients to precisely represent the data streams is high, which induces significant amount of computations. Our work differs in the calculation of PCC. Furthermore, we calculate PCC incrementally over sliding windows, and our framework calculates it precisely for each pair, over each sliding window. Our studies showed that once a pair of data streams is selected as being highly correlated due to a high value of the approximated PCC, a precise calculation of the PCC is required to prove the hypothesis. This operation requires two passes on the data. Similarly to Stat-Stream, our framework supports sliding windows on data streams. We evaluate the possibilities to extend our framework to support landmark windows and damped windows in the future.

StatStream was further improved to handle "uncooperative" data streams in [7], but it still calculates an approximation of PCC only. The proposed technique employs structured random vectors. The experimental results show that the proposed technique outperforms linear scan and the Discrete Fourier Transformations, proposed in StatStream [6]. Our framework, similarly to this work, updates the required statistics in fixed amount of time. However, it differs in PCC calculations, whereby DCS calculates PCC of the pairs of data streams *precisely* for each sliding window and avoids the need to be calculated later and at a higher cost, once a pair is selected as being "promising".

Detecting similarities between data streams can be achieved through correlation identification techniques. Four different distance measures for similarity of data streams were proposed in [18]: "Autocorrelation Distance (ACD)", "Markovian Distance (MD)", "Local Distance Distribution" and "Probabilistic Local Nearest Neighbor". *ACD* is the version of similarity metric used in our work (PCC), but used for self-correlation, i.e., when a data stream is correlated to itself, whereby one of the windows starts with a lag from the other one. All discussed methods are used to find the first nearest neighbor (1NN) of given data stream only. Our approach, however, identifies all pairs of correlated data streams and is not limited to 1NN only.

Anomaly detection over data streams can also be used as a correlation identification method. A solution is presented in [8] uses the *MD* approach, listed above. Specifically, the presented solution relies on a twofold approach, whereby data streams clustering is combined with Markov chain modeling. The former identifies groups (or clusters) of similar data streams. The latter conveys a possibility for the system to identify anomalies in the data streams in each cluster. In the context of the system, anomalies are considered to be transitions in the Markov chains, which have probability below a certain predefined threshold. Our work may not only be adjusted to identify anomalies, whereby an anomaly is a pair of windows with PCC below a certain threshold, but it also provides analysts with insights about the data. This is done by employing cheap incremental computations, avoiding computationally expensive operations such as building Markovian transition matrices.

6   Conclusions

In this paper, we presented the complete Detection of Correlated Data Streams (DCS) framework, which offers effective solutions for detecting the correlation of data streams within a micro-batch of a fixed time interval for specific analysis requirements. Specifically, we first discussed our novel *PriCe-DCS* algorithm, which combines (1) incremental sliding-window computation of aggregates and (2) intelligent scheduling, driven by a utility function. Then we discussed how the *DCS* framework facilitates the implementation of different policies that tune the utility function in order to meet the exploration and exploitation requirements of analysis tasks.

We implemented and evaluated nine policies that initialize/tune the utility function of *PriCe-DCS*. Other policies could potentially be specified. As opposed to the policies that address explorative objectives, such as *Blind* and *X% Probing*, the policies that address an exploitative objective, such as *P-Alternating*, *Informative*, and *Untouched*, use the result of the preceding micro-batch analyses as part of the initialization of the analysis of the current micro-batch.

Our experimental evaluation using real world dataset showed that the policies that address explorative objectives (i.e., *Blind* and *X% Probing*) detected more unique correlated data streams. It also revealed that for low PCC τ, *PriCe-DCS* with *X% Probing* outperformed the rest of the policies in terms of *detection-recall*, and for high PCC τ values, *PriCe-DCS* with *P-Alternating* performed the best.

Acknowledgment. This paper was partially supported by NSF under award CBET-1609120, and NIH under Award U01HL137159. The content is solely the responsibility of the authors and does not represent the views of NSF and NIH.

References

1. Kalinin, A., Cetintemel, U., Zdonik, S.: Searchlight: enabling integrated search and exploration over large multidimensional data. PVLDB **8**(10), 1094–1105 (2015)
2. Orang, M., Shiri, N.: Improving performance of similarity measures for uncertain time series using preprocessing techniques. In: ACM SSDBM, pp. 31:1–31:12 (2015)
3. Zacharatou, E.T., Tauheedz, F., Heinis, T., Ailamaki, A.: RUBIK: efficient threshold queries on massive time series. In: ACM SSDBM, pp. 18:1–18:12 (2015)
4. Lee, D., Sim, A., Choi, J., Wu, K.: Novel data reduction based on statistical similarity. In: ACM SSDBM, pp. 21:1–21:12 (2016)
5. Shafer, I., Ren, K., Boddeti, V.N., Abe, Y., Ganger, G.R., Faloutsos, C.: RainMon: an integrated approach to mining bursty timeseries monitoring data. In: ACM SIGKDD, pp. 1158–1166 (2012)
6. Zhu, Y., Shasha, D.: StatStream: statistical monitoring of thousands of data streams in real time. In: VLDB, pp. 358–369 (2002)
7. Cole, R., Shasha, D., Zhao, X.: Fast window correlations over uncooperative time series. In: ACM SIGKDD, pp. 743–749 (2005)
8. Jankov, D., Sikdar, S., Mukherjee, R., Teymourian, K., Jermaine, C.: Real-time high performance anomaly detection over data streams: grand challenge. In: ACM DEBS, pp. 292–297 (2017)
9. Zoumpatianos, K., Idreos, S., Palpanas, T.: Indexing for interactive exploration of big data series. In: ACM SIGMOD, pp. 1555–1566 (2014)
10. Idreos, S., Papaemmanouil, O., Chaudhuri, S.: Overview of data exploration techniques. In: ACM SIGMOD, pp. 277–281 (2015)
11. Feng, K., Cong, G., Bhowmick, S.S., Peng, W.C., Miao, C.: Towards best region search for data exploration. In: ACM SIGMOD, pp. 1055–1070 (2016)
12. Petrov, D., Alseghayer, R., Sharaf, M., Chrysanthis, P.K., Labrinidis, A.: Interactive exploration of correlated time series. In: ACM ExploreDB, pp. 2:1–2:6 (2017)
13. Alseghayer, R., Petrov, D., Chrysanthis, P.K., Sharaf, M., Labrinidis, A.: Detection of highly correlated live data streams. In: BIRTE, pp. 3:1–3:8 (2017)
14. Sakurai, Y., Papadimitriou, S., Faloutsos, C.: BRAID: stream mining through group lag correlations. In: ACM SIGMOD, pp. 599–610 (2005)
15. Yahoo Inc.: Yahoo finance historical data (2016)
16. Kalinin, A., Cetintemel, U., Zdonik, S.: Interactive data exploration using semantic windows. In: ACM SIGMOD, pp. 505–516 (2014)
17. Mueen, A., Nath, S., Liu, J.: Fast approximate correlation for massive time-series data. In: ACM SIGMOD, pp. 171–182 (2010)
18. Mirylenka, K., Dallachiesa, M., Palpanas, T.: Data series similarity using correlation-aware measures. In: ACM SSDBM, pp. 11:1–11:12 (2017)

Towards Dynamic Data Placement
for Polystore Ingestion

Jiang Du[1]([⊠]), John Meehan[2], Nesime Tatbul[3], and Stan Zdonik[2]

[1] University of Toronto, Toronto, Canada
jdu@cs.toronto.edu
[2] Brown University, Providence, USA
{john,sbz}@cs.brown.edu
[3] Intel Labs and MIT, Cambridge, USA
tatbul@csail.mit.edu

Abstract. Integrating low-latency data streaming into data warehouse architectures has become an important enhancement to support modern data warehousing applications. In these architectures, heterogeneous workloads with data ingestion and analytical queries must be executed with strict performance guarantees. Furthermore, the data warehouse may consists of multiple different types of storage engines (a.k.a., polystores or multi-stores). A paramount problem is data placement; different workload scenarios call for different data placement designs. Moreover, workload conditions change frequently. In this paper, we provide evidence that a dynamic, workload-driven approach is needed for data placement in polystores with low-latency data ingestion support. We study the problem based on the characteristics of the TPC-DI benchmark in the context of an abbreviated polystore that consists of S-Store and Postgres.

1 Introduction

In many modern applications such as the Internet of Things (IoT), time-sensitive data generated by a large number of diverse sources must be collected, stored, and analyzed in a reliable and scalable manner. This is critical to supporting accurate and timely monitoring, decision making, and control. Traditional data warehousing architectures that have been based on separate subsystems for managing operational (OLTP), data ingestion (ETL), and analytical (OLAP) workloads in a loosely synchronized manner are no longer sufficient to meet these needs. As a result, new approaches such as data stream warehousing [14], near real-time warehousing [27], lambda/kappa architectures [1,2,12], and HTAP systems [5] have recently emerged. While these approaches architecturally differ from one another, low-latency data ingestion (a.k.a., streaming or near real-time ETL) is seen as a critical component of the solution in all of them.

In our recent work, we have designed and built one-of-a-kind transactional stream processing system called *S-Store* [20]. S-Store is a scalable main-memory system that supports hybrid OLTP+streaming workloads with well-defined correctness guarantees including ACID, ordered execution, and exactly-once processing [26]. While S-Store can be used as a stand-alone system to support

© Springer Nature Switzerland AG 2019
M. Castellanos et al. (Eds.): BIRTE 2015/2016/2017, LNBIP 337, pp. 211–228, 2019.
https://doi.org/10.1007/978-3-030-24124-7_13

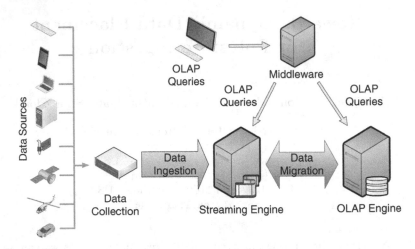

Fig. 1. Architectural overview

streaming applications with shared mutable state [7], we have also shown, within the context of the BigDAWG polystore system [11], how S-Store can uniquely enhance OLAP-style data warehousing systems with near real-time capabilities [21].

We believe that streaming ETL in particular stands out as the killer app for S-Store [19]. More specifically, S-Store can easily be programmed to continuously ingest configurable-size batches of newly added or updated data from a multitude of sources, and apply the necessary cleaning and transformation operations on them using its dataflow-based computational model. Furthermore, it provides the necessary scalable system infrastructure for processing ETL dataflows with transactional guarantees. A crucial component of this infrastructure is the database-style local in-memory storage. S-Store's storage facilities can be used for multiple different purposes, including: (i) temporary staging of newly ingested batches and any intermediate data derived from them as they are being prepared for loading into the back-end data warehouse, (ii) caching copies of older data fragments from the warehouse that will need to be frequently looked up during ETL, (iii) serving as the primary storage for data fragments which are subject to frequent updates. In general, since our streaming ETL engine has all the capabilities of an in-memory OLTP database, it can take over some of the responsibility of the back-end warehouse. For example, it can be directly queried to provide fast and consistent access to the freshest data.

Figure 1 shows a high-level overview of the streaming ETL architecture that we envision. All data newly collected from the sources (time-ordered, append-only streams as well as arbitrary insertions in general) and requests for in-place updates or deletions on older data are ingested through a transactional streaming engine (S-Store). The streaming engine in turn populates a back-end OLAP engine with updates on a frequent basis, through a data migration component. The migration component is bi-directional, i.e., data can be copied or moved between the two engines transactionally, in both directions. Meanwhile, all OLAP query requests to the system are received by a middleware layer that sits on top of the two engines. This layer maintains a global system catalog, which keeps track of all the data fragments and where they are currently stored. Based on this information, it determines where to forward the query requests for execution. Query results received from the engines are then returned back to the user. We have built a working prototype for this architecture based on Kafka [17] (data collection), S-Store (streaming ETL engine), Postgres (OLAP engine), and BigDAWG (migration + middleware layer) [19]. This architecture raises a number of interesting research issues in terms of cross-system optimization.

In this paper, we study how different data placement strategies perform in the presence of mixed (read and write) ETL workloads: Given a data fragment (i.e., the lowest level of data granularity - part of a relation), it can be stored in the streaming engine, in the OLAP engine, or in both. While the main-memory streaming engine can generally handle look-ups and updates faster, it has a limited memory budget. In contrast, the OLAP engine has larger storage capacity, but is slower to access. Furthermore, both engines are subject to dynamically changing workloads which consist of ingestion and query requests. Thus, given a mixed workload with different types of data, operations, and performance needs, data ingestion is affected greatly by the decisions of (i) which data fragments to store in the streaming engine, and (ii) whether to copy or move the data fragments between the database engines. As we will illustrate based on preliminary experiments on the TPC-DI benchmark [23], this decision can have significant impact on ETL latency.

2   Background

In this section, we provide brief background on two core systems that underlie our work: the BigDAWG polystore system and the S-Store transactional streaming system.

2.1   BigDAWG

When it comes to database systems, it is commonly believed that "one-size no longer fits all" [25]. Specialized databases have become the norm. Some systems are designed specifically for unique types of data such as arrays or graphs [3,8]. Others specialize in data formatting such that analytical queries can run extremely quickly [24]. Many workloads, however, require multiple of these specializations to execute efficiently.

Intel's BigDAWG represents a polystore of multiple disparate database systems, each of which specializes in one type of data (e.g., relational, array, streaming, etc.) [11]. BigDAWG provides the user with querying and data migration across these systems, essentially abstracting the individual systems into one unified front-end from the user's perspective. BigDAWG accomplishes this by separating databases into several "islands of information", each of which contains

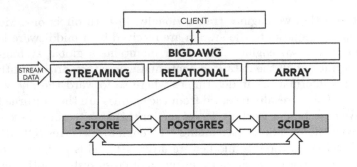

Fig. 2. BigDAWG 1.0 architecture

multiple systems that share a common query language. For instance, relational databases such as Postgres and MySQL are connected to "relational island," which is queried via SQL statements (Fig. 2).

While operations are delegated to the appropriate specialized system, Big-DAWG also contains the ability to run queries on one engine which requires data from another engine. To facilitate this, BigDAWG contains the ability to efficiently migrate data from one engine to another. One specific scenario that data migration makes possible is the ingestion of streaming data into an analytical data warehouse. Such a scenario is best served by a data stream management system performing data cleaning operations on the streaming data before migrating the data to the OLAP engine, as discussed in Sect. 1.

2.2   S-Store

S-Store is a streaming system that specializes in the correct management of shared, mutable state [20]. S-Store models its dataflow graphs as a series of transactions, each of which has full ACID properties inherited from OLTP. S-Store also provides the ordering and exactly-once guarantees of a modern streaming system, ensuring correctness from the perspective of the dataflow graph.

S-Store is built on top of the main-memory OLTP system, H-Store [16]. Transactions are parameterized user-defined stored procedures, each of which passes output data along a stream in a dataflow graph to be used as the input parameters of the next downstream stored procedure. Each transaction executes on an atomic batch of tuples, the size of which is defined by the user. Batches are ordered by their time of arrival, and that order is maintained throughout the dataflow graph. Transactions in a dataflow graph typically execute independently, meaning locks on shared state are released between consecutive transactions in the graph.

3   The Data Placement Problem

In our data warehousing setting, the workload consists of a mix of ingest requests and query requests. These requests must be served on a continuous basis with low latency and high throughput. Ingest requests may generally consist of any changes to the data in the warehouse including insertions, in-place updates, or deletions. Feeds from streaming data sources (e.g., sensors, stock market) are typically in the form of appends (i.e., only time-ordered insertions). Ingest requests are primarily served by S-Store, whereas query requests can be served by both S-Store or Postgres depending on the location of the needed data fragments.

S-Store transactionally processes ingest requests in small, atomic batches of tuples in order to apply ETL transformations. The resulting data fragments are then asynchronously migrated from S-Store to Postgres. This migration can be in the form of periodic pushes from S-Store to Postgres, or on-demand pulls by Postgres. Since S-Store has its own local storage, it can store a data fragment temporarily until migration, or even thereafter if that fragment will be needed by S-Store. While the natural direction of migration for newly ingested data is from S-Store to Postgres, we also support migrations in the opposite direction. It can be useful to bring older data fragments back to S-Store, such as when an ETL transformation needs to look up older data for validating new data or when a certain data fragment starts receiving a burst of in-place updates on it. Note that all migrations within our system are transactional.

In general, while a data fragment is being migrated from one engine (source) to another (destination), there are two options with respect to data placement:

1. *Move.* Delete the migrated data fragment from the source engine as part of the migration transaction (i.e., the destination engine becomes the one and only location for the fragment).
2. *Copy.* Continue to keep a copy of the migrated data fragment at the source engine (i.e., the fragment gets replicated at the destination engine).

These options can have advantages or disadvantages under different circumstances. The Move option keeps a single copy of a data fragment in the system, which avoids redundant storage and, more importantly, removes the need to maintain transactional consistency across multiple copies in case of updates to the fragment. However, data access may take more time if the desired fragment is not available in local storage. On the other hand, the Copy option incurs an overhead for storing and maintaining multiple replicas of a data fragment in the system. This is largely due to the transactional overhead of two-phase commit. However, efficient, local data access to the fragment is guaranteed at all times.

While these are generic tradeoffs between Move and Copy for any given pair of engines, there are additional considerations specific to our setting. More specifically, our front-end processor, S-Store, and back-end warehouse, Postgres, differ in their system characteristics. Being a main-memory system, S-Store can provide fast data access, but has limited storage capacity. Furthermore, it is optimized for short-lived, read and update transactions (e.g., no sophisticated techniques for large disk scans). Postgres is disk-based, and can support large-scale, read-intensive OLAP workloads better than S-Store.

In order to achieve high performance for a given mix of ingest and query workload, data fragments must be placed carefully. Both workload characteristics (e.g., frequency of reads vs. updates) as well as the tradeoffs discussed above must be taken into account. Furthermore, as the workload dynamically changes, placement of data fragments should be adjusted accordingly. Next, we will illustrate the problem using an example scenario taken from the TPC-DI benchmark [23].

4   An Example: Streaming TPC-DI

TPC-DI is a data integration benchmark for evaluating the performance of traditional ETL tools [23]. It models a retail brokerage firm that needs to extract and transform data from heterogeneous data sources. The original benchmark does not involve streaming data. However, some of the data sources are incremental in nature and can be modeled as such. For example, Fig. 3 shows the trade data ingestion portion of the benchmark remodeled as a streaming ETL scenario. In this dataflow, new trade tuples go through a series of validation and transformation procedures before they can be loaded into the *DimTrade* table of the warehouse.

A Case for Copy. One of those procedures (*SP4*) involves establishing foreign key dependencies with the *DimAccount* table. More specifically, when new rows are defined within the *DimTrade* table, reference must be made to the *DimAccount* table to assign the *SK_AccountID* key along with a few other fields. In other words, for each new batch of trade tuples to be ingested, the ETL dataflow must perform a lookup operation in the *DimAccount* table. Assume that an initial load for the *DimAccount* table has already been performed via S-Store (the ETL engine) before the Trade dataflow starts executing. In other words, *DimAccount* already resides in Postgres (the OLAP engine). Unless a copy of the *DimAccount* fragments were kept in S-Store after this initial load, *SP4*'s lookups would require migrating the relevant *DimAccount* fragments from Postgres to S-Store. This in turn would incur high latency for the trade ingestion dataflow. In this scenario, keeping a local copy of *DimAccount* fragments to be referenced by the trade dataflow in S-Store would be a good data placement decision.

A Case for Move. Next, assume that S-Store occasionally ingests update requests for the *DimAccount* table. For *DimAccount* fragments that are replicated in S-Store, such updates must be transactionally applied on both engines in order to ensure mutual consistency. In this scenario, Move might be a more desirable data placement strategy for frequently updated *DimAccount* fragments than the Copy option. This way, S-Store would only have to locally update a single copy for those fragments.

OLAP Queries. Now further assume that, while the above ingestion scenarios on *DimTrade* and *DimAccount* are taking place, a query request on the *DimTrade* table arrives. The query requires the system to scan the whole *DimTrade* table and calculate the total and average difference between bid and trade price values for each trade. Trade data is streaming into the system at high frequency and is being ingested into Postgres through S-Store via periodic, push-based migration. As such, the larger portion of *DimTrade* (which accounts for older trades) is

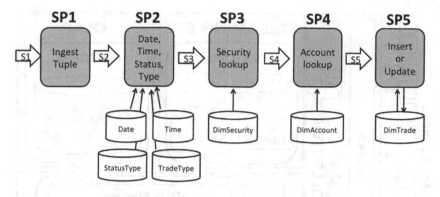

Fig. 3. TPC-DI trade data ingestion dataflow

stored in Postgres, while the smaller, recently ingested portion is stored in S-Store. Therefore, this query cannot be answered in its entirety on either Postgres or S-Store. The query planner has multiple different options to ensure the most complete (and thus, the freshest) answer to this query. For example, Postgres can issue a pull request to migrate *DimTrade* fragments from S-Store and then execute the OLAP query in Postgres, or the middleware layer can execute the OLAP query on S-Store and Postgres in parallel and merge their results into the full answer. We have analyzed some of these options in recent benchmark studies [19,21]. The main takeaway is that data placement can also have significant impact on query performance. Therefore, the ETL workload must be considered in conjunction with the query workload in making data placement decisions.

5   System Prototype

We have created a prototype for streaming data ingestion [19]. This prototype uses a combination of BigDAWG and S-Store, in conjunction with Kafka (a publish-subscribe messaging system [17]) and the relational database Postgres (Fig. 4). New tuples arrive from a variety of data sources and are queued in Kafka. These tuples are batched and pushed to S-Store. As a streaming system with ACID state management, S-Store is particularly well-suited for streaming data ingestion workloads. Streaming data can be ingested and transformed in a dataflow graph, with intermediate state being maintained in a transactional manner.

For each stored procedure that requires access to data, S-Store checks the data catalog in BigDAWG through a **Fragment Selection** module. Data catalog in BigDAWG maintains all information about data fragments including the data placement. If the required data fragment only exists in Postgres, the fragment selection module will instruct the data migrator in BigDAWG to migrate the fragment from Postgres to S-Store. Meanwhile, the fragment selection module is also responsible for deciding whether the migration should be **Move** or

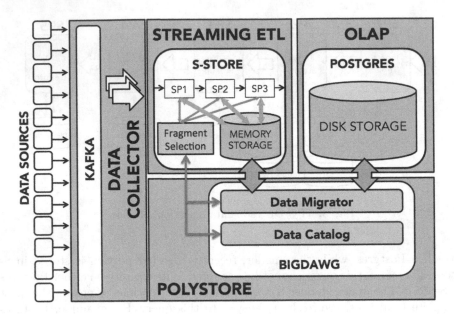

Fig. 4. System prototype

Copy, and if the total size of the fragments exceeds the storage limit of S-Store, which fragment(s) should be evicted.

Once the final tuples have been created, they can then either be stored directly in S-Store, or migrated to a data warehouse.

6   Preliminary Experiments

6.1   Setup

To evaluate the effect of Copying and Moving data in the presence of multiple database systems, data must be distributed between at least two engines. Our experiments simulate a streaming data ingestion workload, and thus we use our streaming data ingestion prototype described in Sect. 5. In the implementation, data can be migrated between S-Store (the streaming ETL engine) and Postgres (the OLAP engine), and queries can be run on either system.

We executed the experiments on an Intel® Xeon® machine with 64 virtual cores and 132 GB memory. S-Store is co-located on the same node as Postgres for ease of communication and migration. We warmed up the S-Store cache for ten seconds before collecting statistics.

To motivate the use of multiple systems in tandem, we implemented a sub-set of TPC-DI as a streaming workload (Sect. 4). Specifically, our experiments involve the ingestion of the *DimTrade* and *DimAccount* tables from their respective flat files. Each of these ingestion processes was modeled as its own dataflow graph consisting of multiple SQL statements. These SQL statements perform

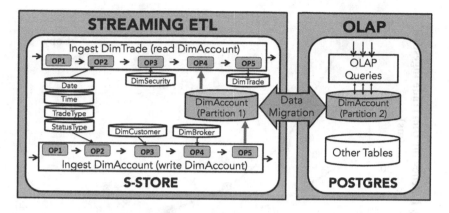

Fig. 5. Experimental setup (*DimAccount* in TPC-DI)

lookups on a variety of other tables to retrieve normalized foreign keys before inserting the finished tuple into a final table (Fig. 5).

In the case of *DimAccount*, incoming tuples represent in-place updates to existing rows in the database. *DimTrade* tuples, on the other hand, are always inserts, but require a lookup on the *DimAccount* table to generate a foreign key. S-Store is configured as single-sited and single-partitioned. Since there are no distributed transactions for this configuration, we chose to implement the ingestion of *DimTrade* and the update of *DimAccount* each in one stored procedure.

We generated heterogeneous workloads that contain changes to both *DimAccount* and *DimTrade*. In each experiment, the workload varies in terms of the percentage of operations that write or read from *DimAccount*. We partition *DimAccount* into ten fragments of equi-width. We notice that the ingestion of *DimTrade* from the *Trade.txt* flat file only accesses five of the ten fragments. For the update to *DimAccount*, we randomly generate a sequence of in-place updates by selecting the *account-id* that falls into the five fragments that are read during the ingestion of *DimTrade*. We then mix the in-place updates with the data ingestion source from *Trade.txt*. We measure the average latency of each operation (in-place update or ingestion) for the heterogeneous workload.

For simplicity, most tables in this experiment are considered to be cached in S-Store. The *DimTrade* table is considered to be entirely located in S-Store. The *DimAccount* table, on the other hand, is primarily located in Postgres. In the following experiments, a percentage of *DimAccount* is either Copied or Moved to S-Store, depending on the scenario. For all of the experiments, we measure the average latency of each operation (ingestion or update) in the workload that includes necessary data migrations.

6.2   Results

Read-Intensive Workloads. As shown in Fig. 5, the ingestion of *DimTrade* contains five operations, with OP4 retrieving the *account-id*, *broker-id* and

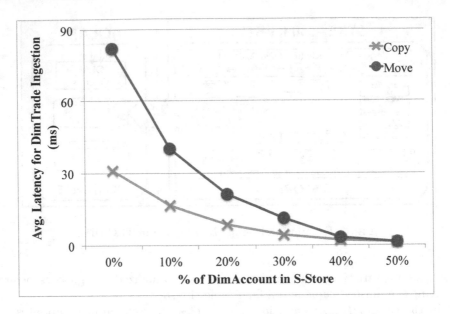

Fig. 6. A read-only workload (100% Read + 0% Write)

customer-id from table *DimAccount*. Executing this lookup process locally in S-Store (i.e., Copying *DimAccount* from Postgres to S-Store) can generally improve the performance, but S-Store only has limited storage space (or *cache* as we call it in this paper). In this experiment, we study how the storage limit of S-Store affects the performance for lookups (to table *DimAccount*) during data ingestion (of table *DimTrade*). The workload we generate for this experiment contains only data ingestion to *DimTrade* and no update to *DimAccount*, i.e., this workload contains 100% reads and 0% writes to *DimAccount*.

Figure 6 demonstrates the benefit of Copying tables to S-Store when there are lookups in the ETL tasks. As we clarified in Sect. 6.1, the y-axis represents the average latency of the ingestion, including necessary data migrations. When the cache size in S-Store is 0, for each lookup to *DimAccount* during the ingestion to *DimTrade*, the fragment of *DimAccount* that contains the key (*account-id*) must be migrated from Postgres to S-Store. Typically the migration incurs prohibitive cost. When the cache size increases, the fragments that have been migrated to S-Store can be stored locally for future lookups during the ingestion, reducing the number of migrations. We employed least recently used (LRU) to evict fragments from S-Store when the size of Copied fragments exceeds the cache limit. When S-Store has a large enough storage and is able to cache all the fragments of *DimAccount* table that are required in the ingestion of *DimTrade* (in this experiment, five out of the ten fragments are accessed during the ingestion of *DimTrade*), the latency of the ETL ingestion to *DimTrade* is minimized.

In this scenario, the average latency of the workload for Moving is more expensive than Copying for most cache sizes. The reason is that when the cache

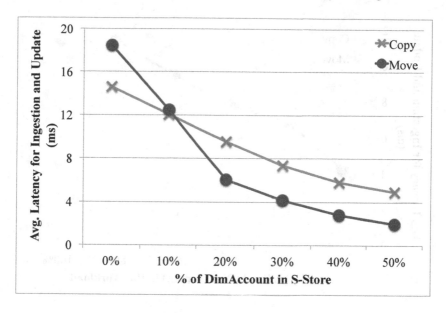

Fig. 7. A write-intensive workload (1% Read + 99% Write)

in S-Store is full, and a fragment required is not in the cache, a new migration must be issued. Copy only has to migrate the required fragment from Postgres to S-Store, while Move has an additional step to migrate the evicted fragment from S-Store back to Postgres.

Write-Intensive Workloads. When migrating data from Postgres to S-Store, Move implies that there is always only one copy of the data in the database engines, while Copy implies that there are two copies of the data in the system: one in S-Store, and another in Postgres. The workload in this experiment contains 99% in-place updates to *DimAccount* and 1% ingestions to *DimTrade*, generated as described in Sect. 6.1. In order to guarantee the transactional safety, the updates are executed synchronously in S-Store and Postgres. When an update is issued to S-Store, if the fragment of the data that this update accesses exists only in S-Store, the update is executed and finished in S-Store. If the fragment of the data exists in Postgres, S-Store will issue the update to Postgres for execution and stalls until Postgres finishes the execution.

S-Store is built on top of H-Store, a system that is designed to speed up transactionally safe updates, and hence for such operations, S-Store has a much lower latency compared to Postgres. Figure 7 shows that when the cache size increases, more fragments are migrated to S-Store, and since Move only keeps one copy of a fragment in the system, Moved fragments exist only in S-Store. Thus, there are no additional steps for updating the data in Postgres, which would increase the cost. Therefore, for a write-intensive workload where updates are

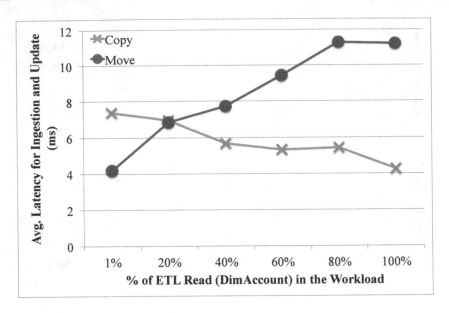

Fig. 8. Heterogeneous workloads

the majority, the average latency decreases quickly when the cache size increases if we choose to Move the data between S-Store and Postgres.

On the contrary, Copy keeps the data in both S-Store and Postgres. As we have explained, the cost of updates in Postgres dominates the synchronized update process, and thus the curve of the average latency for Copy does not change much when the cache size increases. We also notice that when the cache size is less than 10% of the size of the *DimAccount* table, Copy performs better than Move. It is not difficult to see that in such cases, a large amount of migrations are conducted because of cache misses (i.e., the required fragment is not in the cache). For each cache miss, Copy only has to migrate the required fragment from Postgres to S-Store (and delete the evicted fragment from S-Store), while Move must execute two migrations, one for the required fragment from Postgres to S-Store, another one for the evicted fragment from S-Store to Postgres.

Heterogeneous Workloads. We have seen that for read-intensive workloads, Copy often has better average latency, and for write-intensive workloads, Move usually has better average latency. Here, we experiment with workloads that are heterogeneous. In this experiment, we generate a series of workloads for which read operations (ingestion to *DimTrade*) make up from 1% to 100% of the total workload. We fix the cache size to 30% of *DimAccount*.

First, Fig. 8 confirms our previous observation that when the percentage of reads is relatively small (<20%) where the workload is dominated by writes (transactional updates to *DimAccount*), the latency for Move is lower than that

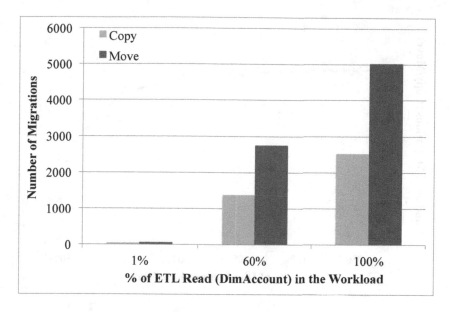

Fig. 9. Number of migrations for different workloads

for Copy, and when the workload is dominated by reads (ETL lookups to *DimAccount*), the latency for Copy is better than that for Move. Secondly, in our experiments, the cost of reads is much cheaper than that of writes (in-place updates); thus, for the Copy scenario, the average latency of all reads and writes to *DimAccount* in the workload decreases as the percentage of read in the workload increases. Thirdly, we notice that the average latency for Move increases when the percentage of read in the workload increases. This is because for cache misses when the cache is full, Move is much more expensive than Copy, as we have explained above. The additional migration cost for Move offsets the benefit brought by cheaper read. The figure shows that the curves for Copy and Move meet in a workload that contains about 20% of read operations in this setting as a confluence of the factors cited above.

We collected the number of migrations that are conducted during the execution of three workloads that we described in the above experiment (Fig. 8), containing 1% of ETL-read (write-intensive), 60% of ETL-read, and 100% of ETL-read (read-intensive) respectively, with cache size fixed to 30% of *DimAccount*. Figure 9 shows that in all of the three workloads, the number of migrations for Move is about twice as that for Copy. When the number of migrations is small (1% of ETL-read), although the cost of each migration is high, it does not affect the performance of ingestion significantly. When the number of migrations is high (100% of ETL-read), the cost of migrations dominates the total cost for data ingestion, and Copy shows an advantage because it only incurs about half of migrations of Move.

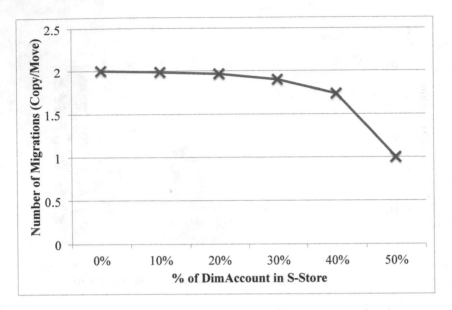

Fig. 10. Ratio of the number of migrations for the write-intensive workload

Furthermore, we repeated the same experiment for a write-intensive workload (1% ETL-read) executing with different cache sizes. Figure 10 shows that when the cache is large enough to store all accessed fragments (i.e., x = 50%), the number of migrations for Move is the same as that for Copy. However, when the cache size decreases, the number of migrations for Move increases quickly to about twice as that for Copy. This implies that Move is more sensitive to the change of cache size than Copy. We observed a similar pattern for read-intensive and heterogeneous workloads.

Takeaway Messages. We notice that the migration cost between database engines (S-Store and Postgres) is very expensive compared to the cost of local reads and writes in a workload. The migration cost is frequently not negligible during the execution of a mixed workload. For instance, although local reads are much cheaper than writes in S-Store in our settings, an ETL read may incur a data migration from Postgres to S-Store, and it may increase the average latency for data ingestion by up to two orders of magnitude. This implies that for certain circumstances, migration cost could be the dominating cost for a workload, and minimizing this migration cost may be a good enough objective function for an approximated optimized design. For other circumstances, considering only migration cost is probably not enough. For instance, for a workload that contains only writes, it may make sense to migrate the data from Postgres to S-Store, so the transactional writes are executed faster in S-Store, even if it means paying the additional cost for migrating data between the database engines.

7   Related Work

Data placement was previously studied in traditional multi-database systems, including federated and distributed databases. In federated databases like Garlic [15], the focus is on unified, cost-based querying over heterogeneous databases, each of which is autonomous in their internal data placement and query processing policies. This is in contrast to our polystore setting, where on-demand data migration across engines in the form of Move and Copy operations can be utilized to optimize data placement. In distributed databases, distribution design involves both fragmentation (i.e., how to divide tables into partitions) and allocation (i.e., how to place fragments onto nodes) [22]. For best results, the two should be tackled together, which makes the problem more complex. In our case, due to volatile and mixed nature of streaming ETL+OLAP workloads, we focus on a dynamic, workload-aware data placement solution.

There is extensive literature on physical database design tuning, including online approaches that are sensitive to workload changes [6,10]. The focus of these works has mainly been on tuning indexes, materialized views, or partitions of a single database system. More recently, new techniques have been proposed for physical design tuning in multi-store systems. For example, MISO determines where to store data in an HDFS-RDBMS hybrid storage system based on materialized views [18]. Our work extends these efforts further by considering data placement requirements of near real-time ingestion in a polystore environment.

Caching has been used as an optimization technique in many settings including databases. In IBM's DBCache, data from back-end database servers is replicated on front-end database servers in order to enhance data access performance of dynamic web applications [4]. Memcached is a distributed memory caching system to speed up dynamic database-driven web services [13]. Anti-caching is a technique to move colder data to disk in main-memory OLTP databases [9]. Our Copy-based migration is similar to caching in spirit, whereas our Move-based migration resembles anti-caching in that the system maintains a single copy of data with hot fragments residing in main-memory S-Store and colder ones residing in disk-based Postgres.

As we briefly mentioned earlier, our near real-time data ingestion support for data warehouses has also been followed by others in different contexts [2,5,12,14,27]. Stream warehouses such as ATT's DataDepot focus on ingesting append-only streams into a historical warehouse focusing on leveraging temporal semantics for consistency and data partitioning [14]. Near real-time warehouses focus on micro-batch ETL by invoking ETL pipelines at higher frequencies to maintain a more up-to-date data warehouse [27]. More recently, big data companies have proposed new architectures that integrate near real-time and batch processing in a way to ensure low latency for the former and high throughput for the latter [2,12]. Finally, HTAP systems such as IBM's Wildfire tightly integrate OLTP and OLAP support in order to support near real-time analytics including ingestion [5]. Our polystore environment contains elements from each of these different approaches, but emphasizes the use of a transactional streaming database infrastructure for near real-time ingestion and a polystore backend for OLAP, in which dynamic data placement plays a critical role.

8 Summary and Ongoing Work

In this paper, we have discussed the problem of data placement and caching in a distributed polystore. Our belief is that data ingestion in this setting presents some unique challenges that require further study. Our solution involves an integration of a stream processing system with an analytics back-end provided by the BigDAWG polystore. This paper is a first step in that direction.

While caching and data placement are not new ideas, the context of a polystore changes their performance characteristics in such a way as to require a complete rethinking. In this paper, we have considered Copying results in the ingestion engine to make subsequent reads faster. Copying requires making or retaining a copy in the streaming engine or in the home storage system of the data. Any update to that data would have to be realized in all locations, making writes very expensive. To address this, we also allow Moving the data, which simply moves the data to a new location (including perhaps the ingestion engine). This paper has studied the problem of how to best match the workload to the appropriate Moves and Copies.

While the work described in this paper involves two systems that each run on a single machine, the data placement problem is further complicated once the individual systems within the polystore are distributed across multiple machines. In this scenario, it is not enough to consider the system-level location of the data, but also the location of the data on physical hardware. It is likely that distribution properties of individual systems must be considered when determining data locations at the polystore level. Additionally, while this paper focuses on only two systems for simplicity, the data placement problem becomes much more difficult in a configuration space of three or more systems. As the number of systems in a polystore increases, so do the possible trade-offs considered when deciding when to Move or Copy data. These are interesting research problems, and we leave them as future work.

In the future, we envision a system that dynamically Moves and Copies the data in response to a particular workload. In order to accomplish this, we will need several things.

- A cost model that can estimate a relative cost for various placement plans. The cost model will be used to compare the effectiveness of multiple plans and must account for the extreme expense that is incurred when migrating data from one system to another.
- A more robust distributed catalog that, among other things, keeps track of where a particular piece of data currently resides.
- A tighter integration with the BigDAWG query optimizer that uses the cost model to choose the best query plan, which here amounts to picking the best copy and using it at the best point in a distributed query plan.
- A comparison between different data partitioning strategies. This will help us to understand how data partitioning affect the performance of data ingestion.

We are currently working on these research issues and intend to perform a thorough experimental evaluation using several benchmarks, including TPC-DI and an application furnished to us by a major credit card processing company.

Acknowledgments. We thank Renee J. Miller and Boris Glavic for reviewing the work. We also thank the anonymous reviewers and the BIRTE 2017 workshop attendees for their helpful suggestions. This research is funded in part by a Bell Canada Fellowship, NSERC, the Intel Science and Technology Center for Big Data, and the NSF under grant NSF IIS-1111423.

References

1. Kappa Architecture. https://www.oreilly.com/ideas/questioning-the-lambda-architecture
2. Lambda Architecture. http://lambda-architecture.net/
3. Neo4j. https://neo4j.com/
4. Altinel, M., Bornhovd, C., Krishnamurthy, S., Mohan, C., Pirahesh, H., Reinwald, B.: Cache tables: paving the way for an adaptive database cache. In: VLDB, pp. 718–729 (2003)
5. Barber, R., et al.: Wildfire: concurrent blazing data ingest and analytics. In: SIGMOD, pp. 2077–2080 (2016)
6. Bruno, N., Chaudhuri, S.: An online approach to physical design tuning. In: ICDE, pp. 826–835 (2007)
7. Cetintemel, U., et al.: S-Store: a streaming NewSQL system for big velocity applications. PVLDB **7**(13), 1633–1636 (2014)
8. Cudre-Mauroux, P., et al.: A demonstration of SciDB: a science-oriented DBMS. PVLDB **2**(2), 1534–1537 (2009)
9. DeBrabant, J., Pavlo, A., Tu, S., Stonebraker, M., Zdonik, S.: Anti-caching: a new approach to database management system architecture. PVLDB **6**(14), 1942–1953 (2013)
10. Du, J., Glavic, B., Tan, W., Miller, R.J.: DeepSea: progressive workload-aware partitioning of materialized views in scalable data analytics. In: EDBT, pp. 198–209 (2017)
11. Elmore, A., et al.: A demonstration of the BigDAWG polystore system. PVLDB **8**(12), 1908–1911 (2015)
12. Fernandez, R.C., et al.: Liquid: unifying nearline and offline big data integration. In: CIDR (2015)
13. Fitzpatrick, B.: Distributed caching with memcached. Linux J. **124**, 5–5 (2004)
14. Golab, L., Johnson, T., Seidel, J.S., Shkapenyuk, V.: Stream warehousing with DataDepot. In: SIGMOD, pp. 847–854 (2009)
15. Josifovski, V., Schwarz, P., Haas, L., Lin, E.: Garlic: a new flavor of federated query processing for DB2. In: SIGMOD, pp. 524–532 (2002)
16. Kallman, R., et al.: H-Store: a high-performance, distributed main memory transaction processing system. PVLDB **1**(2), 1496–1499 (2008)
17. Kreps, J., Narkhede, N., Rao, J.: Kafka: a distributed messaging system for log processing. In: NetDB Workshop (2011)
18. LeFevre, J., Sankaranarayanan, J., Hacigumus, H., Tatemura, J., Polyzotis, N., Carey, M.J.: MISO: souping up big data query processing with a multistore system. In: SIGMOD, pp. 1591–1602 (2014)

19. Meehan, J., Aslantas, C., Zdonik, S., Tatbul, N., Du, J.: Data ingestion for the connected world. In: CIDR (2017)
20. Meehan, J., et al.: S-Store: streaming meets transaction processing. PVDLB **8**(13), 2134–2145 (2015)
21. Meehan, J., et al.: Integrating real-time and batch processing in a polystore. In: IEEE HPEC (2016)
22. Özsu, M.T., Valduriez, P.: Distributed database systems: where are we now? IEEE Comput. **24**(8), 68–78 (1991)
23. Poess, M., Rabl, T., Jacobsen, H., Caufield, B.: TPC-DI: the first industry benchmark for data integration. PVLDB **7**(13), 1367–1378 (2014)
24. Stonebraker, M., et al.: C-store: a column-oriented DBMS. In: VLDB, pp. 553–564 (2005)
25. Stonebraker, M., Cetintemel, U.: "One size fits all": an idea whose time has come and gone. In: ICDE, pp. 2–11 (2005)
26. Tatbul, N., et al.: Handling shared, mutable state in stream processing with correctness guarantees. IEEE Data Eng. Bull. Special Issue Next-Gener. Stream Process. **38**(4), 94–104 (2015)
27. Vassiliadis, P., Simitsis, A.: Near real-time ETL. In: Kozielski, S., Wrembel, R. (eds.) New Trends in Data Warehousing and Data Analysis, pp. 1–31. Springer, Boston (2009). https://doi.org/10.1007/978-0-387-87431-9_2

Author Index

Printed in the United States
By Bookmasters